THE CENTER FOR TEACHING & LEARNING

THIS ONE IS A KEEPER

SUPER COURSES

SUPER COURSES

The Future of Teaching and Learning

Ken Bain

with Marsha Marshall Bain

PRINCETON UNIVERSITY PRESS

PRINCETON AND OXFORD

Published by Princeton University Press
41 William Street, Princeton, New Jersey 08540
6 Oxford Street, Woodstock, Oxfordshire OX20 1TR

press.princeton.edu

Library of Congress Cataloging-in-Publication Data

Names: Bain, Ken, author.
Title: Super courses : the future of teaching and learning / Ken Bain with
    Marsha Marshall Bain.
Description: Princeton, New Jersey : Princeton University Press, 2021. |
    Includes bibliographical references and index.
Identifiers: LCCN 2020036521 (print) | LCCN 2020036522 (ebook) |
    ISBN 9780691185460 (hardcover) | ISBN 9780691216591 (ebook)
Subjects: LCSH: College teaching. | Education, Higher—Curricula. |
    Curriculum change. | Learning, Psychology of.
Classification: LCC LB2331 .B343 2021 (print) | LCC LB2331 (ebook) |
    DDC 378.1/25—dc23
LC record available at https://lccn.loc.gov/2020036521
LC ebook record available at https://lccn.loc.gov/2020036522

British Library Cataloging-in-Publication Data is available

Editorial: Peter Dougherty, Alena Chekanov
Production Editorial: Terri O'Prey
Text Design: Karl Spurzem
Jacket/Cover Design: Matt Avery (Monograph LLC)
Production: Erin Suydam
Publicity: Alyssa Sanford, Kathryn Stevens
Copyeditor: Kathleen Kageff

This book has been composed in Arno Pro with DIN Pro display

Printed on acid-free paper. ∞

Printed in the United States of America

10 9 8 7 6 5 4 3 2 1

Dedicated to Adam, Nathan, and Junhui

CONTENTS

ACKNOWLEDGMENTS

This book began with an idea that Marsha had about studying examples of invitational syllabi. We collected some brilliant examples from around the world, and we are grateful to everyone who offered their work. But the original notion morphed into something different, and better, after Peter Dougherty invited us to lunch one day in August 2017. Peter had just retired as director of Princeton University Press, and, as he put it, had taken on a new project: the development of a comprehensive list of books on higher education. He wanted to know if we might have something to contribute.

That fall, we drove to Princeton from our home in South Orange, New Jersey. Over "French, European, vegetarian friendly, and gluten free" options at Cargot Brasserie, located in the former Dinky train station on the edge of the university campus, we began to explore what we might offer to that project. We mentioned the syllabus book, to which Peter quickly added, "You're looking for Super Courses." It was the first of numerous contributions that the editor made to our endeavor, a title that captured our work brightly and brilliantly and drove our thinking in a whole new direction. We are deeply grateful for all that Peter gave us, gently guiding us toward the book you have in your hands.

Other people also provided rich resources that made the work better. We want to thank all of the great educators along the way who spent valuable time discussing their imaginative pedagogical creations, including all of those whose work doesn't appear here because space limited the possibilities. From those conversations, and from the rich materials educators shared with us, we continued to see a pattern in their work that the natural critical learning environment and Peter's delightful title captured well.

Not every provocative course we encountered, however, reflected that Super Course model, but even those that didn't helped us understand the special power and uniqueness of those that did. Furthermore, they helped us see the full scope of the changes that are brewing. We want to thank and applaud everyone who has or will contribute to this revolution, including you.

Special thanks to Sue Triplett for her encouragement; Brena Walker for reading parts of the manuscript and providing technical assistance with language; Tonia Bain, Al Masino, Marshall Bain, and Alice Yuan Bain for their inspiration and encouragement; Adam, Nathan, and Junhui for providing their stories; Anthony Rossi and Christopher Barker, physicians who (along with their staff) shepherded Ken through his battle with cancer in the midst of the work on the book; and all of the wonderful people at Princeton University Press and its affiliates for their myriad contributions. It takes a big community to produce a book like this.

PART I

THE IDEA

Prologue

We are in the midst of a profound revolution in teaching and learning. This change has come in the form of a new breed of "Super Courses" that have emerged in the humanities, social and natural sciences, arts, professional fields, and other areas. While these new experiences have appeared in all stages of education, they have made their biggest difference in undergraduate colleges and universities. These dramatic changes have also appeared in high schools and medical institutions.

These new kinds of courses are altering the nature of what students encounter in school. While fostering deeper and more widespread learning, they have redefined what it means to become educated and the conditions most likely to produce that end. When Harvard University Press published our *What the Best College Teachers Do* in 2004 and *What the Best College Students Do* in 2012, the nature of this revolution had already become somewhat clear, but it has continued to grow, transforming itself and the landscape around it.

We've Come a Long Way

For decades, many educators simply focused on finding "superior minds" and helping them to develop. These teachers assumed that the best way to educate was to give students facts to digest. Yet the innovations of which we speak are now demonstrating that traditional classrooms have too frequently left most students far short of their potential, even those who score the highest marks. Furthermore, our methods of measuring learning have long been inadequate. It's tough to detect and appraise the changes that go on in people's minds when they learn. Sometimes students have received praise for largely empty accomplishments. Other times some marvelous progress has gone undetected by our antiquated methods of assessment.

In the traditional classroom, instructors might laud the power of comprehension, critical thinking, creativity, and problem solving but often test for memory. Only with improved understanding of evaluation can teachers from grade school to the university focus more clearly on deep learning, adaptive expertise, and the ability to take an idea and realize its implications in a large variety of settings, some far distant from each other (what we sometimes call "far transfer"). Only then can we appreciate the importance of living at the edge of our own cultural perspectives and constantly exploring the problems we might face in accepting whatever we believe.

New technologies have certainly affected change, but they have not been the driving force that so many observers assume. The strongest influence has come instead from research on human learning. True, we have often pinned our hopes on our machines, and a variety of technologies have made it easier to create transforming learning environments. Yet sophisticated gadgets do not create better schools without advances in how we comprehend and measure learning and motivation. Indeed, the emphasis on technology as a savior of education has led to some false starts and pedagogical dead ends. Even in the spring of 2020, when a pandemic forced thousands of classes to go online, insights into how our minds grow, not computers or the internet, determined success or failure.

Our brains work in elaborate and often mysterious ways, but studies in a collection of fields we might call the learning arts and sciences have shed a bright light on those processes. As a result, we have come to recognize that learning is far more than rote memory. We know that teachers must master their subject before they can teach well, but that isn't always sufficient. Professors can become experts in, say, biology or history or any other subject yet never grasp what other people may need to achieve a similar level of understanding. That's a tough pill to swallow for some whose prowess in their field has been so outstanding, but recognize it we must in order to benefit from the new Super Courses.

The sea changes in schooling come at a time of both great promise and a growing sense of crisis. Many critics have lost confidence in formal education. Some people have even urged students, especially in college, to drop out, follow the example of Bill Gates and Steve Jobs, and seek their fortune in entrepreneurship. Yet the emerging Super

Courses could solve many of the problems that have long bedeviled elementary, secondary, and higher education. These new opportunities are so profound that they foretell a bright and productive future for human beings, unless something derails the process. At minimum, they change the debate about schools and learning.

Several factors threaten the future of Super Courses. Despite their achievements, far too many educators cling to outmoded thinking and practices, often unaware of the brilliant advances that have emerged. Others know of these developments only as a perplexing and off-putting wilderness of terms like *flipped classrooms, team-based learning, gamification*, and *role-playing*. Meanwhile, still others who have tried to join the upheaval have misunderstood the secrets that power its achievements, often focusing on a single component.

To save and advance the merits of this leap forward, we must understand what makes these Super Courses tick. How can teachers replicate these educational successes, or, more important, use their insights into human learning to create their own innovations? In the pages that follow we'll explore both some powerful examples of these remarkable inventions and the principles that underpin them. We hope this investigation will inspire the next phase of the movement.

But our book isn't just for professional educators. Even casual readers can enjoy comparing Super Courses to their own school experience. Parents and students should pay attention as they make choices about schooling, from kindergarten to graduate school. Any high schooler searching for the right college should become acquainted with this revolution and use it to measure the places they consider. When taxpayers and political leaders ask questions about the value of public commitments to education, they must take these innovations into consideration. The whole debate has shifted.

Two important points to keep in mind. First, we've chosen a relatively few examples of Super Courses, but we don't want to imply that these are the only possibilities, or even necessarily the "best" college and high school courses in the world. No ranking system is intended or offered. We could have chosen other examples to illustrate our point. But the collection we offer you does exemplify some of the major trends in the movement and the rich diversity of ideas that have emerged in a variety of schools and disciplines.

Second, none of these courses is perfect. Indeed, their architects are acutely aware of the opportunity for continued improvement as new research and ideas emerge. We'll explore some of those efforts to find better ways to create what we call a natural critical learning environment.

What Now?

When the pandemic erupted in 2020, the movement gained more converts and took new forms as the shift to online education exposed old weaknesses in traditional teaching. Faculty members who had never tested the Super Course ideas frequently had only one question: How do I record my lectures and post them on the web? It was like going back to the dawn of the automobile age and asking, how can I hitch old Dobbin to that new vehicle? If professors simply brought to Zoom their old methods of fostering learning, they didn't work so well. Without the charms of personal contact or the power of extraordinary speech, the deficiencies of the traditional approach became glaringly apparent. Students and parents began to protest.

For others, the crisis has become an opportunity to innovate. The models we will explore here have become blueprints and inspirations for the future of schooling—in the classroom, online, or in the community—but they are the beginning of the process, not the end.

CHAPTER ONE

Pinning Our Hopes on Our Machines

One day in 1999 some children playing in the streets of Kalkaji, New Delhi, found a computer fixed in a wall that separated their poor neighborhood from a rich office district. It might have been a strange sight for these young residents of such disadvantaged circumstances, but within hours they had mastered some basic workings of the device and had begun surfing the web.[1] The man who put the machine in the crevice, education engineer Sugata Mitra, later told the world in a series of web articles and TED talks, "within six months the children of the neighborhood had learned all the mouse operations, could open and close programs, and were going online to download games, music and videos." When Mitra discovered that the kids had taught themselves how to work the magic box, he saw it as proof of his favorite educational theory: If you let children follow their own curiosity, they will learn by tinkering about, discovering something new, and teaching each other.

Mitra called this process "Minimally Invasive Education," and after he showed his "Hole in the Wall" experiment before television cameras in 2007 and again in 2010 and 2013, more than seven million people eventually downloaded and watched the excited Indian professor bubble with enthusiasm. Mitra told stories of Tamil-speaking and poverty-stricken children learning English *and* the biochemistry of DNA replication in a matter of months. While they played with a computer he had placed under a tree, a twenty-two-year-old woman looked

over their shoulders and occasionally vocalized little signs of encouragement: "Well, wow, how did you do that?" (in the fashion of a doting
"grandmother," as Mitra put it). Without conventional teachers, these
poor children with so few worldly advantages had outperformed rich
kids in a traditional school.

When the effervescent researcher spoke about his experiment on a
TED talk, his live audience gasped, laughed, and applauded, and around
the world, internet viewers contemplated the wonders of letting children
follow their own curiosity and the alleged fascination of computers.
One of those viewers in faraway northern Mexico taught in a conventional school located next to a foul-smelling garbage dump in Mata-
moros, Tamaulipas, just south of Brownsville, Texas.

Sergio Juárez Correa, a thirty-one-year-old teacher who had grown
up in similar circumstances, stumbled onto Mitra's videos one day, and
they changed his life. How they did so, however, has been seriously misunderstood, even by the *Wired* magazine editors and writer who made
Correa and his students somewhat famous. Indeed, as we will see, many
people have misunderstood what took place with both Mitra and Correa and the role that computers did and did not play in teaching and
learning. In the process these commentators have created a serious mis-
understanding about the nature of our emerging Super Courses.

In a story that has become part of the lore of the computer industry's
promise to the world, Correa decided to do his own version of Mitra's
experiment. It would be quite a challenge. But for one twelve-year-old
girl it would reveal the "extraordinary abilities" of a budding genius.
Paloma Noyola Bueno, a thin young girl with long black hair, lived in a
world where a foul smell "drifts through the cement-walled classroom,"
a world where her father scavenged for little pieces of scraps he might
sell to eke out the barest of existences, and where cement and wood
"homes had intermittent electricity, few computers, limited Internet,
and sometimes not enough to eat." On their daily trek to school, Paloma
and her classmates would walk along beside a sewage-filled ditch and
sometimes find dead bodies on the streets, victims of a drug war shoot-
out the night before.[2] They didn't have a generous and inventive bene-
factor like Mitra to set up a magic box for them.

In the fall of 2011, on the first day of class, Correa put his students in a circle, sat down with them, and told them they had as much potential as anyone. He invited them into a world where they could "build robots and airplanes" and "write symphonies." The young educator then asked that powerful question, "So, what do you want to learn?" That was a radical change. No more would he follow some fixed curriculum handed down from on high. Those traditional lessons often wore the tattered clothes of their nineteenth- and twentieth-century origins, and Correa would have no more of it. From now on he would simply follow the whims and inquisitiveness of the kids in his class. Or so it seemed.

The results were astounding. In June 2012, when his students took the national standardized exams that Mexico uses to find out how schools and children are doing, Paloma made the highest math score in the country, even better than rich kids in major cities who attended posh private schools. Some of her classmates did almost as well. Ten placed in the 99.99th percentile in math, and three did so in Spanish. In the weeks to come, television and newspaper reporters showered Paloma with attention.

A popular TV show sent a variety of gifts, and even a year later, *Wired*, the industry-favored magazine that celebrates technological advances, called her "the next Steve Jobs" and put a somber-looking picture of the young girl on its cover. Since Jobs made no major contributions to mathematics, it wasn't at all clear why the magazine didn't label her the next Albert Einstein, or, better yet, the next, Emmy Noether. But the comparison with the Apple founder fit the narrative that *Wired* seemed to push: it's the high-speed processors that made the difference.

But was it?

It's easy to read these stories and agree with that assessment. Sugata Mitra even fell into that trap and once proclaimed, "If you put a computer in front of children and remove all other adult restrictions, they will self-organize around it, like bees around a flower."[3] He should have known better, and we suspect he did. After all, the South Asian scholar was not the first person to pin his hopes on our machines. But the general move in that direction has not always gone well. The *Wired* article by Joshua Davis that made Paloma something of an international celebrity got much of the story right, but it littered its tale with too much unrelated noise about computers and technological progress, rather than focusing on the news about changes in the way we understand and foster learning.

Devil in the Wired City

Contrast for a moment the stories you just read with this one. In the 1980s Jeffrey Hawkins dreamed of putting a computer in everybody's pocket. Make it small enough, and the costs will go down, he once told us, bringing near universal access to the world.[4] Surely that vision could support Mitra's. By the early 2000s, such miniature computers existed, and Hawkins's Treo company was one of the first to build such devices. They were called smartphones. Apple, Samsung, and other companies have sold them by the billions.

Yet their presence didn't always boost learning. Educators began to worry that the little demons distracted more than they helped. Researchers found that even a cell phone sitting on a table could diminish the quality of conversations—and learning. If someone picked it up and used it, the damage grew. A recent study in the classroom found that not only did use of cell phones damage learning for the user; it also hurt long-term retention for others in the same room.[5] Studies of both students and workers, as James Lang noted in the *Chronicle of Higher Education*, have found that when people are interrupted by a ringing cell phone, it takes them, on average, almost thirty minutes to refocus and fully engage in what they had been doing.[6]

But the potential damage of pocket computers goes much deeper. Two brain scientists from California have developed a powerful way to understand how the devices can harm our learning. Human beings are highly curious animals, Adam Gazzaley, a neurologist, and Larry Rosen, a psychologist, explain.[7] That thirst for knowledge is part of our ancient DNA, and we can't avoid it. You might think then that smartphones and the internet would feed that hunger to the delight of everyone. But not so fast. The speed of the new devices has introduced an element that creates unprecedented problems.

To understand those difficulties and dangers, the brain scientists used studies of animal feeding behavior in the wild. Humans search for information the way beasts forage for food, they argued. When squirrels find a tree full of nuts, for example, they will stay with that patch of food until the supply runs low. But when will they give up on a walnut grove and move on to a new source of nourishment? That depends on how many nuts are left and how far it is to the next tree. If it is close by, the furry rodents will abandon ship when a limb still has some fruit left because an even bigger supply of nuts is a mere leap away. If the new source is, however, across a meadow on the other side of a river, they will exhaust every opportunity before leaving the first tree.

Same for humans looking for knowledge. If it is easy to get to a new source of information, we will go there even before we deplete our current supply. Someone with a smartphone can jump quickly from one information load to another, but it is the thrill of *moving on* that soon rocks our boat, especially if the new is often glitzy, surprising, loud, or even violent. As a result, we get addicted to the bang of finding something new, always jumping from one webpage to another rather than harvesting everything from a current location.

That tendency to forage like animals has been passed down to us over millions of years as ancient forms of life evolved into new ones, and it is now written into the core of our being. But it was our smartphones, social media, and the internet that deeply reinforced the practice of jumping around. Or so these researchers argue.

That habit of switching rapidly became embedded in our brains through a process that the twentieth-century psychologist Burrhus Frederic Skinner called "intermittent reinforcement."[8] Not every new email or Facebook post yields something interesting and rewarding, but it is actually the uneven pattern of rewards that keeps us coming back and embeds the habit of flitting about deep in our brains. If we don't know what the next click will bring but it sometimes gives us a real charge (intermittent reinforcement), we'll keep probing, especially if we can't predict when the payoff will happen. A fear of missing out (FOMO) on something really good drives us into a frenzy of fast-paced clicking, and that addiction stays with us longer than it would if we could predict when the rewards would come.

You can see the results in the way people often use their smartphones and computers. One study of Stanford University students, for example, found that they switch screens "roughly five times a minute."[9] More alarming still, researchers took those measurements while students were supposedly studying. Other investigators have found similar results. We've become a world of hopscotching media users. Such habits make us impatient and anxious, always looking for that next intriguing find on the internet, afraid we will miss out on something big. Millions of students interrupt their own work and seldom stick with one task long enough to enjoy or appreciate it. They become easily bored because they have become addicted to constant change—and it is an addiction. As numerous studies have found, the quality of learning goes down.[10] The iPad and smartphone junkies understand less and remember little.

In this fast-paced world, we try to do more by attacking two tasks at the same time, but our ancient brain structures can't really read email and learn chemistry simultaneously. Multitasking is a giant illusion. It isn't just hard, as a student contended recently; it's impossible. At best, our brains don't really do two things at once; they switch rapidly back and forth between two or more mental actions, harming the quality of each one. (Compare writing all the letters in the alphabet followed by the numbers from 1 to 26. Then do it by "multitasking." Write A1, B2, and so forth. You'll find the second way much slower and more prone to mistakes.) With heavy episodes of FOMO, people become more anxious. It is not at all surprising that depression and anxiety levels among students at all levels have skyrocketed in recent years.[11]

Some of the increase may arise because more high school and college students believe they have little control over their lives, a trend that began long before Steve Jobs even dreamed of iPhones.[12] But you put the two historical developments together (changing technology and the rising sense among students that they've lost the locus of control), and that double whammy mixes like a psychological Molotov cocktail, ready to explode in the lives of millions. Indeed, a study in Taiwan found that the declining sense of control makes people more susceptible to smartphone addiction and "techno stress." The result is more anxiety and increased compulsive use of phones in a frantic attempt to keep from feeling hopeless, guilty, and depressed.[13] Meanwhile, "our brains," Gazzaley and Rosen conclude, "struggle to manage a constantly surging river of information in a world of unending interruptions and entice-ments to switch our focus."[14]

How Do People Learn?

How then do we explain Gazzaley and Rosen's research and reconcile it with the successes of Paloma and her classmates and with the children who found Sugata Mitra's computer in a wall? The answer to that ques-tion can tell us a lot about the nature of the Super Courses we are going to explore, and perhaps keep us from following false gods.

Despite Sugata Mitra's vision of honey pots that lured children into learning, it wasn't the computers that turned the trick. The magic boxes sometimes became a bountiful grocery store where curious people could find the nourishment they craved, but it was the food (or the in-formation and questions) that enticed them, not the delivery system. Indeed, in Paloma's case, she didn't even have a computer.

She and her classmates feasted instead on the opportunity to explore, to ask questions, to control their own education, to hear the inquiries and problems the teacher invented, and to play with the ideas they en-tailed. Sergio Juárez Correa dangled delicious morsels in front of their noses, ears, and eyes and invited the children to enjoy, making sure the best food came in the right portions and at the proper time (and with-out coercion, but more on that later). If Gazzaley and Rosen are correct, Paloma may have been better off without a personal computer or smartphone.

Correa would pose questions and then sit back and let students struggle with a problem and invent ways to solve it. The chance to spec-ulate became part of the inducement, as we will see in other contexts. While his ideal educator, Sugata Mitra, had urged schools to give stu-dents access to computers, Correa didn't have that luxury. No one had one of the magic machines at home except the teacher. If the children asked about something he didn't know, he'd search for an answer on the internet that evening and report back the next day. The process proved slower but had some advantages as his students anxiously awaited the outcome of his daily diggings.

If you listen carefully to Mitra, Correa, and other purveyors of minimally invasive education, you learn that they act like someone paddling a canoe downstream, not like a rudderless boat or hapless bystander adrift in a sea of ignorance.[15] Only occasionally would Correa stick his oar in the water to keep the boat headed in the right direction and away from dangerous shoals, but paddle he did. He guided the discussion and didn't rely on some invisible hand of education, often raising intriguing questions that his young pupils would probably never invent on their own.

One day, for example, he challenged the children to add all the numbers from 1 to 100 as fast as possible. Paloma quickly recognized that if she added the top and bottom number (1 plus 100, 2 plus 99, and so forth) she would have 50 sets of 101, or 5,050, and then she helped her classmates understand the same idea. It was the first day her teacher began to consider the power of pupils fostering learning in other students. In the days to come he teased the class with fascinating mind games. We'll see in a variety of Super Courses how different instructors did their own paddling.

Sugata Mitra didn't leave his Tamil children to wander aimlessly in a sea of porn, urban legends, and mindless ignorance. Rather he loaded his machine with "all kinds of stuff from the Internet about DNA replication."[16] It wasn't just everything but a limited body of information where he wanted the children to focus. He also raised problems, posed questions, and invented games. He placed among some Telugu-speaking Indian children a voice-recognition computer that could understand only neutral British accents. After challenging the kids to get themselves understood by the device, he went away, leaving them to their own curiosity and ingenuity. In two months, their speech changed, and they all began talking like a Newcastle English professor.[17]

Even Mitra admitted that, at times, "intervention is required to plant a new seed for discovery, such as 'Did you know that computers could play music? Here, let me play a song for you.'"[18] We call what the Indian professor did "scaffolding," that is, building structures that facilitate students' exploration and even guide them in certain directions. Now, we have to imagine how something similar could be done with history, chemistry, psychology, mechanical engineering, philosophy, and a host of other subjects. We'll return to the art of scaffolding later in the book.

It Isn't the Shoes

When he was three years old, Adam took a fancy to his mother's iMac and soon taught himself how to surf the web. He found a site called Starfall, which used phonetics to help children learn to read. Within a few weeks, the young boy had moved quickly through the learn-to-read lessons with their enchanting songs and colorful graphics, and by the time he was three and a half, he began reading books and even helped write a poem about the origins of mac and cheese ("Did it grow on trees"). At his preschool, he sometimes helped the teacher by reading aloud to his classmates, and when he entered kindergarten, he continued in that role. His precocious progress seemed quite natural to him and his friends, and when he reached seven, he expressed concern about his younger brother. "I'm worried," he told his father one day; "he's four years old and can't read a word." By the time Adam reached the eighth grade and beyond he applied those reading skills to advanced texts in math, science, and history and to novels and short stories.

Nate had learned to read by the time he was six, without much input from Starfall, and soon consumed books with a mad passion. By the time he was ten, he read far above his grade level, plunging through an array of novels, short stories, and nonfiction. In the fourth grade he fell in love with the saxophone and every night after school found lessons on YouTube where he could learn how to play the instrument. He advanced rapidly with that computer-assisted tutoring and soon mastered a whole string of songs, claiming first chair in his school band and flooding his house with the sounds of Charlie Parker. In the fifth grade, he started writing a graphic novel, filling it with a wondrous tale and illustrations he'd learned to draw with painstaking precision, again with the help of lessons he found on the web.

Junhui came to the United States from rural China when he was eighteen months old and quickly became engrossed in YouTube videos of tractors and earthmovers. The iPad he found on his new parents' couch became his favorite toy, filling long sessions with him sitting in someone's lap watching big machines transform a construction site. While that fascination soon faded, the English he began learning in the process stuck with him and grew. So did his enchantment with building stuff. By his sixth birthday he could wield a hammer, drill, and screwdriver like a master carpenter, and he had his own set of advanced tools and workbench where he crafted an array of toys from pieces of lumber. The young boy lived in an old neighborhood undergoing a facelift. New buildings sprang out of freshly dug holes while ancient houses sprouted replacements for rotting timbers, broken windows, and missing bricks. Some of the row houses on his block grew third stories and displayed a rich palette of paint colors. The parade of changes sparked his imagination and wonder. He became a keen observer of small details and could discuss the intricacies of joints and joists with the best of them.

His parents restricted his "iPad time" but found other ways to tickle his fancy. For his annual birthday party they brought something special to each event. One year a snake handler exhibited an array of reptiles. The next, a "science is magic" show displayed the wonders of nature to the delight of neighborhood playmates.

Learning often flows from a rich milieu in which a smartphone, iPad, or computer *could* play a role, but it isn't the electronic device that makes or breaks the education that happens any more than Michael Jordan's shoes explained his extraordinary jumping ability. Something far more subtle and complex has built the new Super Courses that we will examine. For the past two decades, we've explored highly engaging educational experiences and repeatedly found a collection of practices and conditions we have dubbed a *natural critical learning environment*, and it is that educational ecosystem that we must explore and understand if we are to comprehend and replicate the successes of the phenomenal new breed of Super Courses.

CHAPTER TWO

How We Learn

To understand the power of natural critical learning environments we must, first, explore the research on how people learn and what can go wrong. We often act as if learning is a simple process of remembering ideas and information, but it isn't that easy. Even if we toss understanding into the mix, we still haven't captured the complex undertaking involved in human learning. While the bold research on the brain and its function has offered fresh insights, even that mechanical exploration hasn't fully captured what it means to learn deeply. For more than a century, people have pieced together insight into what takes place. Let's take a quick tour through some of the most important discoveries. In that excursion we will begin to understand the nature and power of the Super Courses that are transforming higher education and are even re-shaping some corners of secondary and elementary schools.

Let's start with how our learning begins. When we are born, light, sound, touch, smell, and taste bombard our senses. They are our only contact with the outside world. We take that input and try to understand it, noticing patterns and building mental models of reality in the process. We then use those resulting models to understand any new sensory stimulations that come along later.

Someone walks into a room, for example, and an electromagnetic field called light tickles the retina of that person's eyes. We label that sensation "seeing," but it isn't the electromagnetic field alone that informs. Rather the individual takes the sensory input and wraps it around some already existing models and understands the room in terms of those frameworks constructed years ago. The person already has a concept of tables and chairs, rugs and walls long before the light zings the eyeballs. Students hear a lecture or read a book and interpret the sounds and sights with some existing paradigm, comparing and contrasting the new information with what they already "know." The memories that humans hold shape what they see, hear, and learn.

Thus, we understand the present in terms of some earlier experience, and that ability and habit serves us well. We can go somewhere we've never been and still make sense of the place. Otherwise, we'd live like Drew Barrymore's character in *Fifty First Dates*, always forced to start from scratch with each encounter. But that practice of depending on past experiences also proves to be our greatest challenge as learners and educators. Why? Because we often, especially in deep learning, want our students to build new models of reality, or at least have the capacity to question their existing ones. In the humanities we often say that educated people realize the problems they face in accepting whatever they may believe. Our friends in the sciences will sometimes go further and encourage their students to abandon certain models—say, that the earth is the center of the universe—and form new ones. Either way, we are asking people to do something quite unnatural. Indeed, when Sam Wineburg wrote about the phenomenon in his own field, he called his book *Historical Thinking and Other Unnatural Acts*.[1] While his discipline asks people to use evidence from the past to understand a former time, many will rely only on the mental models they have constructed about their own world.

By the time students arrive in middle school, high school, and college, they have constructed thousands of models that will have more influence than anything a professor tells them. They may know nothing about a subject, but if they make any attempt to understand it, they will use something already constructed in their brains to do so. They will compare and contrast, looking for analogies and differences.

Even if their current ideas are faulty, however, people find it quite hard to abandon an existing concept and build a new one. We can even become emotionally attached to our mental models, afraid to give them up because the unknown is a little scary and any changes suggest that we didn't do such a hot job in the first place. But those difficulties don't always show up in standard assessments. A story we told in 2004, at the beginning of the second chapter of *What the Best College Teachers Do*, illustrates the point.

In the mid-1980s two physicists at Arizona State University asked this important question. Does my introductory course change the way students understand motion. If it doesn't, you have two possibilities. Either they didn't need to study that material because they already understood it, or the course had failed them.

To grasp learning in their classes, Ibrahim Abou Halloun and David Hestenes devised an instrument to measure someone's conception of physical motion. They called their invention a Force Concept Inventory and administered it to approximately six hundred students coming into four different sections of an introductory physics course. On the front end, they discovered that most students began their study with what the Arizona professors called a commonsense theory of motion, "a cross between Aristotelian and 14th-century impetus ideas."[2] Without going into the physics details, let's just say that if this were the primary way we understood motion today, we wouldn't be able to put a satellite in orbit or even build a highway around a curve without sending cars into a ditch.

But that's before students took the course. Once they had done so, Halloun and Hestenes gave them the Force Concept Inventory again to see how much their understanding of motion had changed. Guess what. For the overwhelming majority of students, the shift was small if any. Even people who made high grades in the course often kept their original mental models. When the researchers approached some of the students with additional questions, many of those pupils refused to change their view, argued with the researchers, and engaged in all sorts of mental gymnastics to keep from confronting a challenge to some deeply held paradigms.

Those people had constructed a mental model of motion, using everyday experiences, and they refused to let go. But this attachment to existing paradigms doesn't happen just in physics. It occurs in history and every other field where people study because it is a human habit.

We will seldom rebuild major concepts unless we face repeated challenges to our current models. Merely telling a class that their existing ideas are wrong will not usually turn the trick. Students must enter a space where their paradigms do not work and care that those models come up short. People can then begin to grapple with those pregnant moments and build new ways of looking at the world. We call those experiences "model failures." In the old days, we just called them "intellectual challenges," but the new term better captures what happens. Our brains anticipate something because of the models they hold, but they get a surprise instead.

It's tough to get humans to pay attention when any paradigm doesn't work because we face too many breakdowns to notice all of them. The model failures must be bold and a little shocking. They should spark concern, but not too much. So the successful learning environments often jolt students just enough to trigger their interest without plunging them into a cycle of worry, despair, anxiety, and depression. That is a delicate matter that makes teaching more like the art of playing the violin than the science of mixing chemicals. The best teachers raise questions that challenge but do not threaten—or, at least, not too much. They intrigue and fascinate, perhaps serving some need to know. Surprise, love, and mystery often fuel the emotions that motivate deep learning and any conceptual shifts.

Many teachers can't raise those good questions, however, because they suffer from what we call the "expert's curse." Think of it this way. As a scholar in your field, you are currently interested in certain questions because you were once intrigued with another inquiry. You took up that previous problem after battling with a still earlier query, and so forth, back up through your own intellectual journey that may have begun when you first asked your parents, "Why?"

While you are currently deep underground digging at what you know to be valuable intellectual or professional ore, your students are standing on the surface wondering why anyone in their right mind would be so far underground. To reach them, experts must retrace their intellectual steps and find questions that will capture learners' interest and ultimately pull them into a more advanced conversation. That's not easy to do. But it is the power of questions and problems that drives deep learning.

Any learner must remain highly motivated to stick with the arduous process of building a new paradigm and thinking about its implications and applications. To maintain such dedication, students must believe that their learning will make a difference to themselves and others. The change should have a purpose that satisfies intellectually and emotionally. People are most likely to attempt deep learning approaches when they are trying to answer questions or solve problems that they regard as important, intriguing, beautiful, or fun. Altruism, a concern for others, can play a powerful role in stimulating the hard work necessary.

To learn deeply we must intend to do so. Humans are born with insatiable curiosities. But here's the rub. Our desire to do something will go down if we have the feeling that someone else controls us. Every effort to force students to pay attention and reexamine their existing paradigms will backfire. Extrinsic motivators (for example, grades) tend to suppress internal desires. Maybe we are just ornery creatures, but we don't like to lose what psychologists call a locus of control. We also don't like to do something when we believe we can't do it. One way of thinking about this process is that the motivation to learn has at least three components: purpose; a belief that we can learn; and the conviction that we control when, where, and what we decide to learn.

In school not all students will even try to understand and to think about implications and applications, to theorize about possibilities. Many of them will focus instead only on passing the course ("surface learners") or making the highest grade ("strategic learners"), and neither of these types has the intention to learn deeply. Students become a particular type of learner because of conditioning, however, not as a result of their personalities or intelligence. Maybe they didn't have parents who invited a snake charmer to a first-grade birthday party or read to them every night. Maybe instead an aunt, uncle, or teacher hammered them about "being smart." Perhaps a whole series of teachers fostered a focus on grades rather than learning. The conditioning occurs throughout our society. A barrage of movies, songs, television programs, economic pressures, and even friends can stimulate those surface or strategic approaches. The path students take isn't written into their DNA or a reflection of their abilities. Some highly capable humans can develop predominantly strategic or surface intentions with the wrong experiences in life.

Schools make big contributions to this phenomenon. Some kinds of assessment can leave the impression that learning consists of recognizing correct answers on multiple-choice exams. Highly competitive emphasis on grades can deny students a sense of control over their own education and reduce their motivation to do the hard work of deep learning. Without deep intentions students resort to memorizing correct answers and procedures that will have little sustained, positive, or substantial influence on the way they will subsequently think, act, or feel.

Even when students build perfectly acceptable mental models, "learning" doesn't always produce good problem solving. When people learn some new information or ideas, they do not necessarily develop the capacity to use it in different kinds of situations. Medical students who memorize reams of information on the body and can even explain physical functions in gory detail cannot always use that knowledge to make a proper differential diagnosis or devise a novel and effective treatment for a complex ailment. This "transfer problem," as learning scholars call it, can bedevil the most dedicated students. Knowing a body of information needed to solve a problem does not necessarily entail the capacity to unlock its puzzle.

It is, of course, easier to solve problems someone else has already mastered. We can go to school on their work, learning to apply standard answers to known types of difficulties. But we live in a world of rapid change with new kinds of trouble no one has seen. Back in the 1980s some Japanese theorists saw two kinds of experts: routine ones who know many if not all the standard answers, and adaptive wizards who also know those common routines but have additional powers. They have both the ability and the attitude to recognize and relish the opportunity and necessity for invention. The adaptives like taking on those unique difficulties, and they are good at it.[3]

How then do people learn to become that kind of expert? Practice and feedback. Lots of opportunity to speculate with problems *they* have never encountered before.

Imagine, for example, two math classes. In one, the instructor performs algebra in front of the students (that's what often happens in many math classes). The pupils take notes and then try to apply the procedures to equations they encounter on their homework and tests. In the second type, the teacher gives students conceptually rich and fascinating problems that are slightly more advanced than anything they've tried before and invites them to invent their own solutions, perhaps working in groups. They haven't encountered the problem, and no one is there to solve it for them. They are invited to become adaptive experts. The teacher becomes a guide by the side rather than a sage on the stage, ready to ask a question to help students think past some conceptual difficulty rather than performing the problem for them.

Manu Kapur, at the National Institute of Education in Singapore, discovered the secrets of what he calls "productive failure."[4] Students "who engaged in problem solving before being taught," he concluded from an elaborate comparison study, "demonstrated significantly greater conceptual understanding" than did people who received "direct instruction" on how to do problems. Furthermore, the ninth graders who struggled to invent solutions, made mistakes and corrected them, could more easily solve "novel problems" than could "those who were taught first."

All the learning we have discussed involves memory. But people are most likely to remember what they have used and maybe invented, not what they have had drilled into their heads. Marshall and Albert began learning French in the sixth grade, but six weeks into the fall semester, Albert's parents moved to Paris, taking the young boy and his sister with them. By the time he graduated from high school, Marshall had taken six years of French, memorizing vocabulary and usually acing the exams. His parents drilled him, using all the sophisticated procedures of spaced repetition. It doesn't take much imagination or insight, however, to guess which one of the two boys read, spoke, and wrote French with almost perfect fluency when they met for a reunion right before going off to college, and which one struggled to keep up with the chatter.[5] People learn deeply by doing in authentic situations.[6]

Students are more likely to remember what they understand. When we comprehend we make rich associations between ideas and information, and the network of connections we lay down in our brains enhances our memories. If through speculation, someone has invented a solution, that person can more easily recall its steps and why you should take those steps than if the person had picked up the solution from watching someone else perform the process.

To engage in the difficult business of learning deeply people often need help. This is a tricky matter because it doesn't mean simply providing them with "correct answers." That's largely what traditional lectures do. Rather students require assistance in constructing insights and inventing ways to solve problems. Maybe the help comes as a question that sparks thought and understanding, rather than as an explanation. Students need an opportunity to try, fail, and receive feedback. Novice learners who have recently struggled with the same problems can often provide the best assistance to the absolute beginner. Those novice learners remember the tough parts while experts have forgotten the potholes along the route. The scholar often uses shortcuts in thinking while the neophyte may need to think through every step. But students also need far more than intellectual assistance. Emotional help is often crucial, not simply because humans harbor anxiety and misgivings, but also because struggling with deeply held paradigms can prove traumatic.

If learners must meet new standards, they may require assistance in understanding them and practice in applying the criteria to their own work. To remain motivated, people need to believe that their work will matter and that it will have lasting consequences for themselves and perhaps for others, and that the standards will be applied honestly and fairly. That process begins with clearly defined standards and lots of practice in comprehending the criteria.

Going Bad

What can go wrong beyond those pitfalls we've already mentioned? Let's explore threats that emerge from a couple of strong social forces. You may have noticed that we've made no mention of "intelligence" as a factor in learning, even though many traditional educators have relied almost exclusively on that concept to explain who succeeds and who comes up short. "It doesn't matter what I do in class," a math professor in the Courant Institute of Mathematical Sciences at New York University once told us. "The gifted students will get it, and the weak ones won't." This genius theory of education pervades schools on all levels, but it doesn't set well with everyone, or with some important research on human development.

When Carol Dweck finished her doctorate in psychology at Yale in 1972, she had one burning question on her mind. Why do some people melt in the face of failure while others zip right through adversity, even using it to improve their work? "I grew up in an . . . era that worshipped IQ," she told her campus newspaper recently, "and thought that" it largely determined your future. "My sixth grade teacher even seated us around the room in IQ order."[7] After more than forty years of research, the Lewis and Virginia Eaton Professor of Psychology at Stanford University has found that people's *conception of intelligence* has more influence than does anything you might measure as an IQ. "If you believe your intelligence is just a fixed trait," Dweck explained, you're likely to develop a sense of helplessness. If you think you don't know and can't learn, you're not apt to try something. But that feeling of helplessness can also emerge among people who think they are smart and also believe human brains can't grow.

Imagine a kid who has heard all his life, "You're really brilliant." He may then build his whole self-image around being a genius. Soon he may grow afraid to try anything new for fear he will fail and prove he's not so sharp after all. In contrast, "if you think . . . your talents, abilities and intelligence . . . can grow" then "you want to jump in and develop them," Dweck summarized. That can make a huge difference in someone's learning.

Thus, people who believe their intelligence is fixed for life often have difficulty embracing failure. They tend to recoil from their mistakes rather than learning from them. If a teacher tries to put them in a situation where their mental models do not work (creating a "model failure"), they resist and learn little because they cannot stand to fail. Meanwhile, students flourish with challenges to their thinking if they believe intelligence can grow.

Fortunately, Dweck and her colleagues have found that fixed and growth mindsets, as she calls them, come from conditioning, not from any innate qualities of someone's brain or personality. They can change. In a series of powerful experiments, she and her colleagues discovered certain experiences that cause children to develop one mindset or another. People who hear a steady stream of *person praise* ("how smart you are"), for example, often grow a fixed view of intelligence and a feeling of helplessness, while those who encounter task-oriented feedback ("you must have worked hard on this") build a strong growth mindset. In her research, Dweck found that students with the fixed view gave up easily, sometimes complaining that they were "not a math person" (or "writing person"), and growing easily bored with school, especially if they failed. Furthermore, and this is probably the most disturbing result, their abilities actually decline in the face of failure. Meanwhile, students with growth perspectives sail right through adversity and often deliberately seek hard challenges.[8]

None of this means we've discovered a magic cure. We continue to face enormous problems in changing anyone's mindset, especially as people grow older. Yet some of the Super Courses we will explore have devised some innovative approaches with promising results. They deserve additional trials and careful research to find out what works and what doesn't.

Stereotype Threat

Joshua Aronson and Claude Steele found different social forces shaping learning outcomes.[9] If you are a member of a group about which there is a popular negative stereotype, that common belief can influence your performance in school and elsewhere even if you personally reject it. Obviously, if you accept the negative idea that "people like you" can't do something, you will give up easily. Failure will become a self-fulfilling prophecy. But you don't have to accept the negative stereotype for it to affect you. On a subconscious level it may simply bother you that others think of you in terms of that popular image, even if you never internalize a sense of inferiority. In a silent and unspoken dash to exonerate yourself and others, tensions grow. Nervousness increases, and your academic performance tanks.

Margaret Shih knew that research but asked a brand new question. We have lots of stereotypes in our culture, she noticed. Some positive. Others more negative. Many people believe, she pointed out, that women can't do higher mathematics as well as men can. At the same time, many Americans also think that people of Asian descent possess some kind of "math superiority" gene. But what about Asian American women? Which stereotype, negative or positive, will influence their performance?[10]

To find out, she created three comparable groups of Harvard undergraduates. They were all females and Asian Americans, were majors in mathematically oriented fields, and wanted to attend graduate school in their discipline. In other words, she had fairly reliable evidence that if she gave the advanced portion of the Graduate Record Examination in math to everyone in her sample, the group performances would be statistically indistinguishable. But that's not what happened. Shih's intervention changed the outcome. It was her experiment.

She asked each woman in her three groups to fill out a questionnaire before taking the test. It looked fairly innocent: name, telephone number, and so forth, about a dozen items of seemingly innocuous questions. But the first group had an inquiry designed to trigger a subconscious reminder of their gender. The second group didn't have that question but had another one meant to prompt a reminder of ethnicity. Psychologists call this process making something salient. The third group had neither of the subconscious triggers. You now have the data you need to predict how the three groups did. The group that had the reminder about ethnicity performed better than the other two; the one with the prompt about gender came in last. Little things a teacher does can have a huge influence on students' learning, lives, and academic performance. So much for the genius theory so popular at places like the Courant Institute![11]

PART II

THE COURSES

Prologue

With all these concepts and research considerations in mind, we can easily predict the kinds of Super Courses that have emerged. You will see the key components repeatedly as we examine specific examples in part 2 of this book.[1] They are the same elements that Paloma, Adam, Nate, and Junhui experienced. Computers played only a supporting role at best, and sometimes no part at all. In the chapters that follow, these conditions manifest themselves in multiple ways, and it is a rich and generous use and combination of these ingredients that make each course work. Sprinkling one or two of them over a standard syllabus would no more turn the trick than would dusting a liver sandwich with brown sugar turn it into a cherry pie.

Essential Elements

1. Center the course—not on topics—but on big, fascinating, important, and often beautiful questions and problems. These inquiries should spark intrinsic interest. What causes wars? How have societies dealt with pandemics before? How can I become more creative? Why do businesses fail, or succeed? What causes change in human history? Why are there so many different species of plants and animals? How can I understand myself? What is my purpose in life? How do you calculate the area under a curve? Why are some people (and societies) rich and others poor? Can human life on earth survive, given the changes in the environment? How does the physical universe work? What is the biggest question your course and discipline will help students to address? Where and how are students likely to encounter the question or problem? What caused that disaster, or windfall? As we frame the question, keep in mind the "expert's curse" we talked about in chapter 1. Frame the question with words and images that speak to your learners.

Use problem or project-based approaches in which students tackle those questions in steps within small heterogeneous groups while each person has the opportunity to display his or her own thinking.

2. Let students try, fail, receive feedback, and try again before anyone makes a judgment about their work (grades them). Encourage productive failure. In short, give them the same kind of environment professors expect for their own learning when they do research.

3. Allow, encourage, and facilitate collaboration with other learners struggling with the same problems. Build groups heterogeneously not homogeneously.

4. Let students speculate even before they learn, inventing ways to solve problems.

5. Find out what kind of paradigms the students already hold that you will want them to question or abandon, and give them repeated explicit yet friendly challenges to those mental models (put them in situations where their existing paradigms do not work).

6. Give students emotional, physical, and intellectual assistance when they need it.

7. Help them care when their fundamental paradigms do not work.

8. Explicitly try to give students a sense of control over their own learning. Give them meaningful choices.

9. Make sure their work is considered fairly and honestly.

10. Help them believe that their efforts will matter to themselves and others.

11. Explicitly encourage people to believe that intelligence and abilities are expandable.

12. Show faith in students' ability to learn and act as if your job is to foster each individual's educational growth rather than to divide the sheep from the goats. Help people in the class believe that they can learn.

13. Recognize the rich diversity of backgrounds class members will bring to the questions and problems, and integrate those into the course.

14. Give students a chance to do the discipline before they fully know it, discovering the basic information while they engage in problem solving, analyzing, synthesizing, evaluating, theory making, and the discovery of ambiguities and contingencies in anything they study. Get them physically, emotionally, and mentally involved in the process.

15. Give them chances to learn inductively not just deductively, moving from the specific to the general rather than the general to the specific.

16. Appeal to their emotions as well as to their intellect.

17. Help them to help other people to learn.

18. Invest students with a goal that is larger than the class—maybe even bigger than the discipline—and in the process of pursuing that objective, they learn. We call that educational circumstance a "passion-driven adventure."

Supporting Elements

19. Bring multiple disciplines together to address the questions and problems.

20. Use the arts to raise the questions.

21. Deliver most of the information and ideas learners will need with reading opportunities rather than lectures. Then help students learn to read deeply using a social reading program like Perusall (see chapter 9).

Most important, in a Super Course version of a natural critical learning environment, student groups tackle questions and challenges they find intrinsically interesting, important, and beautiful. The challenges put them in a situation where some important paradigm doesn't work as well as they thought. People in the class learn to think critically, which means to reason from evidence and concepts, examine the quality of their own thinking, make crucial decisions, and defend them rationally and articulately. The whole experience leads them to ask probing and insightful questions and make improvements in their reasoning as they think.

Learners receive feedback on their efforts, develop the ability to provide meaningful responses to themselves and others, and—when they sometimes come up short—can try again. In that environment, everyone receives respect and encouragement for the unique perspectives, qualities, and creativity that each person brings to the conversation. We'll continue to expand the ideas of this potent learning experience as we examine the role of what one teacher called the dynamic powers of our minds.[2]

We live in troubled times. As Cathy Davidson put it, all our efforts to plan "will be wasted" if we do not recognize "that our students are learning from a place of dislocation, anxiety, and trauma. So are we." The Distinguished Professor of English at the City University of New York wrote in 2020, "Before we even think about a syllabus, think about what it means to be a student. Now."[3]

CHAPTER THREE

A New Kind of University

One day in the 1940s, according to a widely repeated academic story, Albert Bandura, a psychologist at Stanford University, watched as people learned how to handle snakes. When they practiced on toy reptiles, nearly everyone mastered the technique—grab it by the back of the neck. Yet when they switched to real serpents, some students couldn't do it. To make it work, people needed to learn the right procedure, but they also had to believe that they could use it with precision before they would try and succeed.

Bandura saw in this carnival scene a broader pattern of human behavior and attitude. He noticed that some people believe that with the right effort they can influence and even control the challenges they face. Bandura called those beliefs "perceived self-efficacy."[1] People with those conceptions focus on how to solve a problem and how they can learn to do so. Others think about what they can't do and how tough it will be to find an answer. They often fail and give up easily.

In more than fifty years of research Bandura and his colleagues have found that people with high measures of self-efficacy take control of their own education and learn deeply while others don't. They also found—and here's the big point—that teachers and schools can influence how much of this powerful quality students develop.[2]

What if you took what the psychologists have learned about self-efficacy and used it to design new and better college experiences for students? Maybe even a whole new kind of higher education institution? That's precisely what a group of engineering educators in

Massachusetts began doing in the early 2000s. They also listened carefully to the research on human motivation. Why do some students stop caring while others remain highly driven? Why do some people become deep learners, fascinated with what they study, while others turn into strategic players at best, focused only on making high grades or just passing the course?

All teachers worth their salt have longed for classrooms full of learners who take a deep personal interest and drive themselves to do well. Those self-starters often seem like mythical creatures to many academics. "You're either born with that ambition, or you're not," concluded one professor, "and I haven't encountered many in my classes who have it." The Massachusetts pioneers, however, thought they could use the research on motivation and self-efficacy to cultivate students with strong desires to learn deeply, rather than just waiting for them to show up. Perhaps most important and revolutionary, they turned to the work of Edward Deci and Richard Ryan, two iconoclastic psychologists.

The Olin Experience

With a huge endowment, Olin College of Engineering emerged in the early 2000s on seventy-five acres it purchased from Babson College in Needham, Massachusetts. Richard Miller, former dean of the College of Engineering and professor of mechanical engineering at the University of Iowa, became employee number one in 1999. As president of the emerging school at Olin, he had this idea that learning environments ought to be created around the research on human learning and motivation. What a novel idea for an institution built on the power of research.

Jonathan Stolk and Robert Martello both came to the experimental institution early in its history but with very different backgrounds. Stolk studied materials science and engineering at the University of Texas, while Martello went through MIT's program in the History and Social Study of Science and Technology. They both wanted to use the science of learning to address some of the challenges of education, and like most of their colleagues at Olin they had found great results in project-based learning (PBL). After ten years of teaching classes with PBL principles, Stolk teamed with his historian colleague to address a serious challenge many educators face and engineering professors encounter in spades.

Simply put, the problem is this: we live in a rapidly changing world. In engineering that means that technology is evolving so quickly that no student can rely solely on what he or she picks up in college. Engineering students and professionals must become lifelong learners, constantly updating skills and knowledge. In other words, they must be able and driven to take control of their ongoing education and find ways to learn throughout life.

In other fields, this may mean simply that no one can possibly learn enough in a measly four years. If a college education doesn't leave people with a driving curiosity that feeds a lifetime of study, creativity, and contributions, it stunts their growth and robs them and society of their potential. Any course that doesn't leave students with a burning desire to learn more and the facilities to do so has failed in ways that may not always be recognized.

These matters weighed heavily on Jonathan Stolk's mind as he prepared to teach an introductory materials science course at Olin. So did another child of constant change. By the early twenty-first century, if not long before, engineers could no longer ignore the long-term consequences of their inventions. Technological change flowed so fast that any results could trigger an avalanche of problems. In the early twentieth century, major cities, for example, needed faster transportation and an end to the twenty thousand horses that yearly dropped dead on the streets of New York City alone, but the solution, the internal combustion gasoline engine, spawned air pollution and a host of deadly issues. The history of technology abounds with numerous other examples of one answer causing a new problem.

Stolk and Martello knew these stories and wanted to address them. They spoke to us of the "societal contexts of technologies" and of "ethical decision" making.[3] They also recognized that if you teach only the techniques of engineering, you can strip the discipline of its broader appeal and increase the chances that students will not take a deep interest and approach. The Olin colleagues put it this way: traditional engineering classes "often present technical topics in a completely de-contextualized manner." It's not surprising then that students "may have difficulty identifying either personal or societal value in their learning tasks."[4] Therefore, people who go through a traditional engineering curriculum frequently will not emerge as lifelong learners filled with a strong desire to learn and to contribute to society.

Furthermore, the problems of engineering had become so complex, no one person could solve them alone. Much the same could be said about any intellectual or artistic endeavor. Great ideas and creative works emerge at crossroads where artists, philosophers, historians, scientists, and others can feed on the results of many perspectives. Such a world requires good abilities to communicate along with the more traditional engineering skills from math and science. In short, Stolk and Martello wanted their students to emerge with a lifetime commitment to learning, an ability and desire to work in teams, superior "contextual understanding," excellent communication powers, and "rigorous quantitative and qualification skills," as they put it to us.

And they wanted them to have fun doing so. That last part about fun turned out to be more important than you might suspect.

The Motivation Trap

For many centuries, humans believed that the best way to increase any activity was to reward it—or punish people who failed. Lots of institutions built themselves on that bedrock. Schools certainly did. Teachers used grades to honor students who studied hard and passed the tests, and to reprimand those who didn't. As we noted earlier, "It will be on the exam" became a common way to command attention and push interest in a subject.

Some of the social science research coming out in the mid-twentieth century seemed to support that practice. Under the influence of Burrhus Frederic Skinner, one of the major scholars of psychology, researchers had been doing experiments on rats running through mazes. When they gave the rodents cheese (a reward), the little critters seemed more motivated and found their way through the puzzle more quickly. From his post as Edgar Pierce Professor of Psychology at Harvard University, Skinner defined orthodoxy on motivation: to move someone to action you need rewards and punishments.

In the early 1970s just as Skinner neared retirement, a young scientist at the University of Rochester began poking holes in this behaviorist thinking that Skinner had defined and led for so many years. Edward Deci had two simple yet revolutionary ideas. Let's skip the rats and do experiments on human beings, and let's look not just at the immediate results of some carrot-and-stick approach but at what it will do to a person's long-term motivation. Sure, someone might act if promised a big reward for doing so or punishment for not. But what will happen to that subject's interest later on? After receiving their "cheese" or feeling the lash of their "whip," will students or workers grow more fond of the activity and take it up spontaneously? Or lose interest?

A sizeable body of culture handed down through moral teaching, poetry, and little sayings had taught, as Alexander Pope put it in 1734, "Just as the twig is bent, the tree's inclined." To many people that meant a literal bending that forced children to conform. "To my parents," reported one colleague, "the bent twig ended up across my backside if I didn't do my homework." Beginning in the 1970s Deci and an army of researchers who soon followed him uncovered considerable evidence that the old carrot-and-stick approach actually diminished long-term interest.

When Richard Ryan came into Deci's lab as a graduate student a few years later, the mentor and his chief disciple fashioned a broad theory of human nature that would help explain the behaviors they were seeing in multiple experiments. The dynamic duo from upstate New York had made what seemed like an outlandish claim that humans are naturally curious creatures who love to learn.

But how then do you explain classrooms full of bored and disengaged students? "Why do so many enrollees display no interest in anything," more than one teacher has complained "Why do I have to browbeat them and threaten their grades to get them to read daily assignments?"

The answer to that key question lies in understanding human nature and how it interacts with society. People have three basic psychological needs, Deci and Ryan explained, that go beyond the biological drives for sex and food. We are animals who like to feel competent at doing something. People are ornery enough that we love to control our own lives (which is not the same as wanting to be a lone wolf, operating independent of anyone else, and it's certainly not a reflection of some innate selfishness). Finally, we have a burning desire to relate to other people, to be a part of something larger than ourselves. In our drive to relate, we tend to help our fellow human beings; and in our desire for autonomy, we want to choose what we do, how we get it done, when, and with whom.

When those basic needs of competence, autonomy, and relatedness get supported and nurtured, the Rochester duo concluded, humans get all sorts of benefits, including happiness and a healthy curiosity about the world. When they get crushed and denied, people can lose interest in nearly everything, including school. Deci and Ryan identified two types of motivation, one that came from deep in your body and brain. In that type, to paraphrase an old adage, "if you lead a thirsty horse to water, it will drink because . . . well, it's thirsty." As they explained in 2008, "people are by nature active and self-driven, curious and interested, vital and eager to succeed because success itself is personally satisfying and rewarding." They called this type "autonomous." You don't need to spark it in students; it just happens if you show them something they find interesting, and they feel in control, related, and competent.

But you can kill or diminish it with the other type of stimulus, which they called "controlled." Humans can be "alienated and mechanized," the Rochester scientists wrote, "or passive and disaffected," and that's likely to happen if they feel manipulated by those controlling motivations: a teacher who simply threatens them with punishment (a low grade) if they don't learn something, for example.[5]

Their theory and research identified a powerful struggle "between people's inherent active nature and the social environments that either support or thwart that nature." Human beings "need to feel competent, autonomous, and related to others," they proclaimed while standing on a mountain of empirical evidence and inductive reasoning. When the learning environment helps people satisfy these "three basic psychological needs," it will foster "optimal motivation." Students will be happier, more engaged. When the learning environment doesn't, they will become grade-grubbing strategic learners at best and alienated and depressed dropouts at worst.

Think about how we often react if students "don't get the work done." We pile on the punishments, lower their grades, and wonder why the class has lost its initiative. We assume that if students have an interest in something, we can spark even more fascination with our "requirements" and "assignments." Even the language we use suggests that teachers, not personal curiosity or intrigue, dictate learning.

Yet when Deci stood before the Canadian Psychological Association in 2007, he could point with pride at the more than one hundred published studies that supported his theory: external incentives usually decreased long-term internal motivation "across a range of ages, activities, rewards, and reward contingencies,"[6] especially when people feel manipulated and controlled by those prizes and penalties.

Does that mean you can't give students feedback or correct their mistakes? Not at all. It all depends on what you intend, which will influence how students feel about your "help." If people in your class think you just want to dictate their lives and education with assignments and requirements, if they see you as a "control freak" who wants to make yourself look good, your feedback will likely diminish their interest. If they feel supported by your "informational" comments, their fascination and commitment could zoom. In other words, does the feedback feel like helpful information or a judgment?

The master from Rochester summarized the research this way: "when people are rewarded, threatened, surveilled, or evaluated, they tend to feel pressured and controlled, and that diminishes satisfaction of their autonomy needs." Other researchers talked about people feeling a shift in the "locus of control." We love the way psychologists talk, but we might put it a little differently: If students feel manipulated and controlled, their long-term interests will decline.

Sometimes something as simple as giving people choices can make a huge difference. So can the opportunity to try, fail, receive feedback, and try again. It's all part of changing the "social climates" that can seem either "pressuring and controlling" or "supportive and informational."

In the classroom, teachers are often like weather gods who create those climates, not so much as willful acts but through the power of their own conceptions and attitudes.

If teachers believe that students are fundamentally lazy and must be forced to learn, for example, those conceptions will shine through everything they say and do and foster the negative social thunder clouds against which Deci and Ryan warned. In short, the ability to see a vibrant five-year-old inside everyone in a class makes all the difference.

Teacher Beliefs Play a Big Role

We started this chapter with a promise to look at Super Courses at Olin College of Engineering. Professors Jonathan Stolk and Robert Martello still wait in the wings to show us what kind of courses they created, but before they make their grand entrance, one more important idea from the research on human learning.

What teachers believe about the people in their classes will affect the students' motivation, grades, and learning. When we did our initial research on what the best teachers do, we certainly found that pattern. "The key to understanding the best teaching," we wrote in 2004, "can be found not in particular practices or rules but in the *attitude* of the teachers, in their *faith* in their students' abilities to achieve, in their *willingness* to take their students seriously and to let them assume control of their own education, . . . and from a mutual respect and agreement between students and teachers."[7]

When Mary Murphy, a professor in the department of psychological and brain science at Indiana University, and her colleagues tackled the issue more recently, they uncovered a similar pattern. They found that science, math, and engineering professors who subscribe to the genius theory of learning—that either you are smart or you're not—"inspire less student motivation in their classes" than do those who think that mental abilities can grow.[8] The people in the classes of genius theory teachers do less well than do the pupils who study with people who believe that intelligence can increase. These students have less motivation and probably learn less.

The pattern prevails regardless of almost any way you might chunk the student body: "race," ethnicity, gender, or family income. "On average," the researchers concluded, "all students performed more poorly in STEM courses (science, technology, engineering, and math) taught" by professors who believe that people "have a certain amount of intelligence, and they really can't do much to change it."[9] That lower performance emerges regardless of the nature of the students. But underrepresented minority students incur the biggest negative blow. Why? That's where our earlier discussion of "stereotype threat" comes into play.

Remember from chapter 2, we mentioned the research finding that negative beliefs within your culture about "your kind of people" can harm your performance even if you reject those popular prejudices. On a subconscious level, it simply bothers you that other people may think of you in terms of some negative cliché. Your tensions grow, and your physical and mental abilities suffer.[10]

In addition to other disadvantages you may face (poverty and lack of adequate schooling, for example, and other obstacles), the old bromides your broader culture may have about you and your community can cut into your learning. African Americans, Hispanics, and Native Americans in the United States live in a society filled with popular views about which social groups are more or less likely to have ability in STEM. Females can face centuries of ideas that their gender is ill-suited to the rigors of science. Even European American males who come from families without much money can suffer the sting of prejudices. When society asks, "if you're so smart, why aren't you rich," the implication is clear. If you are poor, you must not be as bright as others. Such hackneyed ideas can deflate performances.

If you want to do well in school but you also know that some people do not expect you to excel, you face extra tensions to prove that you can learn. The more you care, the more you feel the strain. For many students the additional pressure is simply too much. On average, victims of prejudice get lower grades in STEM classes, not because of some innate deficiency but in part because of the social forces of stereotype threat. A "performance gap" emerges between them and students who don't face the same negative images.

When those same pupils encounter a professor who thinks that intelligence is frozen and then communicates those fixed views in sometimes subtle cues, the negative consequences grow. The performance gap mushrooms. The Indiana study found achievement differences "in courses taught by more fixed mindset faculty were twice as large as those in courses taught by more growth mindset faculty."[11]

Back to Olin

Stolk and Martello have been waiting too long in the wings. Let's bring them out to learn more about how they used these ideas to create a powerful learning environment. The two Massachusetts professors thought they could stimulate greater motivation if courses integrated disciplines together, allowing students to see how the engineering knowledge related to broader issues and vice versa.

"We argue that improving cross-disciplinary connections between technical studies and societal contexts," they wrote, "may help spark the type of student engagement that leads to long-term growth."[12] To become interested deeply, the pupils needed "a sense of personal relevance" and had to see "broader value" for their engineering education. Could they gain both if they studied history and society while they learned materials science?

By the time the students reached the Stuff of History course that Stolk and Martello created, they had already experienced two years of project-based classes at Olin. But they had not engaged in the kind of interdisciplinary environment the Stuff course had in store for them.

On the first day of meetings, the students entered what Stolk told us was a "hybrid lab and project studio space." It had worktables and benches, surrounded by "laboratory equipment, including a fume hood, mechanical testers, and microscopes." Students sat in groups of four or five. Perhaps the most unusual sight was the pile of consumer products—"things you might expect to see going down the aisle at Walmarts, a hardware store, or Target." Tools, clothing, baby toys, and other consumer products piled on a table.

"Please come down to the front of the room," the two professors invite their students, "and select an item for your group that interests you, from the perspective of societal impact, or technology and design." They are told to start asking questions about it. What is it? What's its role in society? What values do we place on it? What economic and environmental impact does it have? What was used to make it? Why?

For thirty to forty minutes or more, students brainstorm about questions they could ask. In the process, they construct a basic outline of a project plan, and they continue that process over the next few days. If you studied this object for the next five weeks, what would you do, the professors asked? What questions would you raise? How would you answer those inquiries? In essence, the pupils plan the class and their learning. When the day is done, they have the option to continue with the object, pick another one, or abandon their learning entirely. No one chooses the latter, but in keeping with the motivation research, they have the autonomy to make choices. The people in the class take charge of their own education.

Stolk and Martello became resources, providing articles to read, both on the materials science and about the broader historical context. But at every step along the way, they were constantly caught in a gigantic struggle between giving students the freedom to learn and offering them the structures they will need to stay on the path toward success. Tipping too far to one side or the other could upset the applecart, sending its luscious cargo tumbling chaotically down slippery slopes.

Students design their projects and decide what they will pursue, what they will deliver, and how they will go about it each time they come to class, but the professors give them feedback, helping them to design something that will be productive and stay on course. The students have chosen to take the class, but can they design activities that will get them to London and not end up in Bristol? The first project is supposed to help them learn about atoms, ions, molecules, bonding, and structure, but will their road maps bring them through those cities?

As they embark on their journey, the class might look like "complete chaos, a free-for-all," with students moving hither and yon even from room to room to conduct experiments or collect data, and "Rob and I are running around like crazy," Jon Stolk recalled recently, "trying to facilitate their learning process." But there was method in their madness. Part of that method centered on the quest for fun.

You could feel it in the attitudes of the professors, in the voice tones and body language they used, in the words they chose, and even in the stories that circulated in the Olin culture. The young school had often mixed serious study with moments of relief and play when students could take a deep breath and relax before going on to the next challenge. At Olin, everyone knew the stories from the early days of the college when the faculty rented bouncy castles one day, placed them on the lawn, and invited students to break from their demanding routines and go a little wild.

But more of their approach centered on the right balance between freedom and the creation of a structure that would seem helpful and "informational" rather than controlling and directive. A key part of that symmetry came with the Weekly Assignment Document, or WAD as it came to be called. "We provide them with an overview of what we think they might need to be doing by this point," Stolk explained. The WAD offered a list of readings, some discussion questions, and "practice problems that will help them understand key concepts."

Notice how the professors discussed these instruments, providing both traditional language as transitions to a new world, and new words that smacked of fun and play, helpful guides, rather than the dreaded "homework" and all the emotional baggage wrapped up in that school-day nomenclature. In that atmosphere, the professors could offer "checkpoints" where students could "submit something to get feedback." During the first week, Stolk explained, "we might, for example, ask them to do some readings on the mechanical properties of their products, the stresses and strains operating." Students reply to a number of different prompts intended to help them understand how the ideas apply to their project. "These are individual submissions, and they receive low-stakes feedback on their answers. The process is highly formative rather than a summative judgment."

Keep in mind also that the course integrated what we have tradition-ally regarded as two separate disciplines: materials science and history. As they explore their modern product, people in the class also examine the "material and societal aspects of an ancient civilization." They re-search historical counterparts to their modern product and the issues that both ancient and contemporary societies have faced around their material culture. Through classroom discussions of Mesopotamia, Egypt, Mayan civilization, and Greece, Martello and Stolk help students see that their interests lie not just in history or engineering but in the chance to think critically about both and to find ways to communicate their thoughts. For five weeks, they work toward a "student presentation in a local art museum."

Over the semester, the students do two more projects. In the process, they gain increasing control over their time and "learning strategies." They also take on more sophisticated inquiries, building their sense of competence gradually. In the second project they analyze modern metal alloys, their structures and properties, and how they are processed, as any good materials scientist might do. But they also investigate Paul Revere's work. The famous American revolutionary had gained most of his notoriety for a supposed ride one night in 1775 to warn town folks in Lexington and Concord about advancing British troops, but much of his value to the rebellion against the Crown came "through his silver working, iron casting, bronze bell and cannon casting, and copper sheet rolling endeavors." As students learn more about material properties and how to analyze modern examples, they "reproduce some of Revere's work, examine the efficiency of his processes," and explore "the social context of one of his metallurgical endeavors."

The Final Project

That progression of greater sophistication and more autonomy contin-ued into the final five-week project. Students picked a contemporary materials science technology and explored why and how it emerged, what it changed, what questions or problems it raised, and how it related to "larger issues." What can we learn from its history? "Why is it significant?" What "environmental and/or ethical impacts" did the technology have?[13]

When they finished, they produced a "deliverable" of their "choosing that educates an audience about [their] technology, its context, its properties, the reasons for its properties, and its larger impacts." They could communicate in any manner they wished as long as they included a "written component" that contained, at minimum, around two thousand words. Choices and an invitation to take control. A rich experience for a lifetime of systematic study and learning.

CHAPTER FOUR

Books Behind Bars

"The humanities are not just dying," wrote Justin Stover, a lecturer at the University of Edinburgh in 2018; "they are almost dead."[1] For several decades, skeptics have made similar pronouncements. Enrollments have slipped. Career-minded students choose fields that promise jobs and high salaries while parents steer their children into medicine, business, law, engineering, or anything other than the humanities. J. K. Rowling, Harry Potter's creator, told Harvard graduates a few years ago that her parents hoped she would study something "useful," perhaps "a vocational degree" rather than the "classics corridor" she chose to travel.[2]

Observers have blamed the decline on everything from sun spots to broad social patterns. Noah Berlatsky, a freelance writer who penned a book on Wonder Woman among other feats, faults the rising cost of education. Because college is so devastatingly expensive these days, he argues, students have less financial independence. They must depend on their parents to help foot the swelling bill. Mom and Dad have always been more career-minded, Berlatsky concludes. With greater financial leverage over their children, they can now impose a "practical" bent on their curiosity-driven sons and daughters.[3]

Even if we dismiss Berlatsky's explanation, it's still clear teachers in the humanities face a tough row to hoe. Yet they are not alone in encountering new challenges. Other fields may not be losing students, but they still face issues that cloud their skies. In the wake of the 2020 pandemic the very existence of organized education has come into play. We live in a world that increasingly asks if school (especially the university experience) is worth the expense and effort. Furthermore, a growing chorus of critics has questioned how much students actually learn from the classes they take. Does that university or secondary education change the way people think, act, and feel? How much does the learning influence the way people solve problems, invent, understand, and communicate? Does it expand or destroy intellectual curiosity, or the capacity to tackle fuzzy problems? Does it foster moral behavior?

A Revolution of Rising Expectations

Even where there is no sense of crisis, a revolution of rising expectations has swept across schools around the world. Demands of our complex times keep indicating that old habits of teaching and standards of learning will no longer suffice. The rush online in 2020 revealed a plethora of problems with the old pedagogy. Because we now know more about how our brains work, professors can envision creating a school experience to achieve far more than we did in the past. An international conversation between scholars and learning researchers has sparked a wave of exceptional innovations. We've personally witnessed that revolution rumbling across Europe, Australia, Africa, North and South America, the Middle East, and East Asia.[4]

We can begin to grasp the revolution that Super Courses have fashioned by looking not at the worst of traditional models but at some of the best. That way we can better see the giant changes that the new breed of educational experiences has created. One prominent scholar of Russian literature and highly lauded teacher from the old school, for example, talks about how he *reads expressively* in class and takes students through key passages in hopes they will understand what is important because they *follow* his process. In that traditional pedagogy students remain passive vessels waiting for someone with golden tones to fill their minds.

With that approach, this professor has won teaching awards and even an endowed chair of teaching excellence. Yet that same educator bragged and complained to us a few years ago, "I get some students excited, but you can't reach everybody. They're too caught up in making money."

Imagine a course that goes beyond the traditional lecture-discussion format and doesn't depend on spiffing up the classroom with vocal razzmatazz, an experience that draws from the research on human learning and motivation. Andrew David Kaufman has created such a learning world with a Super Course in Russian literature at the University of Virginia. The model for what he calls "Books Behind Bars" offers promise for the humanities and other fields, including the sciences, engineering, business, and law, and it illustrates well the kind of revolution that is emerging.

Kaufman's course Books Behind Bars: Life, Literature, and Leadership employs the most powerful elements of the natural critical learning environment, building a beautiful model for service learning[5] courses in almost any discipline and engaging students headed into a variety of careers. We chose this class as a prime model for a Super Course because of its broad and powerful implications.

Fundamentally, it helps undergraduates at UVA learn by becoming teachers, by struggling to foster the deep moral and intellectual growth of other people, and in one of the most difficult environments one might imagine. To achieve that end, the program utilizes a host of ingenious techniques. While we cannot possibly capture all that it does, we can identify several specific principles the course employs.

The Invitation

Much of Kaufman's success depends on a strong invitation rather than stiff requirements, giving students a potent sense of control over their own education. He entices people to grapple with some of the most fundamental questions of life: "Who am I? Why am I here? Given that I will die someday, what kind of life do I want to live?"

If those don't seem like the kind of inquiries that capture college students, look again. When a group of scholars at the University of California in Los Angeles investigated, their seven-year nationwide study found that 80 percent of entering freshmen across the United States wanted college to help them address some of the big "spiritual" questions about the purpose of life. Two-thirds of them said "that it is either 'very important' or 'essential' that college 'helps you develop your personal values' and 'enhances your self-understanding'" in life.[6]

Yet we also know that such questions can go unheard, sparking few if any students to engage in them. Kaufman succeeds because he begins to rebuild the whole structure of motivation within the classroom. Much of traditional education relies on fear and power to stimulate interest in learning ("it will be on the test"). Teachers give assignments and use the grade to coerce students to complete them (even when courses appeal to curiosity, the fear factor is often still there). The research suggests this is a recipe for disaster, or at least for churning out surface or strategic learners.

As we studied Andy's course over the last decade—interviewing him and his students, following their careers, watching films of the experience he creates, reading through the materials he designed for students' learning, and hearing him discuss the class with other faculty members and on national television interviews—it has become increasingly clear that the extraordinary power his course musters rises from a different kind of motivational structure. He takes seriously the considerable body of evidence[7] showing that extrinsic motivators will actually decrease intrinsic interests, especially if people feel manipulated by those outside forces. The UVA professor appeals unabashedly to one of the most internal of possible drives, a sense of altruism, a desire to help other people. And it works.

Consider how the Virginian introduces students to this phenomenal experience and invites them to the table. He asks them, first, to apply to enroll. Thus, he knows a great deal about each student long before the first day of class. When they do seek admission, he sends them a letter with this enticing sentence: "You will grapple," he writes, "in a profound and personal way with timeless human questions by reading and discussing classical works of Russian literature *with youth at a maximum security juvenile correctional center.*"

That last part changes everything, putting students in charge of their own education and in the service of others. They will go into a maximum-security correctional facility, housing people not much younger than themselves who are, for most University of Virginia students, quite different than their usual friends on campus. A sobering adventure. (Virginia calls its young prisoners "residents.") Lots of schools offer courses to incarcerated people. Few put undergraduates in charge of conducting those classes.

The experience offers students an opportunity to help a special population learn deeply, and it is the power of that chance that first drives their interest, commitment, and growth. But the class does not just coach college undergraduates to deliver powerful lectures before a truly captive audience. The people who take Books Behind Bars learn to create a highly interactive environment in which that special community takes control of its own learning. Everybody benefits. Both the UVA undergraduates and the correctional center residents develop a keen fascination with and understanding of the material, while their lives often become transformed on multiple levels.

The process works well because everyone enjoys a natural critical learning environment. Both college undergraduates and residents at Bon Air Juvenile Correctional Center develop new ideas about what it means to learn and how best to foster intellectual and personal growth in others.

The Power of Altruism

A small but growing body of research literature has begun to uncover how selflessness can motivate. You can hear its power reflected in how students describe the Kaufman experience. "We weren't reading to write papers just to sit on some professor's desk," one alum explained, "but to search for key meanings and personal connections," and to help people "who had been marginalized by the justice system."

We've long known that attempts to foster deep learning enhances our own comprehension. How many of us have said, I didn't really begin to understand my discipline deeply until I tried to teach it. Books Behind Bars gives undergraduates that "learning from teaching" experience in spades. Indeed it ups the ante, offering the UVA pupils an even richer dose of that old benefit.

Think about it. In the traditional form, professors deepen their learning because they write and deliver lectures. They perfect their explanations and arguments. In the Kaufman course, these undergraduates must do something even more challenging. They must design the questions and discussions that will help Bon Air residents actively construct a deep understanding, and in that task they expand their own insights. The Virginia undergrads struggle with the richer framework of a natural critical learning environment rather than with building a lecture and toying with the vocal inflections they might employ.

More Than the Spiritual

The UVA Russian professor links the spiritual goals to other ambitions in a potent setting and even gives students the chance to find their own emphasis in the course. Just listen to this robust list of promises:

- learn how to read in a whole new way (gaining powers of enjoyment and learning),
- emerge with leadership and facilitation skills,
- find ways to live creative lives,
- practice managing relationships with diverse groups of people,
- become creative problem-solvers (thinking "on the spot").

Students will face real crises and learn how to overcome them, struggle to find the right but delicate balance between freedom and structure, explore both Russian literature and the juvenile justice system (is it possible to "reform" young offenders; what experiences will do so best?). Both the residents and the undergraduates will discover "the connection between the study of literature and the world around them" and consider what it means to learn deeply and how best to foster it. In essence, every aspect of the experience says that if you take this course, you will not only benefit yourself (yes, even your career); you will also help other people, most of whom have never enjoyed the benefits, privileges, and opportunities that your life has given you.

Let us make clear that this Super Course does not abandon the traditional learning objectives of a college literature class. Indeed, it adds to them in ways that enhance their power and the likelihood that they will be achieved. The additions are like the spices that bring out the flavors of a nutritious meal, enticing a persnickety eater into a wholesome culinary delight. We'll see that same achievement across our curriculum of Super Courses. As they pursue the broader goals of the program, the people in Kaufman's class learn a great deal about Russian literature, the key authors, and the culture and history that produced the classics. But they also learn about themselves and others and develop important skills that can change their lives.

Students learn to do literary analysis by doing it, getting feedback, and helping other people develop the same abilities. In preparation, they read about the historical, personal, and cultural development of key Russian writers. They develop a new way to understand why anyone would study classic pieces of literature. Literary analysis becomes not an end in itself, however, but a means to explore profound questions of life, and to help other people do the same.

While many professors think first and foremost about their discipline, Kaufman begins with ideas about what it means to grow and mature and how his field might contribute to that broader end. The distinction is subtle but crucial. In other words, he starts with the students' educational needs and asks how the study of his field might help them achieve those goals. But he also ignites hidden passions, bringing them to the forefront of how the people in his class think, act, and feel. Perhaps most crucial, he helps them meet standards of thinking and action that are at the heart of living a reflective, moral, compassionate, and critically thinking life.

The students explore the juvenile justice system, the incarcerated population, and the use of arts in the rehabilitation process. They examine ideas on what it means to learn and how best to facilitate that development, digging into the literature on human learning. They consider how to stimulate and assist meaningful conversations and resolve conflicts. At each step along the way, a strong sense of caring about other people in a climate of self-control drives their passionate involvement.

It's More Than a Course

Many of the exercises and activities Kaufman designs for the class flow out of his intentions for the students and the residents. Most important, he wants the questions he raises to become not only the driving force across a semester but a sustained and substantial influence on the way the students will subsequently think, act, and feel. Books Behind Bars, he explains, is a "program that gives university students and incarcerated youth the transformative insights and practical tools necessary to lead lives of greater purpose and fulfillment." The course helps both groups build a new paradigm for themselves in which they constantly return to the big questions as they make important decisions. As these two communities—university students and young people living at Bon Air—struggle with those matters, their battles affect one another in a way that no lecture can achieve, no matter how brilliant and expressive.

Both the differences and the similarities that life brings to all the participants educate everyone. "It doesn't matter if you're a twenty-year-old college student or a twenty-year-old resident of a correctional center," the UVA teacher observes. "You know what it feels like to lose someone you love [or] struggle with family situations. You know what it feels like to try to search for your place in a world that doesn't always make that easy." Books Behind Bars harnesses the power that comes from that shared humanity.

CHAPTER FIVE

Diverse Classes

Every year, the pool of applicants in Books Behind Bars is five or six times larger than the number of places in the program. Students come from an array of backgrounds. Some are the children of privilege. Others worry that their working-class youth might keep them from "fitting in" among more well-to-do colleagues.

Emma, who took the course in its early existence, came from an affluent Maryland suburb. We first met her in our 2012 publication *What the Best College Students Do*. Her parents, both physicians, fostered curiosity and sent their daughters to posh private schools with small classes and lots of attention. She emerged from the Books Behind Bars experience increasingly aware of our common humanity and conscious of how much she controlled her own education.

Josh was the first student to live this educational experience from both sides of the fence. He had grown up in a tough neighborhood, on a diet of stolen cars and illegal drug use.[1] He and his buddies feasted on the narcotics, "fights, anger, [and] boredom." After his arrest and conviction for his youthful crime spree, he'd gone to jail. When he got out, he had enrolled at the university and joined nearly a hundred other people applying for one of the spots in Kaufman's class. He hadn't taken the class while he was in the correctional facility, but he'd heard about it from a buddy and now wanted to experience it from the other side. It was a life-changing endeavor.

It is the rich combinations that enhance the learning. As students look at the opportunities the course offers and the activities it entails, they can easily imagine not only that their vigorous participation and commitment will help them achieve noble ends but that its journey will be fascinating and far-reaching. That's what makes his invitation so effective.

What Happens in the Class

In the weeks before the group first meets, Kaufman sends students a series of documents that helps them comprehend the unusual nature of the adventure before them and the issues they will tackle. "I want to make sure they are prepared for what they will experience and understand its far-reaching value," he told us.

At their first meeting, the literature teacher begins to model the kind of interactions the students will have throughout the semester. They will do most of the talking and thinking when they meet on campus. The residents will later take up that charge. To spark that conversation, Kaufman tells them a brief story, maybe three minutes in length, illustrating how they can do the same once they are teaching. It is about a young man who read Leo Tolstoy's *The Kingdom of God Is Within You*, and how that writing changed his life. Only gradually do students realize that the tale is about Mohandas Gandhi and his path toward nonviolent activism.

Andrew Kaufman then asks the class to think about an art object or piece of literature that influenced them and to share their examples with each other. "The point of the exercise," he explains, "is to illustrate one of the principles of the class: Literature has the potential to change a person's life." Rather than offering a lecture on the beauty, importance, or intrigue of Russian novels and poems, he lets class members convince themselves and each other. In the process they entertain deep and meaningful questions. Rather than lectures or recitations that sparkle with the professor's inflections, Books Behind Bars constantly uses such interactive "exercises."

We do not want to reduce this super professor's approach to a series of techniques, but the brush strokes he employs do make a difference. While other teachers struggle with provoking conversations, Kaufman scores with a simple yet effective sequence that can be used in a variety of settings. His questions are open-ended and captivating. Students often write before they talk. They converse in pairs before opening up to the entire class or the professor. We saw that "think-pair-share" (and sometimes "square") approach across scores of highly effective discussion leaders.

Kaufman does convey some information orally, but he doesn't lecture. Instead, he sets up and stimulates a conversation that they will have. "I explain that Russian literature goes to the heart of some of the big accursed questions of life." He then gives them a list of ten such questions and asks each person to pick two that resonate personally with them and think about why. "That's where they begin the conversation with each other."

Andy has a background in drama. After finishing graduate work at Stanford, he joined the theater scene in Los Angeles, where he became a professionally trained actor. He is well spoken and articulate, and he uses his powers of oral expression to good ends. But he doesn't let that prowess dominate the process. After all, he's trying to help his undergraduates develop their own abilities to think and communicate orally. The people in his class must dominate the discourse and learn to listen to each other and the Bon Air residents with whom they will be working. None of that will happen if he simply performs his own orations, demonstrating the abilities he learned in California.

Preparing to Go to Jail

In the first four weeks of the class, students meet on campus to gear up for their work behind bars. Much of that time is spent exploring the literature, learning to analyze it and to generate conversations with each other. Students think about "themes and other aspects" of each work they read, much like "you would expect in a traditional literature class." Yet this course is different. It also asks students to consider "which characters or themes might resonate with the correctional center residents."

They begin to practice facilitating conversations with each other and then to analyze and question their own efforts. What will provoke "lively group exchanges" with residents of a juvenile correctional facility? How can you "formulate stimulating questions?" When and how should you inject "personal comments?" What can you do if no one talks? It is this layer of thinking about their own thinking and actions that raises the whole experience to such unusual levels of insight.

In book 2 of the *Nicomachean Ethics* Aristotle wrote, "For the things we have to learn before we can do them, we learn by doing them."[2] Over two thousand years later, John Dewey added that only the capacity to "Stop and Think," to examine experience, to free it from "immediate whim and caprice" can empower someone for "intelligent judgment."[3] In essence, we don't learn from experience but from thinking about it.

In the Russian literature class, students develop Dewey's vision of freedom by exercising Aristotle's observation. People "become lyre players by playing the lyre, . . . become just by doing just acts, temperate by doing temperate acts," the ancient Greek philosopher wrote. Students become empathetic, thoughtful, critically thinking, analytical readers and human beings by exercising those qualities as they get ready and then meet with the residents.

Kaufman prepares for his class by becoming acquainted with Russian literature, the scholarship on human learning, and his students. In turn, he asks the UVA undergraduates to understand the people with whom they will be working. During that first four weeks the class makes an initial visit to Bon Air Juvenile Correctional Center near Richmond, where they are fingerprinted and hear correctional officials discuss the residents, theories and practices of juvenile justice, and how to set boundaries and react to surprises.

Later in the semester, a teacher in the German Department and associate director of the Center for Teaching Excellence at UVA conducts an experiential workshop on listening. An official from the justice department talks to the class about how the state of Virginia thinks about their treatment of juvenile delinquency and how the Books Behind Bars program fits into those efforts. In short, the professor makes sure that his university students are well prepared to help other people to learn and to go into a maximum security correctional center to do so.

What to Study

With the growing body of knowledge in most disciplines, professors often feel pressure to "cover everything." Even in a field like nineteenth-century Russian literature, where the size of the content isn't growing,[4] many people see no alternative to stuffing courses with as much as possible.[5] Some educators, however, are now focusing on a different set of questions. Kaufman is one of them. Rather than asking "How can I require more?" they are exploring ways to help students learn to read deeply and to stimulate the desire to do so. In some disciplines that means asking, What are the threshold concepts that students need to understand if they enter the discipline at this level and continue to grow? How can I best choose the set of material with which they can practice what I hope will become a lifetime endeavor? Jeanette Norden, a longtime professor of neurology at Vanderbilt Medical School, puts it this way, "I want to teach less better." Indeed, she found that an emphasis on deep conceptual learning has produced better medical students and physicians, more likely to do an accurate differential diagnosis even with tricky cases, and to maintain a lifetime of constant learning.

Books Behind Bars uses a humanities version of Norden's "teach less better." University of Virginia students and the residents read a baker's dozen of short examples of classic Russian literature that all meet a telling criterion: their length allows all readers "to delve into them deeply." Both groups—the UVA students and the Bon Air residents—find them "interesting, accessible, and provocative." They are entertaining, "have stood the test of time," and "radiate with a moral-spiritual intensity and emotional boldness" that "encourages readers to ponder timeless human questions." The poems, short stories, and novel he picks allow the class to read "slowly, carefully, and deeply," emerging with finely tuned abilities and motivations to feast on a lifetime of literature.

Former students, some of them nearly a decade out of the class, all reported that they continued to devour nineteenth- and twentieth-century Russian fiction long after they graduated. Furthermore, the big questions they explore with the young people at Bon Air continue to animate their lives. Even mundane matters about what job to take or pursue become richly framed in the shadow of Russian literature's inquiries about "who am I" and "what kind of life do I want to live?"

What Happens at Bon Air—and After

For the last ten weeks of the semester, students travel each Tuesday to Bon Air, where they work in pairs to conduct discussions with residents.[6] On Thursdays, the UVA undergraduates gather on campus to review their work, identify problems, and seek solutions. That schedule is part of a pattern of constant review and reflection. So are the journals that students keep about their "thoughts and feelings" as they read, go to the correctional center, and interact with the residents. "You will explore how your discussions affect your ideas," Kaufman writes in their syllabus, "not only about the literature, but about juvenile offenders, yourself, and what it means to read and study literature in a community context."

Notice something about the language he uses. It reflects a pattern we saw consistently across the Super Courses we examined. The instructions avoid words like "required" and "assignments," using them sparingly. Instead, the message is couched in what the class members will do if they decide to accept the invitation. No sense of commanding troops into battle. No play for power. Rather the people in the class receive the respect usually accorded a guest at a dinner party.

The Invitational Syllabus

We first introduced the idea of the invitational syllabus in *What the Best College Teachers Do* in 2004.[7] Maybe a brief analogy can clarify the idea, keeping in mind that we refer not just to the printed pages teachers give students on the first day of class but to everything a professor and students might do in the first few sessions: every word spoken, every gesture, all the activities in the course from lectures and discussions to lab work or research projects. The oral and physical invitational syllabus becomes as important as the written one.

Suppose, for example, a dinner invitation looked like the traditional syllabus. It might read like this. "You are required to appear at our house on Friday night and consume one pound of spaghetti and meatballs." You probably wouldn't come. But if we invited you to join us for dinner and good conversation ("we want to hear your ideas on X, Y and Z"), you might accept—especially if we mentioned the pasta cooked to perfection and smothered in a sauce of onions, green peppers, garlic, and other goodies.[8] (Oh, and did we tell you about the other guests who'll join us, the wine list, the meatballs that melt in your mouth, or the vegan alternative?) Yes, we do have instructions: "You'll need to fly to Newark, where we'll pick you up at the airport." But we leave you in charge.

Compare that with a more traditional syllabus. A few years ago, a colleague organized a course in science for nonscience majors, for example. He didn't invite anyone. His syllabus and early days in class simply told enrollees what they must do. "You are required to spend three hours a week with a research scientist." He then outlined how many points they would get or lose if they did or did not follow his commands to a tee. Once he introduced the legal language of grading, he lost all hope that curiosity or altruism might guide the class members.

In the Russian literature class students learn by helping others contemplate, develop new reading tools and ways of thinking, and explore classic literature. They read and discuss, but they also reflect, write, and then consider the feedback the professor offers to their journals and essays. Writing becomes a key element in what people in the class do. "You'll keep a journal," the professor says. He urges (but does not require) them to write "longhand" in a notebook. It is "your opportunity," he argues, again using the language of invitation, "to reflect, to analyze, to integrate, to explore, and to test the boundaries of your thoughts and feelings related to the contents of the class."

Sometimes they might all write a personal letter to an author or concoct an alternative ending to a story. Other times, they write what they wish—at least one entry each week, averaging several hundred words, and all dated in preparation for a bigger writing project.

Twice in the semester, the students write an essay, once at midterm and another at the end. For the latter, they also create a portfolio of all they have written. It is a chance to reflect on the journey they have taken "through the world of Russian literature and juvenile justice." We cannot emphasize enough how Kaufman frames these activities. They become enticing opportunities to think, and grow, integral to experiencing the class and serving the greater cause. As one student told us, "if you take the class, it makes no sense to skip any of these golden moments." Rather than using the traditional language of commandments, the teacher bathes those precious times in words of freedom and wise advice.

"Although it's not required, I encourage you to come up with a *title or theme* for each entry you've written," he offers. "Past students find this to be an enjoyable creative exercise, as well as a useful tool for grasping the bigger picture, the patterns, and the overarching thrust of your thoughts."

Giving Students Choices over Learning Objectives

Kaufman outlines a number of course objectives, but he does not expect each one to be "equally applicable" to every student. Students can find their own emphasis and define what the grade represents. For some, the exploration of Russian literature and culture becomes paramount. For others, it might be what they learn about the juvenile justice system. For still others, the course opens a window on a whole new concept of teaching and learning. Students can read and discuss Parker Palmer's ideas on the meaning of being educated and the creation of a "community of truth" where people explore questions and ideas rather than just receive facts. Some of them become teachers.[9]

"Each of you brings a unique set of skills, passions, and perspectives to this class," the syllabus notes, "which will be reflected in your unique learning outcomes and demonstrated in the things you choose to write about, the risks you take, and the areas in which you grow the most. There is no one type of 'successful' BBB student." People control their own education right down to the learning objectives they hope to achieve.

Professors in some disciplines counter that they don't have that flexibility. "Every student in architecture must learn to design buildings that don't fall down," one former colleague pointed out. Yet we can all imagine giving students choices and respect. For an engineering professor who offers classes on how airplanes fly, the freedom begins with the decision to take the course. "No one is requiring you to take this class or become an engineer, but if you do, you have a moral obligation to do it right, and here's what's involved," says an aeronautical professor at one prominent university.[10]

A public pledge, a show of hands, could replace Kaufman's application process. "There are many ways you might learn this material; this class is one of them. You decide if it best serves your needs." Freedom and respect plus all the promises made define the learning environment.

Creating the Right Environment

Rather than forcing students to attend class,[11] this unique Russian literature course has provided a compelling experience that no one would want to miss, both because it is a valuable educational opportunity and because students feel a commitment to the community they have joined and are building together. Rather than beating them with how many points they'll lose with each absence, the class builds a community of mutual respect. "I had to think about the residents at Bon Air, and my obligations to them," reported one BBB student. "If I skipped class, I disappointed them."[12]

It's easy to dismiss this Super Course success as a result of working with "naturally polite" Virginia students. "You should try that with the people who take my class," one cynic from an open enrollment school jeered when reading a draft of this chapter. "Lots of luck." Yet when you consider the residents in the room, Books Behind Bars is one of the most diverse and challenging environments one might imagine. "Books Behind Bars models for them the same kind of authentic conversation, respect, and community atmosphere that we try to model in our UVA classroom." And that makes a difference. "Residents feel a sense of honor [being in a class] where they can feel human," Kaufman concludes. "So they monitor the behavior of one another in a way that doesn't always happen [elsewhere in the correctional system]."

A community of respect begins with an invitational syllabus rather than a contractual one. Books Behind Bars sets high expectations for both UVA students and Bon Air residents. But the manner in which those standards are established makes a huge difference. Consider the matter of "Participation." Early in the term, the professor holds a discussion, first asking the students what they mean by the term. After listening to their thoughts, modeling "non-verbal participation" in the process, he shares what is invariably a broader way of thinking about engagement. "Students come away from that discussion understanding that [they have] many opportunities . . . throughout the semester [to engage] in . . . various verbal and non-verbal interactions with one another and the residents." They can take part with their minds and body language even if they say nothing.

Underlying all this discussion, Kaufman explains, "is my emphasis on community and empowerment, letting them know that their participation is important in this class not because it will affect their grade but because it is essential to the very success of the class itself." Andy developed this insight the first time he taught the class. "Students were tremendously motivated by the knowledge that we were co-constructing this class together," and that their contributions were "not just a grade category on the syllabus but an essential principle underlying the success of the class."

Altruism, respect, compassion, intrigue, community, and high standards drive a uniquely powerful Super Course. The message to students is clear: "Every one of you is essential to this learning community, and I have confidence that you will measure up (you were chosen, after all), and I invite you to prove me right. And, voila, they do."

Changing the Approach to Assessment

"In this class our focus is going to be on learning rather than on grading," Kaufman stresses. Before they enrolled in Books Behind Bars, most of the people in the program had worshiped high marks and learned to obey their commands. To wean them from that focus and foster a commitment to deep learning, the class works from both ends. From the beginning, Kaufman does not depend on marks to motivate learning. "Grades are not the primary motivation for your work," Kaufman tells them the first day. "You've been chosen for this class because we know you have a strong desire to be here, that you want to learn and work hard, and that you will succeed," the Russian literature scholar proclaims.

Self-fulfillment theorists and researchers have long held that students are more likely to be interested in a subject if their teachers expect them to be and act as if they are. But such attempts to foster self-fulfilling prophecies can fail if students have no chance to exercise the new perspective on themselves and their education. Accordingly, Kaufman invites them to become deeply involved in assessing their own work. To make that happen they need some help in learning how to measure their growth.

How will they know they're learning? "You'll know because you can observe growth in yourself—in your facilitation skills, in your evolving insights into Russian literature, into the world of juvenile justice, into life itself," Kaufman explains. He invites students to look for something new about themselves that they hadn't noticed before. "Have any . . . expectations or paradigms . . . been disrupted?"

Rather than quizzing them on a predetermined list of items, this Super Course invites students to understand their own learning, analyze it, and make a case (in their reflections and essays) about its meaning, depth, influence, and value. Did you gain a new insight from the way you experienced something—reading, writing, or meeting with the residents—and the way you processed it? "You will take responsibility for your own learning and will be actively involved in the assessment of your own work." Implicit in this approach is the idea that deep learning occurs only when students have thought a great deal about the nature of their own intellectual and personal growth and have begun to formulate profound ideas about its meaning.

In the end, he outlines the "general principles guiding the final grading decision." Paramount in that list is the students' growth and improvement. How do you learn from your mistakes and shortcomings? Such an approach "helps to ensure that you . . . take intellectual and creative risks." You cannot guarantee perfection with everything you try, but you control "the effort you put into your work and the diligence with which you address challenges and opportunities," he reminds the class. In every aspect of the "grading policy" the course encourages and rewards honest reflection on "successes and failures." Students can experiment with their writing and facilitation, come up short, and still pull the chestnuts out of the fire, but they can't slough it off until the end. "What I do hope to see," Kaufman writes in the syllabus, "is a *pattern* of effort and diligence over the course of the whole semester."

We'll see this practice of helping people learn to assess themselves across our body of Super Courses.

Humanities and the Poor

If you search for Viniece Walker on the web, you won't find much. Yet the former inmate of the Bedford Hill Correctional Facility sparked one of the most splendid educational innovations in recent years, and it extends the conversation that Andrew Kaufman has fostered. It happened one day in 1994 when a journalist came calling on the high-security prison for women just north of New York City. Earl Shorris was writing a book on poverty and collecting insights from ordinary people. He'd talked to over six hundred Americans before quizzing the short "fair-skinned and freckled African-American" woman who sat before him in her sartorially subdued green dress and jacket. A high school dropout, she'd been in prison since she was twenty. She was now approaching forty. "You got to begin with the children," she responded when asked how you cure poverty.[13]

Walker spoke rapidly, Shorris reported, clipping out her words with "streets sounds" and "rhythmless" phrasing.[14] "You've got to teach the moral life of downtown to the children. And the way you do that, Earl," she pronounced, "is by taking them downtown to plays, museums, concerts, lectures. . . . And then they won't be poor any more."[15] To drive her point home, she repeated with what some would see as a touch of anger in her voice. "And they won't be poor *no more*."[16] But it wasn't anger. She was the Oracle of Delphi, the modern-day Pythia, delivering her message wrapped in an enigma.

After coming to prison on that manslaughter charge, she had read philosophy and psychology as part of a college program that Superintendent Elaine Lord had started. She would later advance into a master's program. Walker had learned to reflect through her reading of great works of human thought. As Shorris continued to listen, the great oracle became more explicit than did the ancient Greek version of herself, spelling out the details of her vision. "It became clear," the journalist would later write, "that when she spoke of the 'moral life of downtown' she meant the humanities."[17]

At the age of fifty-seven Shorris began to understand something that his years as an undergraduate at the University of Chicago had not taught him, that even his life as a part-time bullfighter in the rings at Juarez, Mexico, had failed to teach. The humanities were a "foundation for getting along in the world, for thinking, for learning to reflect on the world," and becoming better prepared to handle whatever life threw you.[18] They would teach you a morality and way of thinking that would allow you to advocate for yourself and your community. Many well-to-do people experienced an education that ate those ideas for breakfast, and it was that humanistic perspective, that experience with reflection and logical thinking, and political and economic action flowing through their culture, that gave the elite such an advantage. Poor people might at best be trained to operate a cash register or some other machine, while many of the privileged learned to learn for the sake of learning.

Over the next year, with Viniece Walker's inspiration and vision floating through his mind, Shorris organized what he called the Clemente Course in the humanities.[19] It brought history, art, logic, writing, literature, and moral philosophy to poor people in discussion seminars. Today those courses flourish on five continents, where noted faculty pick the readings and conduct the discussions. More than ten thousand people, some young, some old, all from "economic distress" have joined those discussions.[20] Many have gone on to college, graduated, and sometimes advanced to graduate school. More important, they strengthened their "critical thinking so that students are better able to engage effectively in action to improve their communities." In 2014, the program received the National Humanities Medal from the White House.

Imagine injecting the undergraduates from Books Behind Bars into a Clemente Course. In the chapters that follow, we'll continue to explore the power of novice learners helping beginners.

Earl Shorris died of cancer in 2012. Viniece Walker got out of prison around 2003, a "model inmate" and "a wonderful student and inspiration to others." She died of "complication from AIDS" sometime in the obscure calendar of "some years ago."[21]

CHAPTER SIX

From Charlottesville to Singapore and Beyond: Searching for Super Courses

For generations, physicians practiced their healing arts alone. They might employ nurses who collected information, stuck a thermometer in your mouth (or elsewhere), and filled out charts, but the physician made the decisions, assessing the state of your health, and administering treatment (or at least deciding what pills you would take, shots you would get, or procedures you would endure). In that traditional model, your personal doctor didn't usually consult with other physicians, no matter how complex the state of your body. But that model is changing.

Those traditional MDs came out of schools that emphasized acting like a lone wolf. Through exams and study sessions, rising physicians seldom collaborated. Medical schools even pitted their students against each other, grading on a curve and often ranking enrollees from top to bottom. "We needed to know whether each student learned the science and medicine," one faculty member explained to us. But the method these educators chose to do so created generations of physicians who often didn't know how to collaborate. That too is changing.

Today medical practice has become a complex and multifaceted enterprise. "The long-dominant model of patient care by solo practitioners," Dr. Robert K. Kamei and his colleagues wrote in 2012 "is increasingly replaced by care through collaborative teams of healthcare providers that include doctors, nurses, social workers, pharmacists," physician assistants, and others.[1] Kamei realized that to prepare medical practitioners for this new environment and to take advantage of all that we've discovered about how people learn most deeply, his school and others needed to find new ways to educate their students.

In the old model, people who wanted to be healers sat in cavernous lecture halls to hear some learned person spill tons of information, but that didn't always work well. It didn't ensure that students understood basic concepts. Even if people chocked down thousands of facts, they often could not do an accurate differential diagnosis and had no collaborative habits to seek help. While the old medical school approach emphasized "covering" a large body of content, it did not ensure that students even heard the golden words from their professors. At scores of physician-training colleges by the middle of the last century, the pupils could hire someone else to attend lectures and take notes for them. That too is changing.

It is, perhaps, not surprising that some of the earliest and most important shifts emerged at a crossroads where a multitude of ideas and traditions stream together. Singapore sits on sixty-three islands off the southern tip of the Malay Peninsula in southeast Asia. The city-state has become a prosperous melting pot of Asian and world cultures, a global hub located between multiple societies, continents, and oceans. In that polyglot of five official languages, a combination of perspectives and traditions have fashioned new approaches that dramatically improve and deepen student learning. While the Super Course we explore here emerged in a medical school, it has strong implications for classes in virtually every discipline.

A New Way to Educate

In 2005 a US university (Duke) joined with the National University of Singapore (NUS) to pioneer a new way to educate physicians. Robert Kamei and his colleagues pulled together ideas from around the world. He had gone to medical school at the University of California San Francisco to become a pediatrician and later lived in Indonesia, where he became fascinated with how people learn to practice the healing arts and sciences. "In Singapore, a long way from the Duke mothership in North Carolina, we had a chance to build something new," Kamei told us.

Building New Approaches

The Singapore innovators sought not just to help people become good traditional doctors but to improve overall medical practice. They wanted medical students to understand and be able to use all the standard routines for addressing ailments and fostering healthy lives, but they also hoped their graduates could recognize when the customary would not quite do, when new knowledge is necessary, when new perspectives are needed.

"Of course, we wanted students to learn the same content emphasized at Duke," Kamei explained, "but we also sought to foster critical and creative thinking skills, self-directed learning, and teamwork." He might have added, he wanted adaptive experts, not just routine ones.

He also sought medical practitioners who could constantly judge their own level of understanding. Traditional schooling doesn't often help students become good at self-evaluation. Yet that capacity is crucial to learning and a matter of moral responsibility in a profession where ignorance can kill.

"We also hoped that the new approach we chose would inspire their curiosity," Kamei noted. No one can learn enough in school to suffice for a lifetime. Even if they could, ongoing research constantly changes what a physician should understand. Today's lessons may not be accepted tomorrow.

To achieve any great leap forward, however, the Duke/NUS faculty had to think about changing what happened in class during the first year. In the old medical school model (and in lots of other fields), educators assumed that people must memorize facts before they could use them to crack medical cases. Thus, professors spent much of their contact time with students giving them the information they needed to "learn." Kamei and his colleagues realized, however, that the content of medical education was readily available from multiple sources. Students might need help in finding it, but they required far more assistance in thinking about its meaning, applications, and implications, in using it to think critically and creatively to solve problems. The Singapore educators also grasped that people are most likely to remember what they understand. If students have thought about meaning and implications, if they have used information and ideas to solve problems and built rich association with concepts that matter to them, they are most likely to understand deeply—and remember what they comprehend. An experience of learning from doing (as opposed to rote memorization) helps people recall their own understanding and employ it in solving clinical cases. As cognitive psychologist Michelle Miller put it recently, "the way in which you process something in the first place heavily determines whether it sticks or evaporates."[2]

Research on building good memory suggests that learners benefit from pulling stuff out of their brains, not just from pushing it in. If you want to embed something in long-term memory, you will have greatest success if you practice recalling it rather than just hearing or reading it repeatedly. Testing beats rehearsing (retrieval practice).

If those sessions of digging it out of your brain occur over several days and weeks rather than in a single marathon study session, so much the better for long-term retention (spaced repetition). If they happen while you are trying to use the information to solve specific kinds of problems (medical issues, for example), you are most likely to use what you've learned to solve those same types of puzzles later on.

It's the same process humans experience throughout their learning lives. Young children develop their language skills by using words, sounds, and meanings in a natural process of trying to communicate. Most of the time, they are not (if ever) huddled in a corner mechanically flipping through a stack of vocabulary cards. Language grows as people encounter new words and ideas, as they hear and try new sounds and meanings, as they blunder and get feedback, as they learn in the same context in which they will ultimately use their words.

What if medical students came to remember information and procedures because they had struggled to understand and use them. Memory would improve, and doctors would still emerge with a huge body of knowledge, but, more important, their capacity to think critically and creatively would mushroom. Their ability to do an accurate differential diagnosis would improve significantly. To rise to that new level, the students needed to take control of their own education, and the school had to encourage and facilitate that process. That meant the neophyte physicians must recognize gaps in their own understanding, learn to listen carefully, understand concepts and principles (not just remember information), and solve problems with what they learned.

While traditional professors spent the precious time they had with students delivering information and concepts, the new medical school in Singapore built ways for people to encounter the facts and ideas on their own so they could work on solving problems during class time (flipped classroom). In that redesigned environment, the learners could try, come up short, recognize the difficulties they faced, practice working together to solve any problem, but always have the professor available for a key explanation or questions when needed. The activities in class would ideally deepen understanding and improve memory, but they would also increase the chances that students' new knowledge would be used to analyze a problem and devise a response.

Team-Based Learning

The Singapore educators turned to a process that Larry Michaelsen, an organizational psychologist, had pioneered in his own classes at the University of Oklahoma and later at Central Missouri University. They then added their own ingredients to the process. In a format they called TeamLEAD (Learn, Engage, Adapt, and Develop), professors would write learning objectives for each lesson, and express those goals as concepts and principles the future doctors would need to comprehend as they considered applications and implications. The instructors carefully chose or created materials that would help students achieve those aims.

Sometimes faculty members worked in teams to write something for students to read or view at home. For some content they assembled video recordings of lectures delivered at the Duke School of Medicine in North Carolina, and material from websites, journal articles, and books.

When the students came to class on Monday and Thursday mornings, they had already encountered the content and thought about it not just as a string of isolated data points but as parts of broader concepts. At the heart of the material they had visited at home, they faced an important medical question often embedded in a specific case or story and then an explanation of the concepts and principles that allowed them to solve the problem.

The entire experience was built around what Michaelsen called the four S's, which correspond to key provisions of the natural critical learning environment. The questions had to be *significant*, both to the students and within the medical community they sought to join. That meant framing the inquiry in language that spoke to the learner even while it captured the concerns of the most advanced professionals in the field. The entire class tackled the *same* problem, which could raise delicate issues about how to make a question significant to a diverse group of learners. Students would face a *specific* choice (as we will see) and the responsibility of defending their selection. Finally, teams engaged in *simultaneous* reporting, debate, and discussion.

In class, people sat in teams of seven. Each student had thirty minutes to answer twenty-five "well-written" and "unambiguous" questions in an "individual readiness assessment exam."[3] Often these questions were also case based and asked students to draw conclusions. The questions required far more than memory; they demanded sophisticated reasoning.

Once that process was done, people in class began to talk with their colleagues. "I never tire of watching this transition," a faculty member told an interviewer several years ago.[4] The room would burst into conversations as students began to struggle with the exam again, this time in teams. As students spread themselves and their notes in available space—on the floor, on desktops, or in nooks and crannies, the volume rose in a crescendo of debates and questions, explanations and gestures.

In the team portion, people in each group had to reach a common response, forcing students to explain why they chose a particular answer. As they explained to one another, the ideas "crystalized" in their minds, producing deeper understanding and retention. But questions undoubtedly remained. In the next step, each group confronted the gaps in their emerging knowledge. They then wrote their questions and doubts on the board for others to see. "We next asked another group to respond" to each set of questions, Professor Kamei explained. Students had ten minutes to prepare for a group discussion of all the issues that had been raised. The teachers assigned two people to stand at the front of the room and facilitate that discussion. Students answered each other's questions.[5]

People who are struggling to understand something new are better prepared to explain to a confused peer than are the experts. Novice learners realize the problems they faced to reach a higher level of insight, while the professor has long ago forgotten those challenges. The entire group assessment process allows "students to learn from each other and, as a team, identify any gaps or uncertainties—which opens the student's minds for further learning."[6]

But what if the students have built false models? Won't this kind of class simply spread ignorance? Faculty members remain in the room, ready to correct any false steps and to reassure students when they understand correctly. When the team takes the Ready Assessment Exam, they get immediate feedback from the faculty and can keep taking the quiz until they get it all right. But it is the power of learners helping one another that drives the success of this enterprise.

People in a group struggle with a significant problem collectively, first among seven, then within the entire class. Students take ownership and find out what they don't understand, then identify and confront their gaps together. They're not pulling answers just from rote memory but from all the discussions, from understanding concepts and principles and reasoning through the information they have, from defending their own answers, and from challenging each other. They're learning to listen to their fellow learners, and when a professor intervenes to challenge something that's been said, or offer a summary, they can confront the ways they drew conclusions initially. Those crucial elements turn the experience into a natural critical learning environment in which people move from performing as strategic or surface learners to acting as deep ones.

Practice, Practice, Practice

Finally, each of the smaller groups tackles a clinical case in which the information they encountered earlier plays a leading role. Without this crucial element, some fear people just learn to become good test takers. But with the clinical cases, the students develop as good physicians and adaptive experts.

Sometimes the diagnosis they make depends solely on concepts from the material they read and viewed for that day. Often it also uses ideas from earlier classes. From session to session, students weave in and out of a variety of concepts and principles in a manner that mimics both the life of a physician and the research findings about spaced repetition and interleaving. Over the course, students will encounter key concepts multiple times.[7]

In most traditional medical schools, aspiring doctors spend two years in lecture classes on basic science material. Duke-NUS's TeamLEAD course cut that in half. In their second year, the Singapore scholars go into the clinic. Do they learn as much medical information about the workings of the body in half the time? To find out, they took the National Board of Medical Examiners Comprehensive Basic Science Examination (CBSE) and the United States Medical Licensing Examination (USMLE). In just one year, "Duke-NUS students achieved comparable standards of basic science knowledge achieved by U.S. medical students" after two years of lectures. By the end of their second year the people who had experienced team-based learning "performed significantly higher than the U.S. students."[8] Furthermore, Kamei and his colleagues believe their pupils emerge with better "teamwork skills." They support each other more vigorously and can pursue their own curiosities aggressively. The team-based learners know how to "manage their own self-directed learning to master the core concepts."[9]

Teams Spread

Over the last decade, team-based learning has spread into other medical schools and into undergraduate programs as diverse as literature and anthropology, cell biology and physics. LaTonya Amboree with the Region Four Education Service Center in Houston and others have carried the approach into secondary schools. Most of the programs have cropped up in the sciences, engineering, and business, but a scattering of humanities and social science programs have used the methodology.

It offers a robust way to engage medical classes in active learning and a natural critical learning environment, but it faces challenges. Does it work only if people are already highly motivated, or can it light fires and rekindle long-lost passions? Does it work as well in other schools as it does at a highly selective medical school? Sarah Leupen has had great success using team-based learning in University of Maryland Baltimore County physiology classes, while her colleague Kal Nanes has done something similar in math.

The Answer Is in the Questions

Much of team-based learning's success depends on the kinds of questions used in both the readiness test and the application exercises. In our survey of the methodology, we found an uneven terrain. Some quizzes did no more than prompt students to regurgitate something they read or heard. Others struggled to promote conceptual understanding, analysis, synthesis, evaluation, and theorizing. Few people consciously used Eric Mazur's ConcepTests, which we'll explore a little later. To do so would require professors to determine what mental models and paradigms their students hold that the course might deliberately seek to challenge.

The Michaelsen team-based approach does provide teachers with plenty of feedback along the way so that they can help each person learn, but not everyone lets class members try, fail, receive feedback, and try again before anyone makes judgments about their abilities. In short, while the approach has demonstrated considerable merit in promoting deep learning and natural critical learning environments, its greatest contributions are yet to come.

CHAPTER SEVEN

Self-Directed Learning and Big Questions: From the DIY Girls to Hurricane Katrina

When you ask leaders at San Fernando Senior High School in northeast Los Angeles to list major accomplishments, they often emphasize championships in sports. Most of the students speak both Spanish and English, but not one of the highlights on the school's website hints at their linguistic prowess. Many of their parents struggle with poverty wages and occasional layoffs, but the school doesn't emphasize the challenges that low-income students face, or the academic triumphs they've enjoyed in facing down those obstacles.

Poverty in the Pacoima neighborhood where San Fernando Senior High sits has always hidden itself well, even when unemployment tickled the underside of 15 percent and the rates of impoverishment nearly doubled those of Los Angeles as a whole. "Many of those who are homeless live in hiding," Susan Abram reported in 2015 for the *Los Angeles Daily News*.[1] But that is changing. As the problems grow, they become more apparent.

When Daniela Orozco entered the ninth grade, she remembered seeing just one homeless person each day as she trotted to school. By her senior year in 2016, however, the numbers had increased so rapidly she could no longer miss these people. Homelessness in the San Fernando Valley rose by over seven thousand people in a year's time. Daniela and her schoolmates could see the victims along Fox Street, in the park near the school, or beneath Interstate 5, which ran a few blocks west of the campus.[2]

In early 2016, a graduate of San Fernando Senior High, Evelyn Gómez, appeared in several classes looking for volunteers to join a special educational opportunity she was organizing. Gómez had been one of the star pupils and had gone to MIT, where she studied aerospace engineering, and later got a master's degree from UCLA. Her undergraduate alma mater was holding a showcase for high school engineering teams, and she hoped to mount an entry from San Fernando High. The twenty-nine-year-old engineer now worked as director of DIY Girls, a nonprofit that helps girls from low-income families learn about science, technology, engineering, and math.

In June a dozen female students began defining a project they might enter in the MIT exhibition. Most of the girls didn't know anything about engineering when they began work, nor did they know one another. Yet they all understood the poverty and homelessness on their doorsteps. The students quickly decided to invent something that would make life easier for poor people living on the streets.

Through the summer, the girls plugged away at their work, engrossed in a goal that intrigued them and captured their sense of altruism. They hoped to design a solar-powered tent for homeless people, compact enough to fit in a backpack with wheels that would give it mobility. With the electricity that came from photoelectric cells, the homeless would have lights at night, a small fan for hot days, and a way to cook food. "We couldn't give them money," one student explained, "because our families were also poor even if we had a house or apartment."

The students created for themselves a passion-based learning environment, and it became a powerful motivator. They wanted to complete their endeavor because of their concern for the homeless. To do so they needed to learn about solar panels, to master coding and 3-D printing, to understand a variety of engineering principles, and to learn the programming language C++. If they encountered something they didn't know how to do, they found videos on the web that took them through the process.

No one needed to give them assignments or dock them points if they fell behind. The only tests came naturally when something didn't work and had to be fixed. The girls encouraged one another and set their own schedule. They struggled together to master a new insight or skill, not because a teacher required them to work in groups but because the DIY crew wanted to invent something new. These young people learned engineering not to pass an examination and make a high grade but to help other people. Their altruism came in major part from sympathy and empathy, made more powerful because the rising engineers worried about themselves and their families.

"If your parents miss" paying bills, one girl noted, "you can fall into homelessness, too."

Through the summer and into the fall the girls worked six days a week, skipping winter and spring breaks to finish their creation. Like a proud sports team, the fledgling engineers drove themselves, putting in extra hours to get the job done. When they failed to crack a problem, these San Fernando students redoubled their efforts, confident they could find a solution.

By spring the DIY Girls had created a working model, but they didn't rest on their laurels. These high schoolers began to look for flaws in their creation. How easily would it tear? Could it withstand rain? Would the solar panels break if someone stomped them?

When they finished poking knives through the fabric and other quality testing efforts, their proud creation lay in shreds, a sight that might have discouraged the most determined. But rather than giving up, the DIY Girls used all that they learned to start over, to build a more durable prototype. In June 2017, with support from a grant, the dozen pioneers took their creation to MIT. But why didn't they just quit, especially after their first model proved to be not quite durable enough?

What Makes Failure Productive?

A group of German researchers looked at what they called "favorable error climates" to understand what prompts mathematics students to learn from mistakes.[3] Behind their list of behaviors and subcategories, lies a simple notion. Students need a chance to try, fail, get feedback, and try again without anyone—teachers or students—judging, condemning, ridiculing, or excoriating them. The San Fernando students worked in a climate of mutual support and trust where everyone assumed their neighbors all had the highest devotion and the best intentions. We'll see some of these same themes as we continue our tour through the world of Super Courses.

Passion-Driven Learning

At Olin College of Engineering, Worcester Polytechnic Institute, Harvard University, Southwest Jiaotong University in Chengdu, China, in a few high schools like San Fernando, and scores of places around the globe, educators are building Super Courses around what is often called project-based learning. In many ways it's an old idea poured into fresh and novel bottles then mixed with an assortment of important insights coming out of the research on human learning. We have chosen to emphasize the passion-driven aspect for this kind of Super Course because the most successful engage students in a purpose that is larger than the class, and maybe even broader than the discipline. Students develop a passion for finding answers and solving problems. In the process of pursuing that big, integrated goal, the students learn a variety of disciplines. They may subsequently become intrigued with a particular field of study, but it is a problem, the challenge, and often the chance to help someone else that pulls them into the enterprise.

It's no longer just a literature class, an engineering course, a math curriculum, a political science requirement, or any other single branch of knowledge, but an integrated and compelling adventure in helping other people.

Projects have long been used in upper-level and graduate classes, but they didn't always conform to the research findings on human learning, and they didn't break through the tyranny of the traditional introductory survey lecture course that kept such magical environments away from freshmen. The new Super Courses create natural critical learning environments that engage and challenge learners, bringing them to deeper insights and long-term retention. When Kristin Wobbe and Elizabeth A. Stoddard collected stories for *Project-Based Learning in the First Year*, they subtitled their book *Beyond All Expectations*.[4]

In chapters 4 and 5, we saw altruistic appeals in Andy Kaufman's course Books Behind Bars. On other occasions we've told the story of how Melissa Harris-Perry used elements of passion-based learning environments to fashion a course at Princeton on Hurricane Katrina and American political history. Students came into that class intrigued with the disaster that befell New Orleans in 2005.[5] Their professor wanted them to understand how Reconstruction following the US Civil War influenced subsequent political developments and institutions, especially for African Americans. She entitled the course Katrina: Disaster and American Politics, and students signed up for the class to understand calamities.

With one question, Harris-Perry transformed their interest into hers: When did the disaster begin, she asked the class on the first day they met in the fall semester. Did it first emerge in August 2005 when the storm surge hit the Crescent City? Or did it start in 1866 with the onset of Reconstruction in New Orleans? With that inquiry, she created a passion-driven learning environment that now propelled her students' study. With that question, she transformed their interests into something broader, into something bigger than the learning objectives she had for them as a historian.

When she first offered the course in 2006, the people in the class became so driven by their desire to help Katrina's victims that after the semester ended, they all went to New Orleans to understand better the situation on the ground and to help people put their lives back together.

CHAPTER EIGHT

Peer Instruction and Then Some

By the early 1990s, Eric Mazur, a physics professor at Harvard, enjoyed a sterling reputation as a fine lecturer and teacher. His students generally performed well on examinations. What more could you ask? Then one day, he read the study from fellow physicists Ibrahim Abou Halloun and David Hestenes at Arizona State University. In their well-constructed research, as we reported back in chapter 2, they had found that people could make high grades on examinations and still not comprehend basic ideas in the discipline.

As you will recall, the Arizona researchers had constructed an instrument, the Force Concept Inventory, to measure students' understanding of motion. The undergraduates didn't do well, reflecting little conceptual learning. Even those who made A's in the course held tightly to beliefs they brought to the class. They had built their mental models around so-called commonsense notions about physical motion, and they would not abandon these conceptions even after learning to solve physics problems. When Mazur gave his own students the inventory, he found they did as poorly as, or worse than, the undergraduates in Arizona.

It was an eye-opener that led the Harvard professor over the next few years to create a whole new approach to teaching physics, a pedagogy that has spread into other disciplines with impressive results. His peer instruction (PI) method has now been used in thousands of classes. But it can be seriously misunderstood. To be clear, let's look at one major confusion and how it emerged.

It Isn't the Clickers

A few years ago, we asked a colleague if he had tried the Mazur approach. "Oh, yes, I use clickers all the time in my engineering classes," he replied with pride. Yet when we later asked for examples of the ConcepTests he employed in his class, we got blank stares. For this educator and scores of others, the Harvard professor had simply introduced little handheld devices with which students could report responses to a quiz or survey. That understanding of Mazur's contributions misses many of the rich insights the physicist developed and the teaching techniques he pioneered.

The Ivy League scientist began his work with some simple observations. First, students often have their greatest difficulty understanding key concepts and applying them to the solution of new problems. They can learn to plug the right number into a correct formula without comprehending any of the underlying ideas. As a result, they all too often can't crack problems they've never seen before even if they involve the same concepts as older exercises. (How many times have you heard someone say, "You gave us test problems we'd never had before"?) This is one version of what we sometimes call the "transfer problem."

Second, much of the information that is traditionally conveyed in lectures can be communicated outside the classroom, saving precious time to help learners do higher-order stuff: understanding, analyzing, synthesizing, applying, theorizing, and transferring their insights from one situation to another. College classes typically meet for no more than 150 minutes a week, and that time could most profitably be used, Mazur thought, to foster higher-order work like deep conceptual understanding and application. Otherwise, students are left to do the most difficult part of deep learning—making sense and understanding implications and applications—entirely on their own.

Perhaps most important, Mazur came to believe that students could help each other learn deeply far better than he could. Advanced learners (like professors) have forgotten most of the difficulties they faced when breaking through to some new conceptual understanding. Novice learners don't have that burden. It's fresh on their minds.

In his newly designed course, Mazur gave students materials to read or videos to watch before they came to each class. When they arrived, they encountered a conceptually rich and inherently fascinating problem, what Mazur dubbed a ConcepTest. "The Levi Straus trademark shows two horses trying to pull apart a pair of pants," read one of those puzzles. "Suppose Levi had only one horse and attached the other side of the pants to a fencepost. Using only one horse would: (a) cut the tension on the pants by one-half, (b) not change the tension on the pants at all, (c) double the tension on the pants?"[1]

After giving such a question to the class, the teacher would then ask pupils to "find someone who has a different answer than you do. You have two minutes to resolve your differences." The room would burst into conversations as Mazur bounced up and down the aisles, observing and listening, not just to the answers but to the reasoning. "Mark your answer again," he would instruct after a few more minutes, "and let me know your response."

The whole exercise gave students a chance to improve their learning while it provided teachers with insights into how they were thinking. Each one of the wrong answers in the ConcepTest had undergone extensive research—and that helped turn a garden-variety quiz into a powerful learning experience. Every choice represented a plausible response from someone who entertained some widely held concepts. By looking at their initial retorts, Mazur could know how students thought and better design a comeback—an explanation, question, or perhaps another ConcepTest.

When the Harvard don began using this method in the early 1990s, he distributed color-coded cards so students could indicate their reply. Depending on what colors they flashed, he knew what conceptual understanding his students held and which misconceptions he needed to challenge. He could then ask questions that would put them in a situation where their faulty mental models didn't work. They had to grapple with the inconsistency and build new models of reality consistent with the findings of modern physics. He did not need to waste time on concepts they already understood, and he could focus only on those that stumped them. Even before he offered any explanation, the students helped one another in those two minutes of "peer instruction."

As Mazur explained later, both the puzzles and the chance to discuss them with a peer proved decisive. So did the nature of his quiz. "The question must require higher-level thinking about a concept so students aren't simply recalling something they read or using 'plug-and-chug' with equations." But it shouldn't be either too easy or impossibly difficult. It should challenge how students think but let them "reason to the answer with their existing knowledge."

As we reviewed banks of questions Mazur devised, we noticed that they also had an intriguing flare to them, beginning with something both familiar to the students and maybe a little outlandish (who would hitch two mules to a pair of pants?). The most captivating stemmed from puzzles that surprised and intrigued, taking something that seemed simple and obvious but still a little mysterious. The question reminds you that you may not understand as well as you assumed. "You are looking at a fish swimming in a pond. Is it deeper than it appears, more shallow, or exactly as you see it?"

Each of the "ConcepTests" embodied some important concept in the field. If students understood that idea (which they had encountered in their nightly reading), they could easily pick the correct answers from a list of three or four possibilities (B in our pants example) and *explain their reasoning to a colleague*. But this was not an attempt to measure whether someone did their homework—or to trick them. It was a new way to learn. Mazur created a space where people could struggle with their own understanding as they attempted to explain it to someone else, hear from others, respond, and improve their thinking. But no one kept track of their answers as part of their grade. They received credit for participation only.

Key to the process was a bank of good ConcepTests, those conceptually rich and fascinating problems, but when many people think of Mazur's approach they zero in on a technology that enabled the process rather than the learning environment he created. Because the color-coded cards proved cumbersome, he turned to an electronic technology to replace them. Soon his students carried handheld personal response systems—"clickers"—where they could register their answers. The devices, about the size of a TV remote control, would then transmit their replies to the professor's computer. But it wasn't the use of clickers that made his pedagogy so effective. Rather it was the challenge of the clever ConcepTest and the opportunity for students to struggle together. As Mazur's longtime associate Julie Schell, put it, "They are the fire, so to speak, that draws students' attention and calls them together to engage in the social learning activities that make peer instruction work."

But good ConcepTests are difficult to write. If they merely expect students to spit out some fact gleaned from the readings, the inquiries provide no insights into the ideas that guide the learner's thinking. It must challenge the class to predict, to solve problems that reveal the paradigms that undergird their approach. With the data that emerges, the professor can build a stronger understanding of the often unspoken mental models that students bring to the class. The approach helps learners think about their own thinking, examine it critically, and then move to a new comprehension.

The results of Mazur's approach have been impressive: Conceptual understanding skyrockets (as measured by strategic use of the Force Concept Inventory and other standardized tests). So do students' abilities to solve complex problems and do accurate computations. Most impressive, people in these Super Courses retain their comprehension and abilities in the long term. Finally, they apparently enjoy the experience, suggesting they are more likely than normal to build a lifetime of interest and learning. What more could you ask?[2]

It Isn't Just at Harvard

Some of our colleagues have looked at Mazur's success and attributed it solely to his students. "He's at Harvard," one of them said recently. "I don't have the kind of students he teaches." Yet a variety of evidence suggests that most students, regardless of educational background and accomplishment, will benefit far more from this Super Course than they have from traditional classes. Hundreds of professors worldwide have adopted peer instruction and ConcepTests with great success, bolstering the learning of students who had earlier struggled to comprehend. Even the best students improved.

No student averaged, for example, more than 80 percent correct on the ConcepTests, but nearly everyone's abilities grew after talking to their neighbor. In PI classes, not only are average scores higher; "there are fewer extremely low" marks. At Harvard and at most schools where the full method has been employed, performances improved "dramatically" *across the semester* and faster than in traditionally taught courses.[3] Students who have often struggled with physics and other subjects have shown the greatest improvement with the Mazur experience. After discussing with their neighbor, they moved from wrong to correct answers most of the time while only a miniscule number (6 percent) did the opposite.

It Even Works among Professors— and without Clickers

Several times in recent years, we've watched Mazur try his peer instruction method on professors gathered from around the world. Our Best Teachers Institute brings about a hundred college teachers to a three-day program where the Harvard educator engages them in the pedagogy. On a recent rainy June morning in West Orange, New Jersey, a few miles west of New York City, nearly 120 people from the United States, China, Canada, and South America took the ConcepTest.

"Imagine you have a flat metal plate with a round hole cut in the middle of it," came the challenge. "If you heat the plate, will the size of the hole grow, shrink, or stay the same." About fifty people came from engineering or science departments while others represented the humanities, professional schools, the arts, and the social sciences. Mazur didn't have any clickers available for the group, so he asked people to show their answers by holding up one, two, or three fingers. To make sure everyone responded at the same time and didn't copy someone else, he asked each person to put their hand on their chest near their left (or right) shoulder and to indicate their answer on his signals. When he cried, "now," one, two, or three fingers flew in the air from each person.

As we looked around the room, it became clear that not even all the engineers and scientists had the same answers. They couldn't all be right. "Now find someone with a different response than you have," Mazur instructed, "and take two minutes to resolve your differences." The sense of almost childlike excitement permeated the room, and that giddy enthusiasm carried into lunchtime, as people continued to debate the principles involved, to scratch their heads, and to question, trying to understand why the hole would actually grow. In this case, the participants didn't have any prereading available (equivalent to a class that didn't do their homework), yet the intellectual struggles emerged.

Mazur has found that the method works best when at least 30 percent of people do the reading and come to class with some fundamental understanding, but we've noticed that with both teachers and students who have had no chance to prepare in advance, they come out of the session with a burning desire to understand more. A few years ago, we gave a group of students the reading material *after* they experienced the ConcepTest and the following discussion with their peers, then later tested them again on the same concept plus a new idea embedded in the material they had received. Their understanding of both ideas zoomed. Apparently, the curiosity sparked in the ConcepTest and the struggles with other students led them to read the material we gave them and learn even more.

The Recipe Is Never Done

Over the 1990s Mazur and his colleagues continued to tinker, to test, and to rethink their creation. By 1998, they focused on the most crucial point in the process: What if students don't read or understand the material they were supposed to encounter at night (we suspect it may be this fear that keeps many people from using peer instruction)? As we mentioned earlier, experience had shown that the sessions work best if at least 30 percent of the pupils understand the basic concepts from the reading and easily find the correct answer. When those students explained their new insights to someone else during the two minutes of peer instruction, they solidified their own understanding while others benefitted from their explanations. Everybody won. But if the prereading level of the class fell below 30 percent, it didn't work as well. How could the professor encourage and improve nightly reading?

The usual approach, of course, has been to test them, holding their feet to the fire with grades based on right answers, and making those marks count for enough to make them sting. But that tactic had problems. It could encourage strategic learning, a focus on getting the correct response rather than on deep conceptual understanding and its application. Furthermore, it could also reduce intrinsic interest as students felt the impact of extrinsic motivators. Most damning, the traditional "I'll-punish-you-if-you-don't-improve-your-reading-ability" approach provided no additional help in acquiring advanced reading abilities or problem solving.

After trying various solutions, Mazur and his team struck upon an answer of simple genius. Rather than just pressuring pupils "to do better," the class provided weekly workshops on how to read and begin to solve problems. Then the night before each class, the undergraduates completed two practice ConcepTests and responded to this question: "Please tell us briefly what single point of the reading you found most difficult or confusing. If you did not find any part of it difficult or confusing, please tell us what part you found most interesting."

That exercise not only held the students accountable for doing the homework (again, they received credit for effort, not for right answers); it also gave the instructor enormous data on how they were thinking. Armed with insights into student responses, the teacher could then decide what ConcepTests to use the next day in class. In a traditional course, a professor prepares a lecture, discussion, or other activities based on a mixture of tradition and some vague sense of what he or she thinks the students may need. Often the schedule is drawn up weeks in advance, even before the first day of class, perhaps emerging after hours of poring over standard textbooks. In this Super Course, each day's activities depended on considerable evidence (collected the night before and in class) on how students were or were not learning.

"To choose the best ConcepTests," Mazur and a colleague explained, "instructors need to gauge what concepts are causing student difficulties and what level of question is appropriate for their class."[4] Even the night before class "instructors receive important feedback on their students' knowledge and understanding of the material, enabling them to better prepare." By asking "what concepts are still unclear to you," the routine encouraged learners to think about their own thinking, fostering the kind of grappling that enables them to build new paradigms. Once classes used this technique, reading comprehension improved significantly.

The whole process employs formative assessment for as long as possible, giving people plenty of opportunity to try, fail, get feedback, and try again before anyone makes a judgment about their progress. Yes, this method can still decide who has learned and who has not (summative assessment) before the final grade goes on the transcript; but before that point the emphasis is on fostering learning not on making final and permanent decisions about someone's abilities. It is the kind of learning atmosphere that all scholars and scientists expect for their own research but is seldom extended to students.

Enough Isn't Enough

Mazur now enjoyed enormous success with his pedagogical experiments, winning converts not only in physics but in disciplines far from his own. In 2014, the nonprofit Minerva Institute for Research and Scholarship gave the professor a half-million-dollar prize for his development of peer instruction and its "Advancements in Higher Education."[5] Yet that same year, the celebrated teacher began a major revision of his masterpiece that would address long-standing problems and take his work in new directions.

CHAPTER NINE

Remaking a Super Course

After more than twenty years of success with the Super Course based on peer instruction, Eric Mazur took a leave of absence from his position at Harvard to redesign his pedagogical masterpiece. What he created contained elements of team-based learning, peer instruction, passion-based environments, and altruism as a major motivator.

The innovative teacher didn't know about the DIY Girls, but he and his colleagues created a supercharged version of their experience. Much like the California high schoolers, the Harvard undergrads worked in groups to tackle socially important problems. Because the collegians had more resources (as we will see) they could finish in a month and then take on two additional projects before the semester ended. Twice a week, they would come together for three hours to work on their collective endeavors (and to learn more deeply).

The Los Angeles girls had to scrounge around for answers to any technical and scientific questions that emerged. The Harvard team provided their charges with a textbook Mazur had written and an ingenious high-tech interactive way for them to read it together before coming to class. That computerized assistance in tackling the textbook also helped the Ivy Leaguers learn how to read more effectively (in ways we'll explore shortly). Neither group spent their precious time in class listening to lectures, and neither had any final examinations.

In both cases, students took "ownership of their learning" because they were contributing to some higher purpose and playing on a team. If they didn't keep up, they would hurt not just themselves but the social goals of the endeavor and the success of their group. A passion-driven experience, larger than the class or discipline, engaged them as they learned physics and engineering. While some students took only the fall course, the entire yearlong experience left others with deep insights into mechanics, waves, electricity and magnetism, and circuits and optics. In this complex and detailed learning environment, three aspects of the course stand out. They are all features that anyone can adopt in almost any field.

Motivating through Altruism

Students work in groups of five to complete three projects of increasing complexity. Each one uses altruism, sometimes a game-like competition, or a little zany fun to motivate. The students are given "backstories" for the projects to create that environment. In the final project in the fall course, for example, the people in the class read that they have been invited to support an ingenious charity in Venezuela that uses music and symphony orchestras to change the lives of desperately poor children.

José Antonio Abreu, they learn, founded El Sistema "in Venezuela in 1975 to help the poor children he saw in the streets break out of the cycle of poverty through classical music." The Venezuelan musician and economist thought the classical orchestra represents an ideal society and a "perfect environment in which to nurture a child," the backstory explained. Starting with eleven children, his charity had grown to reach nearly half a million kids "in a growing number of developing" countries.

How could the Harvard undergrads help?

Some of the "younger children in third-world countries" can't afford real instruments and use "make-believe" ones "made from cardboard," the Ivy Leaguers read in their backstory. That defeats the whole purpose of letting music stir the soul because their toy violins, horns, and clarinets don't really make any noise. Sounds come in waves, and the physics students study the behavior of those undulations. The project invites the undergraduates to use their growing understanding in science to invent new kinds of instruments made cheaply from recycled materials.

"Because of your background in the physics of waves and sound, you have been asked to participate in an international conference on Music and Society." The students then work in teams to design, build, and present their newly invented instruments to this important meeting. "Through this effort the conference organizers hope to spread the idea of using music to fight societal problems and unite the world with musical harmony."

The directions stipulate how many notes the new percussion, string, or wind devices must play and how long they should stay in tune. But they also encourage the inventors to find "innovative new approaches that produce unusual timbres and/or involve novel sound producing mechanisms." It is an invitation to mix art and science in behalf of a noble cause, and it serves as the chief motivator for the work. The students eventually share their creation with a written paper and a brief videotaped recording. In other Super Courses we'll see how "going public" with school work helps spark imaginations and changes attitudes and intentions.

We'll also see how students learn to judge their own work and the products of colleagues. The Harvard students work with a "panel of outside experts" to explore the instruments that other teams produce, assess their quality, and pick the ones ready to be pressed into production for Abreu's children around the world.

Offbeat Incentives

In another project the people in Applied Physics 50 build outlandish contraptions, mimicking the convoluted designs of cartoonist Rube Goldberg. From the early twentieth century, the San Francisco artist and engineer had entertained and intrigued newspaper audiences with his elaborate cartoon drawings of wild devices. Those contraptions turned some simple act into a complex (and largely unnecessary) series of steps. Each part of the process contained a great deal of physics, as balls rolled down ramps, knocking over objects that triggered some other action, and so forth. The project invited students to build a "Rube Goldberg" machine to crack an egg. It was fun and challenging, calling on their growing understanding of physics to complete their joke. Once more, everyone worked in teams of five, learning from and challenging each other. Every machine had to demonstrate some principle of physics, and the teams had to calculate the energy used in the process.

The course sequences the projects carefully, each one involving some distinct area of physics and containing increased complexity. The professors don't just throw the class into deep water to design a musical instrument or a Rube Goldberg contraption. They prepare the students with less complex challenges. In the first project, for example, teams build a car out of a model kit, choose how it will be propelled, and then analyze its motion. This is an introductory endeavor to give people a sense of how the class unfolds. At this point in the semester, they have not yet been certified to work in the machine shop available to the class, but the model kit offers them all the scaffolding they need. The experience ends with a fair where teams compete to see how far their motorized buggies will travel on one propulsion, each group trying to get the car to reach at least six meters. High-spirited and good-natured competition drives students' involvement.

By the spring semester, the central project returns to that spirit of fun and competition. "Build a safe that only your team can open," using the principles of electromagnetism to operate the lock. At the same time, they are told to crack open the vault of another group. They must be able to open their safe in less than two minutes but keep competitors out for eight. A panel of judges awards points to boxes that can't be opened and for "the clever incorporation of principles of electromagnetism." Even aesthetics and originality receive extra cookies in the competition. You get bonus points also for every safe you can unlock and for every team that can't crack yours. It's all done with a great sense of fun and excitement. We suspect that its success as an educational enterprise depends in major part on what kind of excitement and enthusiasm the professor brings to the game.

Furthermore, instructions for the enterprise contain a small provision that we imagine plays a key role in building team success. It asks students to get to know each other, to exchange email addresses and telephone numbers, and to draw up a short "team contract." In that document each group spells out how they expect to "work together and what to do to resolve problems and disagreements." By this point, the students have already worked in some teams, so the instructions for the contract ask them to think about problems they have run up against in those other experiences and to spell out how they can avoid them in the future.

Learning How to Read and Flipping the Class

Early medieval universities had no easy way to convey information and ideas to their students. Machines to print words and drawings on paper with ease didn't appear until the middle of the fifteenth century. So professors simply told their classes what they wanted them to remember and understand. That oral communication had some advantages, incorporating a rich vocabulary of gestures, words, and inflections that made the best of lecturers masters at simplifying and clarifying their complex ideas, and for several hundred years, this was the only game in town. But deep learning requires intellectual struggles in which learners try not just to comprehend and remember but also to apply, analyze, synthesize, evaluate, and theorize. With lectures just to say the content of a subject in front of students taking up all the class time, little if any space remained to help them engage in those higher-order—and more difficult—mental activities.

Johannes Gutenberg invented his printing press in the mid-1400s, but for several hundred years thereafter, the primary means of getting information and ideas from the professor to the student remained the oral lecture. In the twentieth century, some teachers began shining light on a wall or screen to supplement the sounds of voices, but that still didn't leave much time in class to help students struggle with the tough stuff of understanding, inventing, solving problems, and so forth. "If you asked students to read before they came to class," one professor observed, "Mr. Gutenberg's invention faced two almost insurmountable problems."

Fundamentally, students just didn't complete assignments because reading was lonely and many people didn't know how to read sophisticated texts. The last time many of them had received any systematic instruction or feedback on how to tackle the written word, they were exploring the lives of Dick and Jane or something similar. If you just used reading tests to prod their out-of-class preparation, you ran into the old extrinsic motivation problem, and undergraduates still didn't always know how to read advanced subjects.

That's where Kelly Miller and her colleagues entered the story. She grew up in Toronto and became intrigued with physics through her fascination with sailing. "My father made sure all of his children learned to sail" in the waters around Toronto, she told us. After college, she took a job teaching in a seafaring high school. Students learned while they sailed "the world's oceans aboard a majestic tall ship." (We'll explore the pedagogy of getting out in chapter 16.) She hadn't taken much physics by that point, but the program needed someone to teach the basic course. She took up the responsibilities, fell in love with the "cool" discipline, and later worked on a PhD under Mazur's guidance.

While still a graduate student around 2011, she worked with a team that included her mentor, and two other people to invent something called Perusall, an online environment that could address the reading problem.[1] "We aim to change the nature of reading," they would later write, "from the traditional solitary experience to an engaging and collective one."[2]

Beginning in 2015, students read the physics textbook within the social media that Perusall offered. As they plowed through the online text, they could raise questions, point out something important, pose puzzles, or cry for help. "It is like writing in the margins of the book," Miller observed to us, except that other students could read and respond to those annotations. Gutenberg might turn over in his grave if he knew, but we suspect he would be delighted.

Perusall changed the nature of reading. Miller even developed, as part of her dissertation, algorithms that gave professors and readers important feedback on the quality of the annotations and their interactions with the text. Students taught students, not just about physics but about how to read, cultivating deep approaches and results.

Active Learning in Class

Students could now spend time in class engaged in active learning exercises that help them understand basic concepts and their application. They don't learn by watching someone perform physics on the board. They deepen their understanding while struggling—sometimes individually and other times in groups—with fundamental ideas. You can see in the appendix detailed explanations of the six types of activities that Miller and Mazur use.[3] Those engaging exercises help class members clarify important ideas, challenge misconceptions, and reinforce insights. On any given day, the professor in charge (Miller in the fall; Mazur in the spring) might use two or three of the activities, depending on the complexity of the material and the difficulties that any particular group faced.

"It's an organic process, constantly growing and changing" Miller explained to us. "I might pick a particular exercise because of comments and questions I saw on Perusall." One readiness exercise could dictate the next one. If students don't understand something, she might pick another activity to help them construct better models in their minds or clean out the dusty cobwebs of misconceptions that clutter the backwaters of their thinking.

Grading

As Mazur changed the course in 2014, he paid special attention to the way grading played out. He knew that you can't force students to take a deep approach, but your system of summative evaluation can certainly eat away at natural curiosity and even the drive to help other people. He and his colleagues developed a complex and comprehensive policy that is difficult to tease apart. Borrowing one or two parts without a broader understanding of the whole could produce much different results than intended. Let's look at two basic principles.

First, the grade in Applied Physics A and B depends on how well students eventually meet detailed and fully explained criteria, not on how they do in comparison with their classmates. If everyone achieves those high standards, so much the better, and they all receive the highest mark. By the end of the course, they should understand complex physics concepts and develop the ability to use that understanding to solve real-world problems (content mastery), often working in teams. But they must also learn how to operate as self-directed learners, to contribute productively to the work and learning of a team, and to display a high level of professionalism. That latter category means they are joining a community of learners and accept their responsibility to make contributions on time, and to act as an ethical person. Anyone who doesn't regularly prepare for each class has not operated in an honorable manner.

Second, students have multiple opportunities to meet those benchmarks, receive feedback, and try again without killing their grades. Only in the end do their performances translate into something that goes on a transcript. In the meantime, the Readiness Assurance Activities and other devices help students learn. They are not there to make judgments about someone's final abilities. In the last chapter, we'll return to the question of grades and the role that they play in the building of a Super Course.

Then Came the Pandemic

When COVID-19 forced colleges and universities to close their doors and go online, the move touched off a firestorm of protests and worry. "The thought of paying the same amount . . . for another semester of lackluster classes is a nonstarter," *USA Today* concluded.[4] Small schools with few resources worried that they might go under, and a bevy of well-heeled institutions faced lawsuits totaling more than a billion dollars for their alleged damage to students. Educators often felt beleaguered and reluctant to try anything new.

Super Course designers, however, often saw the crisis as one more compelling reason to experiment. No doubt, even well-conceived educational experiences benefit when people get together, but that missing human contact isn't the chief problem with moving to distance education. The pandemic has highlighted weaknesses among conventional offerings that many people didn't see before. If the turn of events forces schools to remain online or return there, we believe that Applied Physics 50 and other Super Courses are best equipped to weather the postpandemic academic world.[5]

If you think about all the aspects of this no-lecture, no-final-exam, team-and-project-based course, nothing in its structure required people to get together in the same room at the same time two or three times a week. The groups could still work on their projects virtually, exchanging ideas via phone calls, Zoom meetings, and Skype sessions. Harvard students came from multiple time zones and spread back across the globe when the campus closed in Cambridge, Massachusetts, but they didn't miss a beat, continuing to struggle with the concepts and their applications. The class could still employ Perusall to read the textbook in a social environment, and mutually support and encourage one another in doing so. ConcepTests remained as vibrant as ever, and no worse the wear from their new residence online. So did other exercises and the enticing projects.

Many traditional classes didn't fare so well. A lack of flexibility emerged as one of their major liabilities. They were built around synchronous meetings where professors dispensed information in long lectures. Students then retreated to asynchronous isolated individual sessions, where these learners struggled alone to devour required reading and try to make sense of all the teacher had told them. They often faced reading quizzes rather than the nurturing environment of Perusall. That important sense of being self-directed learners no doubt waned in the face of such blatant extrinsic rewards and punishments. The appeal of those traditional courses often depended in part on snazzy voice tones, compelling gestures, and the charm of personal contact with friends and maybe the teacher. When the pandemic shattered that world, many students felt cheated. In those "online lecture courses," attendance appears to have dropped precipitously as students decided to watch the recorded lectures completely alone.

Super Courses, meanwhile, rested on engaging questions, students struggling together, the chance to try, come up short, receive feedback, and try again. These courses promised intellectual and personal growth. When Mazur surveyed what he and his colleagues had done, he concluded, "after moving [this] course completely online, there are a number of components that I am not going to move back offline—it's been quite a learning experience and an eye-opener."

CHAPTER TEN

Soup of Interdisciplinary Learning

Chengdu is a rapidly growing city of more than ten million people located just east of the enchanted Himalayan ranges of southwest China. The most sacred mountain of Buddhism rises in those peaks and contains an array of red temples and troops of wild monkeys roaming the higher elevations. In Chengdu and on a branch campus in Emei at the foot of that sanctified mount, Southwest Jiaotong University has more than thirty thousand students and a proud history of engineering and scientific prowess. Its curriculum has also included the humanities and the arts, physical education, the social sciences, and a wide range of other disciplines. Local leaders will tell you about the contributions that the school has made to the six-thousand-mile web of high-speed electric trains that now zip through the countryside knitting the nation together. Yet the school has more to celebrate than the railroad museum in one corner of the campus.

In the last five years, the university has produced some remarkable examples of interdisciplinary courses that invest students with a goal that is larger than the course or any of the single disciplines. As these learners pursue that big objective, motivated by its intrigue and potential power, they become self-directed scholars feeding on the fascination and importance of what they find before them, while escaping many of the problems that plague more traditional classrooms. Two women, Li Hao and Fan Yihong, have helped spark this transformation.

Sichuan Province, the most populated in China, is a land of both long tranquility and geological upheavals that shake foundations to their core. The earthquakes that occasionally rumble through this majestic landscape can upend nearly everything, but thanks to a twenty-five-hundred-year-old engineering miracle that split the Ming River and built an irrigation system that still runs on its own, this valley of four rivers has enjoyed centuries free of floods and famine, allowing the culinary culture plenty of time to blend spices and food into a one of the world's great cuisines.

That tradition of integration has spilled over into the educational innovations that have appeared at the university in recent years. When Song Ailing came to Southwest with a degree in physical education, she sometimes worried about fitting into a university of science and technology, In March 2015 she participated in a new faculty workshop that Professor Fan conducted and which introduced her to interdisciplinary education. In short order, she and a few other colleagues began meeting over lunch to fashion a course they eventually called Sports, Science, Technology and Wise Life. Professors from electrical and mechanical engineering, materials science, and marketing joined Song with her background in sports studies as they lunched together.

In Sichuan people usually eat meals gathered at a round table with a large rotating center (Americans call it a "lazy Susan"). As food floats around on the rotating platform, diners choose which dishes entice them. In the intellectual conversations that emerged, these faculty members did more than build their individual plates. They mixed ingredients to create a new learning experience for the whole table. As with all round platforms, no one sat at the head to chair the session. Everyone had equal influence.

They began with a problem. How can the people in their classes learn to think critically and creatively, to communicate ideas clearly and effectively, take concepts and knowledge from diverse fields and integrate them together, and to work collaboratively in doing so. How can they help students improve their ability to become good problem solvers using technical and scientific knowledge? How can those students develop a strong devotion to civic responsibility while beginning to comprehend how both the human body and markets work?

In the years immediately following the Second World War, a Soviet inventor and science-fiction writer began a massive study of creative ideas that would help inform the work of the educators in Chengdu. Genrich Altshuller dug through thousands of inventions listed in the world's patent offices. He looked for patterns both in the creations and in the problems they addressed. The upshot of his work was a "theory of inventive problem solving." In Russian that phrase has the initials TRIZ, and that's the name often given to his creation. The Chengdu innovators wanted their students to learn both design theory and TRIZ as they tackled problems.

As the teachers engaged in their own passion-driven adventure to create a new kind of learning experience for their students, their conception of what it meant to teach began to shift. "We all sensed our own growth together with the students," one of them told us. These instructors could no longer just act as an "imparting person" showing their "own talents at the podium." As they tasted the sour and sweet, the bitter and aromatic dishes that circled the table, these pioneers began to see that they had to create an interactive environment where students would most likely develop new capacities. They had to endow those learners with a passion of their own, something larger than mastering any single discipline and making good grades. In the weeks to come, they created a Super Course where students worked in teams to create engineering products that addressed physical education issues and the good life. In the process of chasing that objective, the students would achieve the diverse learning objectives the educators had identified.

On the first day of class, they invited students to play and find challenges in their games. Professor Song asked the class what athletic activities they enjoyed most and announced that they would experience some of those sports to identify problems that humans face in benefitting from them. "I was surprised by the excitement that shot through the room," Dong Fangfei, a language and literature major, remembered. Rock climbing impressed him and his group most. Others took a fancy to swimming, cycling, badminton, basketball, or other sports. Engineering and liberal arts students each brought their own talents and perspectives to the enterprise. "We could form very compatible teams to invent and make products," argued one young humanist.

After a field trip to a sports equipment center, the students began to brainstorm about the exercise problems they might tackle and how they would do so. One group designed a small, comprehensive workout machine that could be "disassembled" for easy movement. On that device, users could drill their abdominal and chest muscles, legs, arms, and other body parts. In the project Tang Jinhua and other students "learned about the comprehensive properties of materials" and studied "the structure of the human muscle so the equipment can adapt to different people." They used 3-D software to design the size and shape, and they studied marketing principles and research to consider how they could sell their creation. They learned to work in teams, to reason through evidence and ideas, to reach logical solutions, to make value judgments, to exercise aesthetic choices, and to weigh the social and economic implications of their work.

"I not only gained knowledge and abilities, but also friendship from our teamwork," Tang emphasized. "I have a new understanding of life and learning in the university." I must "challenge myself and constantly learn new knowledge." In essence, the students were both building a new community of knowledgeable peers and joining the intellectual groups to which their professors already belonged within their disciplines.

With the help of the marketing professor on the faculty team, the people in the class began to turn their work into a product. Zhou Jilin and her colleagues learned "how to analyze the market . . . and how to sell a product." But that part of the class was more than an exercise in business basics. For Zhou, a self-described "oblivious girl," the experience "built up" her "self-confidence," helping her "amplify" the "potential" she now found in herself. Because they had to share their creations with others, the students learned to communicate clearly and effectively.

As people in the class confronted their special problem, sliced it into the categories suggested by TRIZ, and explored the engineering principles they might employ, they also dug into the physiology of the exercises. How does the body work? What are the physical and chemical processes when you do this activity? What can go wrong? In class, members of the faculty team would circulate through the room, using their "professional knowledge to help" students with their "ideas and solutions."

On occasion, the teachers served tea, "playing music for us to build a relaxed atmosphere," as one student put it. For Jia Chunlin, a mechanical engineering student, much of the magic came from the discussions that the projects prompted. In traditional classes, "we just sat there and accepted knowledge passively." In this one, "we become active participants in the learning." That meant "different voices prompted us to think more deeply."

Most of the students came to the university to study some branch of engineering, but others majored in language, literature, and other non-science fields. For Huang Yanqiu, who studied how to teach Mandarin to nonspeakers, the course was at first terrifying because "there was not enough science knowledge in my head." Yet the collaborative learning experience working with students from electrical and mechanical engineering helped him catch up quickly. Students taught students.

It worked because of the "harmonious teamwork," as Huang put it, that developed among students, within the faculty team, and between the teachers and their pupils. They tackled fascinating problems and trusted one another, recognizing the unique perspectives that each person brought to the enterprise and how each could contribute to the endeavor. For the people taking the class, their projects made discussions more meaningful while their conversations drove their testing, probing, and designing. Through "bumps" and "zigzags," through "theory and practice," the novice engineers tried and sometimes failed, received feedback and questions, and tried again. "We often found a gap between theory and practice," Jia remembered a year after taking the class. They built new paradigms and insights, combining physical and mental exercise. When something worked, it stirred students' excitement and imagination. "When the robot first moves," one class member recalled, "we shouted 'bravo, bravo.' " One quiet student confessed, "I pretended to be calm; actually my heart already lit up as with fireworks."

In April 2018,[1] we brought some of the people who had taken the course back together to share their experiences. Zhou Jilin, a young woman studying mechanical engineering, remembered the "bumpy journey" and how her team felt "more and more frustrated" because each idea they generated had obvious flaws. But she also recalled the day Professor Song came to her group and gently guided them to make a choice rather than "keep digging new wells." It was perhaps a Chinese version of "Don't let perfection become the enemy of the good," or as Confucius allegedly put it, "Better a diamond with a flaw than a pebble without." The message propelled her group forward.

Interdisciplinary Courses in New England: Giving Students Control

When Charlie Cannon turned to creating interdisciplinary courses more than a decade ago, two mid-nineteenth-century young men helped inspire his efforts. In 1857, Frederick Law Olmsted, a thirty-five-year-old park superintendent, and Calvert Vaux, an architect from Great Britain, pooled their talents to offer detailed plans for a new park in what became New York City. They suggested that their burgeoning metropolis on the Hudson River transform some "broken swampy ground into a visual amenity, and a road strategy that would not impair the city's service traffic."[2]

Olmsted and Vaux won the competition to create what became Central Park in Manhattan. As Charlie Cannon wrote, their design triumphed because of "its broad vision and attention to detail." For Cannon, however, the most telling point was what happened next. "Olmstead would spend," the Rhode Island professor summarized, the "next sixteen years organizing thousands of workers, wrangling political support, overseeing engineers and gardeners, and courting the media in order to realize Central Park." That interdisciplinary prowess impressed Cannon, who began to wonder how such abilities could be cultivated in people today. How do you help your students become the kind of creative driving force that turned Olmsted into a legend and the most productive landscape architect in US history? We still need, Charlie Cannon argued, his "unflagging vision, political acumen, organizational skills and technical knowledge."

In 2004, we examined, in part, what Cannon and his colleagues would create at the Rhode Island School of Design. But let's look again at that treatment from *What the Best College Teachers Do*, probing it this time through the lens of a passion-driven adventure, interdisciplinary project-based learning, and a natural critical learning environment. We'll pay special attention to how Cannon began with a project of his own making and got his students to take it over. In the process, we will explore an early Super Course with considerable influence. When a Korean television network produced a multipart series of documentaries on nine excellent teachers from around the world, they focused in part on Cannon's course.[3]

Redefining Learning Objectives

His observation of Olmsted's career and thoughts about his profession in the twenty-first century led Cannon to rethink the traditional learning goals for his students. That standard education had emphasized highly technical expertise in some distinct box of education. You studied to become this or that, but seldom both, and seldom learned how to run something as complex as Olmsted's Central Park project. In the new Super Course, Cannon sought to promote collaborative skills and to integrate diverse disciplines. Students would learn to move outside their narrow field of specialty, considering environmental, social, economic, community, and political issues, and to take a deep approach in their learning.

Cannon created a course in which he chose the project (at times, some would argue, that's necessary) but planned from the beginning for students to take control of it and their own education. He became the facilitator, the guide by the side, rather than the dictator, judge, and jury of their work. In that role, he planned the dinner party and invited his guests to the table, scheduling times and places where they could work together on something big and important. But he ultimately left them with lots of choices and control. Most important, he designed the experience so that if students accepted his invitation, they would invest themselves in a goal that was larger than the class, even bigger than any single discipline. As they pursued that end, they would learn deeply.

That did not mean Cannon could simply pick any project that he fancied. Students had to accept his invitation, and he could ill afford to offer a steak dinner to a group of vegetarians. He had to invite rather than command them to the table, and he needed to be completely candid about both the costs and the rewards. Even on the first day of class, the Rhode Island professor helped students understand the "heavy demands of time they faced,"[4] but the enterprising educator also made clear two highly appealing aspects of the experience.

First, they would be working collaboratively to achieve something valuable, and, second, their efforts in this class could have wide influence: their experience with collaboration and multiple perspectives could help reform a profession traditionally locked in highly individual work, and the ideas they generated on the problem at hand might actually be implemented. They would help define "whose voices are heard in a large-scale public project," and how a clamor "of words and ideas gets turned into something concrete."[5] Human beings love to feel that they are part of something larger than themselves, and Cannon designed his class to appeal to that sentiment.[6]

If he expected students to take control, they had to learn how to collaborate. Few of them had any experience. Cannon couldn't leave them in charge without helping them engage in that kind of work. "You will play shifting roles," he emphasized in multiple ways. One day a student might be a facilitator, the next a transcriber, someone who monitors whether everyone gets included in the discussion, or the person who "attends to the emotional tenor of the group." Students needed to respect one another's work. They are "all in the same boat."[7] None of them yet knew much about the topics they would investigate.

Every year, the big project at the center of this work varied. When we studied his class, he asked students to help evaluate and perhaps plan a proposed waste treatment plant on New York harbor. Such enterprises are often highly controversial and fraught with political, social, and economic pitfalls that can easily ensnare the unprepared. Society needs to treat its waste, but nobody wants a facility in their backyard. It was a devilishly fascinating puzzle with such a variety of issues that could give students rich experiences.

Across the semester, Cannon shifted power to the students until "they had assumed ownership" over the project. While he spelled out what they must achieve, he left them in charge of how they did it. To begin, each student had to pick an individual topic related to the overall project that they would explore thoroughly. "For the remainder of the semester," he told the class, "each of you will become the class expert on your single topic. If we need to know about the migration patterns of rattlesnakes, we'll know who can tell us."[8] When students brought their research findings back to class, they quizzed each other, integrated their findings into a series of large boards, and left them on permanent display in the classroom. That activity formed their first major experience with the kind of collaborative work that would define their educational experience.

Four weeks into the semester, Cannon finally took the class to the site of their project, the place on the New York harbor where the waste treatment plant was supposed to be built. On their trip down to the Big Apple they undertook several side tours, including going to a "town dump" and a "recycling center," and a visit with engineers who "make products out of recycled materials."

"Their book-based learning," Cannon noted, "was suddenly connected to how dirty things might be on the ground." The professor arranged for students to drive around the neighborhood, and he took them to the local library, where they examined phone books to see the kinds of businesses in the area and pored over aerial and zoning maps. With that work behind them, they met with community and environmental activists, New York architects and artists, and a variety of related people. Cannon arranged with some of those individuals to meet with his students in a giant two-day brainstorming session, generating ideas about the design and location of the proposed waste treatment plant.

On the first day they reached no conclusions. "I want them to spell out the broadest array of possible approaches," the professor explained, and "to immerse themselves in the soup of non-conclusion." On the second day, they began to think about implications and to group their ideas into clusters. "They were encouraged," Cannon told us, "to develop ideas that are as physically different from each other as possible so that they could begin to recognize that no one solution is the sole answer to the problem."

The climax of the class came in the "Master Planning State." At that point, Cannon gave up all control and turned it over to the students. He did that with an ingenious message. "It's not likely," he told the class, "that any of our ideas thus far are the right answer. We need to develop design guidelines or philosophies for attacking this work and I want you to come up with those ideas, to decide what direction the studio will go. Work out what the class project will be." They could not design and build a complete waste treatment plant on the East River, but what would they do that would help them learn to live creative and productive lives?

He then left the room. It was a form of Sugata Mitra's noninvasive pedagogy, but knowing exactly when and how to execute that departure comes only with lots of practice and feedback, perhaps from both students and colleagues. It comes with a bit of luck, with a timing and grace discovered accidentally from a part of yourself you didn't know you had. But it also usually comes with growing comprehension of why anyone would use this teaching technique, with a deep understanding of the research and theory on the human need for autonomy, and with a large measure of humility, empathy with your students, and concern for their learning. We suggested earlier that teaching well was a lot like playing a violin. Maybe it is more like playing any instrument in a jazz quartet.

At that key point, the students designed the rest of the course and the problem they would address from that point forward. "Now the year belongs to them." Cannon observed. "They have usurped my limited problem, reframed it, and defined the goals of the studio." From this point on in the course, they are now in charge of their own education, picking their own path through the wealth of learning opportunities before them. Cannon is still there, ready to provide assistance if they need it. The students decide what outside experts they might consult, including their teacher, divide up the work before them, and decide how they would share research and ideas with one another.

In a more traditional studio class at Rhode Island School of Design, the students produce a polished piece of work. The people in Cannon's class can't possibly do that. With all the extra stuff they must digest in this multidisciplinary involvement, with the sophistication and creativity with which they must tackle their complex real-world project, they don't have time to reach a full set of designs. Yet they do develop an array of competencies. They learn how to identify problems and design solutions. When all is said and done, they can work collaboratively to consider a variety of perspectives, do research, and weigh environmental concerns and other long-range results of their work. The students emerge transformed from the experience because it challenges and changes the way they will subsequently think, act, feel, create, and value.

CHAPTER ELEVEN

Integration of Abilities

In the late 1930s a young Texan envisioned creating a new kind of college course. Rather than studying a particular subject, students in his emerging masterpiece would work to find their own creative abilities across all disciplines. "Everybody is a genius,"[1] he kept saying, "and I want to help them find their creative self." This didn't mean that all humans had Einstein's mathematical abilities or scientific imagination, nor did it signal that everyone possessed Beethoven's musical talents. Indeed, the young professor thought each person was unique and that those individual qualities made that person special. He wanted to create an experience that would allow all students to unleash and grow "the dynamic powers of their own mind," whatever those abilities might be.

For Paul Baker, the son of a Presbyterian minister, that process began with a new definition of what it meant to become educated. "To some," he would say, "growth is almost all" about memorizing stuff. To others, "it lies in learning how gadgets work—how to put motors together, how to attach pipes, [and to] mix formulas." That kind of growth, he argued, "is never to develop a new method but to become extremely adept at the old ones." For still others, education would help you gain prestige and position in life. You go to college to make connections, to build relationships so you can count yourself among the privileged. You learn to "join, dictate, slap backs, smoke cigars in backrooms, belong to important committees, become a pseudo artist, musician, actor, prophet, preacher, politician. You drop names and surround yourself with" indicators of status.

Baker wanted to invite people into a new pursuit, one that sought to live a creative life, to discover who you are and how you can use your own unique experiences and the world around you to fashion something fresh and better. For the Texas educator, creative growth could come in any area, not just in the arts, and was as central to human well-being as Edward Deci and Richard Ryan's idea of competency. Your inventive product, he kept emphasizing "could be a sermon, a scientific formula, or a book, but it could also be something you build, a well-planned street system, a beautiful meal, or a well-run gas station." It could be a new way of looking at the world, solving problems, rearing children, treating old people, or resolving conflicts. Fundamentally, it would change the way you lived your life, thought about yourself, and how you conceived of learning, intelligence and ability. Baker believed that all human beings had a psychological need to be creative.

"A lot of people" haven't changed since "they were juniors in high school," Baker declared. "They've got the same concepts, the same ways of looking at conditions about them, the same answers, the same emotional and visual images and pictures that they've always had; there has been practically no change in them."

For the first few years of his early life, Paul had lived in Hereford, a small town forty-five miles southwest of Amarillo in the Texas panhandle. His experience there would profoundly influence his educational philosophy. It was a flatland of cattle and dust storms. "I'm a West Texan!" he would later write. "That means I come from sun-conquered and wind-conquered country. It is a cruel country," he remembered, "and the faces of the old men who have lived there all their lives show the sand, wind, heat and dryness of it all." Yet the land sparked growth.

"As a child, I was overwhelmed by the tremendous sky and great flat land," Baker remembered. "That space bounded by very distant horizons, where flat earth met the sky, seemed to me an infinity of distances. That was the first great space I knew." That focus on space would become central to his educational ideas.

When he turned eight his parents moved to Waxahachie, a green and humid semitropical hamlet southeast of Dallas near the piney woods of

East Texas. When he was eighteen, he went to school at the local college but then did graduate work at Yale, studying with George Pierce Baker (no relation), the legendary dramatist whose classes also included the likes of Eugene O'Neill and Thomas Wolfe.

In that academic and artistic New England culture, Baker had tasted the oysters of a whole new world, then toured England, Germany, Russia, and Japan, studying theater design and production. Out of that mix of cultures, he began to fashion the learning insights that guided his Super Course, which he called Integration of Abilities.[2]

Baker would become a world-renowned theater director who pioneered a mixture of sights and sounds that transformed the stages of the world, even among impresarios who never heard his name. He integrated film and live performers in an ever-moving potpourri of actions and lights, no curtains to interrupt the flow.

He would work with Frank Lloyd Wright to design the only theater the famous architect ever produced, while celebrated actors like Charles Laughton and Burgess Meredith flocked to his studio and classroom. In the 1950s Baker would achieve an international reputation both for his innovative design of Studio One, where audiences sat in revolving chairs and followed action on six stages that surrounded them, and for his forward-looking approach to drama. He integrated cubism into the theater and split Hamlet into three characters. Laughton called his production of Othello "the most exciting piece of theater in America."[3] Yet Baker regarded his class Integration of Abilities as his most important creation.

Einstein and Creativity

Baker came of age in an era that began to prize creativity and to see its connection to everything. The major scientist of his youth, Albert Einstein, had famously championed imagination in an interview that appeared in a popular weekly magazine, the *Saturday Evening Post*. Sitting in his Berlin apartment only a few years before the Nazis drove him to move to Princeton, New Jersey, the celebrated mathematician unloaded his views on learning and teaching. While Elsa Lowenthal, his second wife, served strawberries and other fruits, the man whose last name became synonymous with genius concluded, "I am enough of the artist to draw freely upon my imagination. Imagination is more important than knowledge," he proclaimed. "Knowledge is limited. Imagination encircles the world."[4]

Looking Inward

In the shadow of those pronouncements, Paul Baker fashioned a course designed to spark imagination and creativity. In the arena of his class, the journey toward a creative life began by looking inward and recognizing how different you are. "You come from a certain soil, a certain family," the young Texas educator would tell his class. "You were born in a certain house at a certain time. Nobody else in the world has done so." Students can, Baker emphasized, develop ideas and perspectives that no one else will originate.

"Each of you has your own philosophy, your own viewpoint, your own physical tensions and background." To live the creative life, people must, first, learn to look inward, to understand themselves and find out how their mind works, to explore their own history and begin to pull from those experiences.

But he also stressed the implications of such an idea. If everyone is different, we can all learn from one other. We can benefit from the great ideas—from calculus to cubism, from economics to engineering—that have emerged from human thinking, and from the experiences of the ages. An important part of the creative process, the Texas educator stressed, is the ability to recognize good ideas when we encounter them and to integrate them with our own. But one can't recognize something new unless willing to explore.

Great civilizations develop at crossroads where many perspectives come together. Creative minds emerge at the intersection of ideas and concepts, but if we expect to benefit we must immerse ourselves in the disruptive flow of new perspectives and possibilities, soaking up their refreshing waters. The world becomes our oyster, a soil where minds and ideas can devour the incredible diversity that lies within human history and experience and blend it with the special qualities of our own life. In the process, we can all learn to live the creative life and taste the pleasures of a growing mindset.

Baker's philosophy and course became a powerful rationale and motivation for a broad, deep, and highly integrated education. His class offered a way for students to seize the steering wheel of their own education and to build a new life. Over the next sixty years, thousands of students "found themselves" in the Texas Super Course, first at Baylor and later at Trinity University in San Antonio, crafting a unique creative life in medicine, the performing arts, law, film, history, chemistry, education, science, journalism, politics, music, writing, business, engineering, parenting, and a host of other endeavors.[5] "It was the most important course I took in college," one former student noted. "I learned to learn, to write, to think, to dig deeply into my own brain, to understand myself and the world, to be mindful of how I thought and worked."

Paul Baker came from the theater and did none of the research that distinguished the careers of later learning scientists, yet he began to grasp some important insights into human learning and how best to foster it. Long before Carol Dweck did her pioneering work on growth mindsets, Baker had anticipated the concepts that would make her famous and built a way to foster the transforming liberation of believing that one's brain could grow. On the bonny banks of the Brazos River, in Waco, Texas, the later ideas of Bandura, Dweck, Hatano, Inagaki, Deci, and Ryan hoovered around Baker's shoulders, whispering wild and enticing notions in his ear, even before they pestered the research scientists and theorists.

The Texas director anticipated the insights of self-efficacy, growth mindsets, and adaptive expertise, and he recognized the importance of intrinsic motivation in the way he structured his class. As his students pursued the creative life, they defined an early and highly robust notion about deep learning rather than the strategic or surface quest of academic honors or simply "getting through the course alive."

He even foreshadowed some twenty-first-century findings on the connection between learning and physical exercise. For decades, at the beginning of every Integration of Abilities class, Baker led students in five minutes of physical and vocal gymnastics. "I cannot work with you if you are tired and listless," he told the class. "I want the blood flowing and your mind sharp."

As a group of scientists in Maryland recently pointed out, "A growing body of research suggests that regular participation in long-term exercise is associated with enhanced cognitive function." In their own work, they found that "acute exercise was associated with significantly greater semantic memory activation," including "greater activation in the bilateral hippocampus."[6] Several recent classroom experiments have observed that students who exercise at the beginning of a class do better in the course than those who don't. Wendy Suzuki, a professor of neuroscience at New York University, for example, set up a comparison between a class that exercised at the start of each session and one that did not, and she found the former students did significantly better in the course.[7]

The Opportunity to Grow

"I hope everyone in this class will decide to reach inside themselves, to explore who they are and what they have, and learn to use those inner powers," Paul Baker told his students every semester. "Not for success, not to be seen; that's not important. What is important is that you fulfill your own personal need to keep growing."

In his class Baker created a remarkable world of fun where students could act like children, with all the benefits of youthful curiosity and exploration, yet still learn some tough lessons. His Super Course would have none of the usual pressures of "assignments and requirements," with him almost deliberately avoiding those words. Instead he invited students into this alternative educational universe where their motivations came from within themselves, from their desire to live a creative life and understand themselves. "I'm going to give you some exercises," he would say after laying out his vision of integrated learning and personal uniqueness. "They are a little crazy, but they work."

When he suggested that students write out their "life up to now," and record on paper their reactions to everything they did in class, he stripped away all the trappings of school writing assignments. "Write in pencil," he casually proposed, "or with crayons." He told them not to worry about the usual rules of composition, just to get their ideas and reactions on paper so they could study themselves and see how they think.

Baker wanted those exercises and the related activity to help students to embrace their own mistakes and thereby to appreciate several key ideas about the work of the mind. First, people often latch onto the first thought that comes easily to mind while works of genius require repeated failure and the willingness to keep pushing for something fresh and uniquely yours.

Second, he wanted them to know that an initial difficulty with a subject or task doesn't mean one can't ever do it. It was the same idea that Carol Dweck invoked with her emphasis on a "Not Yet" grade ("You haven't done it yet," a teacher might say, rather than "you failed"). Baker would coax students into envisioning themselves doing a "work of the mind," something that built what Albert Bandura called "self-efficacy."[8]

Third, while external forces can corral the best of intentions, limiting success, internal factors still have more power than we might suspect. Much of traditional schooling and life have given us simple habits in the way we think. To learn is to break free of those old routines, to push ourselves, to build and rebuild, to question, struggle, and seek a better way of understanding and doing something. Although Baker never used this language, he might have said that he hoped to produce what Ellen Langer called "mindful thinking,"[9] that process in which we build new categories, think about our thinking as we are thinking, turning something one way and then another, looking for deeper meaning, and something new.[10]

Students took on two large projects to achieve this goal. First was an exercise in self-examination. The students were told to think about some creative act they'd achieved in the past and begin to exam it. It could be an innovative solution to a math problem, something they wrote, a personal relationship they repaired, a new way of understanding an important idea, or anything that represents a fine work of the mind. What motivated them to undertake the creative act? How did they overcome their resistance to work? What habits did they marshal in behalf of the effort? Which ones did they need to overcome? Did they carry a small notepad to record random thoughts and questions?

They needed to find out what can keep them from working on a creative enterprise. "Get used to the pattern by which things come up in your mind and in your imagination," Baker urged. "Find out when and at what times of the day you work best and what motivates you." What kind of space did they need? What mood worked best? What feelings could stop them? Did they need to walk, sit, stare at the sky or a blank wall, sit in the grass or snow, or work in a particular corner of the library, deep in the stacks where they maintain their own study space?

How did they block out distractions that might keep them from working? Did they need to move around, or find a secure and personal space where they would do all their work? Did they need to eat ice cream before they got started? Could they visualize themselves working hard at something? What led them to that moment? What kept them going? How can they understand themselves and how they work and what keeps them from working.

The second major activity asked students to study a work of art that intrigued them, to become excited about a great creative endeavor of the mind, to recognize innovation and originality in other people, and to poke around behind a product of genius and discover its creative nature.

Explore the way artists work. How do they come to certain ideas? Why do they reject others? What interests and fascinations drive them? Can you find your own passion and let it spark you? "If you are not capable of excitement, you will never produce anything."

Many of his students began to integrate art into their lives, to explore sculpture, dance, drama, photography, paintings, music, and to let it challenge their thinking and stimulate their mind. A physician in Austin told us how that exercise in Baker's class changed his understanding of the arts and the role they could play in his work. It awakened a new passion, spawning an awe with the world and the creative process. It challenged his thinking. As a result, he revolutionized his own medical practice, built a sizeable fortune, then used it to endow new theaters and performance halls, dropping $55 million on the school of music at the University of Texas. Future scientists, political leaders, economists, writers, musicians, social workers, business entrepreneurs, historians, and others took Baker's course and began using artistic creations to challenge their thinking.

Here's the most unusual aspect of those two endeavors, and perhaps a key secret to their success in transforming lives. Baker didn't treat either of these two activities as "assignments," in the traditional fashion of a school course. He didn't say they had to finish the work by a certain day, didn't collect the autobiographies that he suggested students write, or give them letter grades. He didn't give the students long comments on how they wrote, or spill red ink over their efforts. Yet the people in his classes undertook these activities and sometimes worked on them for years, letting them transform their lives, activities, attitudes, and ways of thinking. That doesn't mean that he reached every person who sat in his class, but he did profoundly influence most of them.

That succeeded because of how Baker introduced the projects, appealing to deep intrinsic sentiments and giving students a sense of control over their studies. "This is a class in discovering your own creative ability, and all you will have to help you with your discovery is yourself and getting acquainted with the way you work." The thought of taking a class about themselves intoxicated students. "What you bring to this class is yourself and your desire to participate, and what you do in here depends finally upon that," he advised. "You will fail only if you don't work, and you do not use the exercise to learn something about yourself." He told them to take an interest in who they want to be because that's all they've got. "You are a unique person with much to contribute. You need to find out who you are. There are no right or wrong answers. There is just you," Baker would contend. "How are you ever going to learn about yourself if you don't . . . engage in an inner dialogue," he asked. "You want to know what's going on inside your brain, and that's why you are putting these things down in a notebook."

"I studied in major part," we heard again and again, "because everything I learned, all the ideas and insights, helped spark imagination and made me more productive." Baker took people who came from weak and sometimes disengaged educational backgrounds and helped turn them into highly productive and creative human beings.

Five Exercises

In addition to these two overarching activities, Baker built his transformative experience around five exercises, each one designed to help people understand themselves, including their strengths and weaknesses, and to open up a dialogue with their inner being. The Texas theater director came from a world where words mattered and—along with light, movement, sound, colors, and the silhouette of props—created fantasies, raised philosophical questions, provoked thoughts and feelings, and made people laugh and cry. It should not be too surprising then that he gave students a new vocabulary for thinking about the creative process.

To create, he claimed, one must work with five elements: space, time (or rhythm), motion (direction or line), sound (or silence), and silhouette (or color). Those five components became, for his students, a universal language for the creative process. "We can express everything," one of them would argue years later, "including the theory of relativity, in terms of those elements."

In one exercise they worked with space and movement, thinking about how they approached it. He would invite them to walk across a space displaying tragedy, then do it expressing comedy. In exercises, they reacted to lines and words. Sometimes they let their thoughts flow like a stream, letting their minds run wild. In others, they would "listen to their muscles." They analyzed and played, twisted and turned, flipping ideas over in their minds and looking at them from a variety of perspectives.

Each student, for example, studied a person he or she had known for a long time, exploring every aspect of the subject's life then distilling everything into a rhythm. "About fifteen or twenty times during the distilling process," Baker would say, "you are going to get a quick result. Every time you do so write it out and go back and make yourself start over." He asked them to stop being concerned with a "good result," rather to engage in the process. "When you are building a new kind of life for yourself, this process of discovery is the key to growth." In those words, he defined a new kind of environment and approach that stimulated student engagement.

In the grand culminating exercise, students began with lines and moved to color and language, ultimately creating works of arts coming out of the exercise, painting, molding clay, or whatever pleased them. They might write a play or short story. But as Baker kept saying, it wasn't the product that mattered. It was the process. It was the opportunity to rebuild the way they think and work, to examine themselves, learning to use their experiences but also recognizing how they could use the creative energies and processes of other people to grow the "dynamic powers of their own mind." These were exercises that bolstered a growth mindset, helping students see the potential within them. They sparked self-efficacy and helped students build their own sense of autonomy and self-motivation.

Because the whole experience emphasized embracing mistakes, trying repeatedly, because it stressed the uniqueness of each person, the class fostered a sense of competency. Because students had joined a community of creative people, each one unique, yet everyone connected through the exchange of ideas and perspectives, the integration of abilities said they were part of a grand process that was bigger than any one individual.

In other words, the secret sauce in this unconventional world was learning how to be mindful. In each exercise, students looked at something quite ordinary—a walk across the floor, a branch, a word—from new perspectives and paid attention to how their brain processed stuff. As Baker kept reminding them, the final product didn't matter. It was the process of being mindful that could transform them. How did their mind work? How did they come to understand something, and how could they look at something they'd encountered all their life and see in it something different. They learned to believe in the power of changing how they approached work and their capacity to grow. Carol Dweck's growth mindset and Ellen Langer's mindful thinking danced in their brains.

Much of the literature on learning uses the metaphor of the ladder. In its old-line traditional form, some people appear to be better climbers than others. The geniuses can zoom to the highest rungs while the mediocre and inadequate lag far below. Even Carol Dweck's idea of a growth mindset kept the ladder metaphor firmly in place, suggesting that the key to good climbing skills rested in one's concept of intelligence. If one believed brains could grow, that they were highly malleable, learners would more likely reach a higher plane.

Baker had built his course on the idea of growth but did so around a fundamentally different metaphor, a tree with an array of branches. Any given limb wasn't better than another, just different. There was no mad race to the top, just unique people, each one struggling to develop his or her full potential, and playing off of each other. The tree metaphor eliminated competition for the top spot and left students with the joy of living a creative life, learning about themselves and others, and using the latter not in any exploitive enterprise but in the mutually beneficial process of personal growth. If one student expanded his or her creative capacity, that person became more beneficial to others.

Nothing in any of this philosophy says there are no standards. It does mean that each person seeks to meet a criterion, not to compete with other people, and that all will blossom in their own way, and it does leave open the possibility that one might define a new standard. Students coming out of the course learned to value their abilities to find and explore their own uniqueness rather than basing their self-worth on how they ranked against other people. "I came out of that class," one person reported years later, "understanding that I wasn't going to school for my teachers. They didn't live my life. I was the only one responsible for who I was going to be."

Baker brought students into a world that seemed like play but involved enormous work. Their motivation came from within themselves, from their desire to live a creative life and understand themselves. The experiences of the class helped them understand how a work of art can challenge their thinking and stimulate their minds, how they could discover "themselves and their own creative thinking." Although Baker and Andy Kaufman never met and apparently did not know about each other, both helped students think about works of art and how those creations could change the way each student thought and worked.

The Texas innovator fashioned a space and set of experiences in which students could rediscover the curiosity of childhood and build an adult person with deep intentions. Much of class time revolved around students exhibiting their versions of the five exercises and reacting to one another in a fashion that said anew that creativity was both highly personal and a product of a community of diverse individuals feeding off the energy, actions, and thoughts of other people.[11]

We'll see the ideas of Integration of Abilities reflected in other Super Courses as we continue our tour. We'll also find twenty-first-century variations on the theme popping up in sometimes surprising places.

CHAPTER TWELVE

Fostering Growth Mindsets

Baker's Integration of Abilities course has found a new life on the secondary level and in so doing has sparked answers to one of the major questions coming out of Carol Dweck's work on mindsets. How do you stimulate a growth mindset? We know that's no easy task, and it seems to get more difficult as people get older.[1]

We have come to believe, however, that Baker's course may have some major solutions to this conundrum, and those answers have flourished in a downtown high school in Dallas, Texas. In 1976, Baker left higher education and became the founding principal of the Booker T. Washington High School for the Performing and Visual Arts in Dallas. Booker T. had been the segregated school for "colored students" in the heyday of Jim Crow. Now it would become a magnet institution, designed to help desegregate public education in the North Texas city. Baker brought his Integration of Abilities course as the centerpiece of a comprehensive educational experience that centered on the arts. That course is still the keystone of education at Booker T. and a crown jewel in the Dallas school district.

In the late twentieth century, most of the teachers in the program had taken the course from Baker when he taught it on the university level or in the graduate program at the Dallas Theater Center. When Scott Rudes, a young musician and educator from Indiana became the principal in 2013, he had no experience with Baker's ideas. But he soon realized how central the West Texan was to the success and heritage of Booker T. He reintroduced Integration of Abilities after a three-year hiatus, moving it to the junior year and a central role in the curriculum. Students sing its praises and talk freely about how it transformed their lives.

In the hands of Kate Walker, Karon Codgill, and their colleagues, the Integration of Abilities course has morphed into a twenty-first-century cauldron of creative growth, bringing forward Baker's basic ideas and integrating them with the thoughts of a new generation of artists and educators. What they have fashioned has powerful implications for secondary and college education more broadly.

Walker is no stranger to teaching success. In her first decade at the North Texas high school, she has molded the dance program into one of the premier conservatories of its kind in the United States. The prestigious Julliard School in New York City annually admits only two dozen new dance students into its freshman class, half males and half females, drawn from secondary programs around the world. For any aspiring dancer, it is the cat's pajamas of recognitions and opportunities. In 2017 nearly half the guys in that small elite contingent—five of twelve to be exact—came out of Kate Walker's program at Booker T.

Yet her Integration of Abilities class, with students coming from all the programs at her special high school, ultimately has had more influence. Walker's rendition of Paul Baker's legacy highlights self-discovery. "The more you know about yourself, the more you can be a productive and creative person," she says to her students. Her course helps them dig into their own history, to find out who they are. Every corpuscle of that effort focuses on growth and work, not on finding the geniuses who will shine.

Just look at what happens. The premise of the course, conveyed in multiple ways, is that everybody is unique; students are not divided into "good" students and "bad" ones. It begins with a deep dive into who they are, how they work, what is ideal for them. Students are urged to ask, How do *I* overcome my resistance to work? What ceremonies and rituals do *I* employ before and during my most creative periods? This special educational experience continues with a look outward to find and explore other people whose lives and ideas can inform theirs. The rhythm of the class doesn't center around correcting students' work but on inviting them into a place where they can set their own standards, play with their thoughts and experience, learn to defend their choices, and emerge with a result that keeps growing.

The teacher and each student make pledges to each other. "If they are willing to dive into the work," Walker promises, "and really get their feet wet, then they are going to get a whole lot of information about themselves." She warns the class that it might not be "easy or comfortable or even fun," but they will get "tons of insights about how they work." At the same time, the dance master warns that not everything will click for everyone but reassures students that the total experience has a long history of success and offers them a rich garden where they can find nourishing opportunities. "I promise you will get out of the class exactly what you put in." That assertion is one of a series of statements and experiences that puts students in charge of their own education.

In return, students pledge to become "invested" in the class, to get more out of it because they put more in. Yes, there will be "down days." Everyone has them. But the overall thrust will be toward commitment, learning about themselves and how they work. They are asked to focus on the process, not on the product. Every day, Walker gives each person in the class feedback on his or her effort and involvement, not on any specific results. That's all in keeping with a growth mindset.

Highly important to its success, the class has a grading structure that consciously supports its basic ideas and aims. "It's basically a pass-fail class where effort and engagement tells all," explains Scott Rudes, the principal who brought the course back to life. Students either display commitment and work or they don't. No one tries to evaluate the quality of their creations.

Much of the key difference in Integration of Abilities stems from how the teachers conceive of good teaching and learning, how they define success. In so many circumstances, instructors must set high standards and hold their class responsible for meeting them. After all, the criteria stem from a larger community of scholars, artists, and scientists. The Integration of Abilities experience offers an island where students can focus on understanding themselves and learning how to set and defend their own expectations. The benefits of that singular moment enrich everything else they subsequently do in school and life.

"The more you know about yourself and the way you interact with the world," Walker explains, "the more you can adapt and know what you need to thrive, to learn, to grow. That's true in every field—science, humanities, arts, business, or even how you get along with other people."

Much of the result depends, she contends, on "how invested" students are in the process. That is, perhaps, another way of noting whether they take a deep, surface, or strategic approach to school. "When they come into the class," Walker observes, "they often think only about grades." That's been the focus since the early days of their schooling. It's not surprising then that at first they will ask her things like "How many items do I need in this project?" (Or in another class, a similar inquiry might be "How many sources do I need for this research paper?" Or, "How long should it be?")

Her response begins to turn them around but also "drives them a little crazy." She always says, "I don't know. What do you think?"

In some hands, that can become a sophisticated version of "guess what's on my mind," expecting students to create something that conforms to some previously designed standard with little help in understanding what that might be. For Walker it really is an open opportunity. "It is important for them," she explains, "to make their own guidelines and expectations and then justify them to somebody." It is the ultimate act in a student-centered education, and while they will later face demands that someone else or some external reality will impose, those moments in the sunshine of setting a standard, defending it, and driving themselves toward it, provides valuable experience in taking control of their own education. "I constantly try to get them to think about the value they will derive from [understanding themselves] rather than focusing on the grade."

To achieve that end, Walker casts the whole class as an experiment, a place where students can explore ideas and exercises to see what will work for them. "I try to encourage kids to let IA be a creative playground or laboratory," the dance teacher explains. "We try to experiment and allow them some space and time where they can reflect" on the experiences "to see what worked and what didn't."

In the traditional class, students hear about activities they must do (assignments) and standards they must meet. If they come up short of some teacher-imposed criteria, they are punished with lower grades. The implication becomes clear. A low grade says they obviously don't have the stuff it takes to succeed. In contrast, the Booker T. course conveys a different message.

"I tell them all the time not everything is going to work for every person," Walker explains. People are different, not deficient. Keep trying. Effort and engagement matter.

Without the tyranny of the standard approach in which everything has a score and all the numbers are tabulated to determine whether one is a "good student" or a weak one, people have a chance to grow, to explore what stimulates them to do so. This class, Walker advises, can enhance students' interaction with other people. "It can increase your productivity as a maker and doer of things and as a learner of things. You can recognize where you are coming from and who you are."

Most important, Scott Rudes argues, it stimulates intellectual curiosity. "After they explore their own lives and write an autobiography," he told us, students emerge with an insatiable wonder about the world. "That burst of inquisitiveness feeds their approach" to history, math, science, "and all of their academic courses," which Booker T. students take in addition to their work in the performing and visual arts.

Students write a great deal in Integration of Abilities, but it is all about reflections on their own decisions and habits. They examine, question, and defend the criteria they have identified. They can practice writing on something they know quite well: themselves. But some of the exercises use other means of communication besides words (the "unessay" assignment, as a flood of teachers now call it in a variety of disciplines). In one project, the students lay a big piece of butcher paper on the floor and stretch out on it while a colleague traces their body. Over the next few days, they fill the space with items that resonate with them: colors, words, and pictures cut from magazines. They then write an essay on the choices they made to build their collage, why they picked what they did.

Journey into the Inner Canyons of Your Life

The first project is to write an autobiography. While that endeavor among teenagers may seem premature, it is often life changing. "When we talk," Walker notes, "it's a lot of reflective work remembering back to childhood. It's thinking about your habits and your processes. It's things that resonate with you, things you resist and things that can be really challenging work." Students begin by reading aloud to each other Paul Baker's own self-reflection that we quoted in the last chapter: "I'm a West Texan!"[2] In the days to come, they will use that model, adapted to their own lives, to explore and capture themselves.

Most of the activities in Walker's class came out of Baker's original course in the 1940s. His five elements of the creative process are still there (although Walker has organized them a little differently), and students still explore their own reaction to space, movement, sound, and other "elements of form," as Baker called them. They explore the life of an artist and thinker they admire, probing the ways she or he works, the attitudes their subject harbors, the rituals their subject follows, the concepts he or she holds. In what might be a central piece of the experience, students choose an artist they admire and examine how that person works, collecting statements that person has made that capture his or her approach to work. But Walker has brought other ideas into her classroom, borrowing from artists and educators who have contributed to the conversation that Baker sparked with his original Super Course.

To help these sixteen- and seventeen-year-olds explore their short lives, for example, Walker leans on Twyla Tharp's concept of Creative Autobiography.[3] The celebrated dancer and choreographer has identified thirty-three questions that capture remarkably well the ideas that Baker first articulated in the 1930s and 1940s. What is the first creative moment you remember? What is the best idea you've ever had? What made it great in your mind? And so forth.

Walker brings both Jean Houston's memory exercise[4] and Liz Lerman's critical response process[5] to her classroom. In the former, students work in pairs to recall and record in a notebook experiences from their early childhood, flash memories, going back to before culture had shaped their thinking so thoroughly: a favorite taste, or smell; a scary moment; playing in water; whatever they've got. As students take turns sprawled on the floor while their partner takes notes, they play with the idea that travel through childhood and its earliest memories will strengthen their abilities to conjure up more recent experiences, and even empower the mind to trip through time, imaging themselves observing William Shakespeare watching a performance of *Hamlet* or Lincoln delivering the Gettysburg Address.

With their strengthened memory and imagination, the students can presumably learn about themselves, how they think, how ideas come up in their minds, but also how to trigger their creative brain. As they talk about and explore the rituals and habits of their past creative selves, they begin to consider what works best and what doesn't. They are prompted to remember their earliest creative act. Was it successful? What made it fruitful in their mind? What kind of environment do they want, loud music or complete silence? Do they need to walk around or stay in one place?

Walker's class uses the elements of form to spark a fresh perspective on students' schooling and how they react to it. One day she asks them to think about rhythms. What's the general cadence of their day, the pulse and swing of the people they encounter, the beat and tempo of their classes and teachers. They are asked to think about the rhythm of their academic classes where they perform well; what about the ones where they struggle? They need to see how these things are affecting them. They do something similar with each of the other elements of the creative process: space, movement or line, light or color, silhouette, rhythm, sound or silence, shape, and texture.

Not every group of students will react with the same level of excitement and commitment to each of these exercises, but one activity has perennially captured strong attention. "In the sound of silence," Walker reports, the entire class "sits in silence for six to seven minutes then writes down and categorizes all the sounds we heard." Do people make them? Do machines, or something in nature? Are they constant or sporadic? Do the sounds have a rhythm, or more of a cacophony, a harsh and discordant mixture of noises? Do they come from one place or move around us? Can they hear themselves breathing?

In the days following that exercise each person creates a sound track of his or her life, putting favorite vibrations into a digital playlist. Within that exercise, students begin to collect the sights and sounds that define them and to mull over the implications those stimuli may have in defining how they work and create.

Feedback, Baker and Lerman Style

In so many traditional classes to give feedback means to correct, to mark things as wrong. That seems proper and necessary as students enter and try to understand a new culture in, say, science or other fields. They must first get straight a whole world of facts that centuries of investigation, testing, reasoning, debate, and evaluation have set down as true. To master a huge body of material requires people to comprehend and memorize things that can be marked as right or wrong or partially so.

Yet that approach to learning does not necessarily foster imagination or the creation of fresh perspectives of the kind that Albert Einstein praised. In the years after the physicist and violin player gave his ringing endorsement for a creative mind and the power of the arts in nurturing it, educators fought long battles over what kind of education and feedback should prevail. If learning meant only that students got their facts straight, it made sense to focus on correcting errors. Yet others could not ignore Einstein's embrace of being an artist.

Those struggles nurtured Paul Baker's mind and the emergence of a different kind of feedback approach within Integration of Abilities. In 2003 choreographer and impresario Liz Lerman captured many of the ideas that had floated for years through art schools, Baker's classrooms, and other venues, giving them a systematic structure, and overall sense of meaning and purpose. When we talked to Kate Walker, it seemed clear that both Baker and Lerman had driven the Dallas dance teacher's thinking.

The aim of feedback, Walker heard Lerman and others argue, should be to leave someone eager to get back to work. That approach is a long way from finding all the mistakes and correcting them. It doesn't brutalize people by telling them what missteps they took. Walker had begun to worry—as Lerman did before her—that the traditional way to correct writers and dancers stifled imagination and creativity. Like Lerman, the Dallas teacher didn't want just to clone herself but to help students discover how they could find their own voices and rhythms.

This nonjudgmental yet positive process guided the critiques Kate Walker employed. It was quite similar to an approach Claude Steele had taken in his research. The Stanford psychologist and his colleagues found that people usually responded most positively when the teacher said something like, we have very high standards, but we see in your work reasons to believe you can meet them. As Steele told us, "the combination of high standards and assurance was like water on parched land, a much needed but seldom received balm."

Implications

Just imagine for a moment how the Integration of Abilities course might be complementary to some of the other Super Courses in this book. Think about the engineering students at Olin, Georgia Tech, or elsewhere, experiencing this environment while, or maybe before, they plunge into the science and engineering curriculum (we'll begin to explore Georgia Tech's Super Courses in biomedical engineering in the next chapter). Maybe they look at how an engineer they admire works and compare that with the practices of some artist. Remember that Einstein called himself an artist and scientist.

While strong undergraduate programs at multiple schools pay attention to critical thinking, we often give only lip service to fostering creative abilities and imaginations of all students. Integration of Abilities could help them fill that gap.

CHAPTER THIRTEEN

A Super Course Department

This is the story of a biomedical engineering department at a leading science, technology, and mathematics institution, but it has considerable relevance for teaching and learning in a variety of departments and subjects. Historians, chemists, sociologists, and maybe even artists and a wide variety of others can learn from its struggles. We challenge any field of study to consider its implications and devise inventive and highly effective pedagogical methods that create their own natural critical learning environments and Super Courses. It also has an important connection to the material we just explored about the Integration of Abilities course.

Innovation Begins in Breaking the Usual Rules and Patterns

When the Biomedical Engineering Program emerged at Georgia Tech in the 1990s, Don Giddens and his colleagues took an unusual step. Like most leading universities, the Atlanta school had hired its faculty to do research. That meant their primary job was to learn things that nobody else knew. While they had the background to manage that enterprise at a high level, the professors had another duty for which they had little preparation. They were supposed to foster the deep learning of future engineers and for the most part had no formal study of human learning and motivation to guide them.

"Here I was," one faculty member told us recently, "trying to help other people learn, and while there was this vast and growing body of research and theoretical literature on how people get to know something deeply, I had never read any of it, nor did I have any idea that it would help my own studies."

That's a common situation at research institutions in almost any discipline and even for some undergraduate liberal arts schools. The doctorate in most fields is so intense and extensive that people often emerge from it believing that they already know everything they need to help other people advance in their field. "Be full of your subject and care about your students," an old adage advises, and you can "teach well." In truth, many old-fashioned faculty members don't believe there is much of anything to learn about learning or teaching. As researchers advance in their own discoveries, for some inexplicable reason they sometimes grow even more convinced that they already know everything one needs to create good educational experiences.

To address this issue, many universities set up teaching centers with a kind of central authority on teaching and learning as director. That model works well for most institutions. We've found that teaching center directors usually bring great insights that benefit their faculty and students. Occasionally, however, schools can focus too much on getting "someone who will command the respect of the faculty," as one dean put it recently. While that sounds essential, in essence, it sometimes means hiring a person who has a PhD and a sufficient publication record in one of the subjects that will be taught, and then paying no attention to whether that individual knows much about the scholarship on human thinking, learning, and motivation. It is the ultimate expression of the notion that if you know your subject extremely well, you can help anyone learn.

Advanced research schools, for some reason, seem particularly vulnerable to this practice and attitude. They sometimes appoint a strong scholar in a central field as supreme director of the teaching center and another person with a learning science background to do the daily work. Rare is the top-level engineering, science, humanities, or social science department that actually hires a cognitive and learning scientist as a faculty member.

But that's what Don Giddens vowed to do when he became chair of the Coulter Department of Biomedical Engineering at Georgia Tech, a joint venture with the School of Medicine at Emory University. He and his colleagues wanted a department member whose primary study was in human learning. They found Wendy Newstetter, a cognitive and learning scientist, who would help transform the department. She created a new kind of learning experience for students, a class that would not only jump-start the deep learning of undergraduates but also become a powerful force in faculty development, "a kind of incubator," as one faculty member called it, where experimental approaches would help other professors develop a deeper understanding of teaching and learning. The results would ripple across the curriculum, enriching other courses in the years to come and having "a major influence on some of the faculty," as one professor put it.

A Cool Step and Problem-Based Learning

When Joe Le Doux, an associate professor, talks about the history of the department, he notes with pride how "cool" it was that "as we formed a whole new department, we actually hired a learning scientist" into the faculty. "What she introduced to us," he recalls, "was problem-based learning" (PBL).

Two colleagues at McMaster University in Canada had pioneered PBL techniques and insights in the 1960s. Howard Barrows, a professor of neurology, and Robyn Tamblyn, a clinical lecturer in nursing, had worked out many of the details for the approach.[1] They began with a simple yet often overlooked observation. Traditional education emphasized memory. That's what got tested to decide who advanced and who was eliminated from a program. Yet in medicine, patients don't care one whit how many facts their physicians can regurgitate. They want a doctor who can solve their medical mystery, make good decisions, and come up with the best care.

But surely sick people also want doctors who have their facts straight. Barrows and Tamblyn recognized that while scientific accuracy is crucial to making good clinical decisions, it matters how someone acquires the relevant information and understanding. Humans have this annoying ability to memorize stuff yet fail to recognize its relevance for a given situation. It's the old transfer problem in spades. Yet if medical students encounter the facts while trying to solve the kinds of problems they will tackle later "the learning . . . is much more effective for creating a body of knowledge usable in the future."[2]

Barrows and Tamblyn created a formula for problem-based learning, and the Canadians took it to the medical school at the University of Illinois in Springfield. While they had developed the method to meet the needs of medical learning, it would eventually spread to other subjects, including engineering. "We even had some of the Howard Barrows's folks come in and give us a workshop," Joe Le Doux recalled about the early days at Georgia Tech. Across the last four decades of the twentieth century, PBL filtered through various disciplines, but with mixed results. We'll explore what that has meant.

Problem-Based Learning at Georgia Tech

Wendy Newstetter and her new colleagues took the ideas of Barrows and Tamblyn and applied them in a way that enriched the process and created a Super Course of considerable influence. But as Barrows and Tamblyn pointed out in their early writing, the approach doesn't just give students some problem and then ask them to solve it. It is "a very specific approach to education, . . . supported by tools designed to facilitate a specific teaching-learning process," Barrows would write. "It is a rigorous, structured" plan of attack to learning "based on considerable experience and research."[3]

When Wendy Newstetter came to the project, two major observations triggered her thinking. "In a program like Engineering, students are put into a lot of required courses," she noticed. "But no one ever bothers to help them understand why they are taking" all those "background" prerequisites. That's something that happens in many fields—not just engineering. Second, she had noticed that most of the ongoing learning that emerges in science and most other fields develops because someone had a problem they needed to solve, a question they wanted to answer.

That's the nature of research (learning), she concluded. For twelve years she had funding from the National Science Foundation to investigate "research labs like an anthropologist," as Newstetter put it. "We asked questions about the nature of cognition and what does learning look like on the frontiers of science." She brought that experience to the design of her Super Course at Georgia Tech. "Science advances when people have problems they need to solve." They might be questions about understanding something, or "practical" matters that help achieve a particular end. "Problems drive learning. Scientists and scholars have questions that unfold in their thinking and they set out to address them," she argues. As we've noted before, people are most likely to take a deep approach to learning when they are trying to solve problems or answer questions that they have come to regard as important, intriguing, or beautiful.

Yet in school, as Newstetter increasingly recognized, the system too often simply herds learners in one direction or another. Take this. Then that. Complete these requirements before going to the next step. "It's like learning some game," one student observed recently, "by following a formula without ever understanding the ultimate goal." That process often tends to foster strategic learning at best. Newstetter hoped to change that environment.

She planned to plunge students into problems that they had little preparation to solve. They would not emerge from her course as highly trained and educated specialists, but they would come out with abilities to identify problems and break them down into smaller chunks. They would learn to ask questions, to work in teams, to create physical prototyping, and to engage in "model-based reasoning." Most important, her course would help them learn to identify and appreciate what they didn't know and what they needed to learn. In short, the experience would set up all that followed in their engineering education, instilling them with skills and motivations that would power them through every class that followed.

Such a forum would require a great deal of scaffolding. As people in the room encountered an authentic issue from the field, they would need help in breaking it down, in identifying the key issues in the puzzle, in deciding where to begin. They would require skills they did not yet possess, and relatively convenient ways to acquire those abilities as they focused on the problem.

The students must realize the power of Aristotle's observation that "For the things we have to learn before we can do them, we learn by doing them," and develop the comfort to exercise that wisdom. Newstetter called her approach "learning forward." As students tackled specific problems in biomedical engineering, they would begin to evolve new abilities—in math and statistics, for example—that would guide and direct their studies for years to come. More than anything else, they would learn *about* those disciplines like someone tasting and testing the soup of a good book. A spoonful now that would whet the appetite for more to come. The approach would help revolutionize biomedical engineering education at Georgia Tech.

In any semester, 136 students take the class, distributed into seventeen groups. On the first meeting, the pupils receive a syllabus that helps bring them into this new kind of experience. It reminds them that typical engineers in biology and medicine design medical devices and offer help with their use. "But what is it like to work on and solve a multi-faceted problem" that requires "physiological understanding, design, engineering analysis, modeling and building?" Most of the challenges students will face in their career, they hear, begin with a "vague medical" issue. How will they move to an "appropriate design solution?"

To answer those questions, the students "experience the world of biomedical engineering by tackling a current problem" in a systematic way. It was the learning of that orderly process that became the most valuable result of the course. All the topics come from real experiences, straight out of someone's medical practice. "Sometimes we pull something from the pages of the *New York Times*," Joe Le Doux explained. "But it must be an authentic problem for which there is no known solution."

In 2018, for example, Newstetter asked physicians what challenges they faced with Parkinson's patients. They told her that it's often difficult to predict how much medication any one person will need and when they should take it. "You will apply knowledge from physics, math, science, physiology, [and] electrical engineering," to address an important question.

Much of the power of this approach came from the selection and design of the problem. It had to be conceptually rich, ill-structured, and consequential, not just a question of how to fix a squeaky refrigerator at a local sandwich shop. Students must see that they have the opportunity to make a significant contribution. No one has solved this problem yet, and they have a chance to tackle it. "If students sense that they are not just taking courses but actually participating in important projects and research," Newstetter observed, "the motivation level can be very high." In the end, they will produce an actual product, and that becomes the bait that seduces them.

In essence, the department rejected the old notion that you must first "learn the facts" in rote memorization before you can begin to think creatively and critically about them. And it certainly turned down the standard idea that students must listen to some learned person say all the key facts in front of them before they can advance. The Georgia Tech professors created a carefully scaffolded environment that sparked a "need to know" and then offered "just in time" opportunities for students to acquire the information and abilities they would require to solve their problem. At the end of the class, students still needed extensive additional experience with some of the key skills, but they emerged with important powers and an integrated understanding of why they must study various disciplines like, say, statistics, to become a good engineer. In essence, the students in Atlanta learned to be good engineers by being good engineers.[4]

A Special Kind of Room for PBL

Perhaps the most important contribution to PBL that emerged at Georgia Tech was the creation of a novel kind of classroom where the methodology could play out.[5] Because they had formed a new department, Newstetter and her colleagues had advantages that older schools did not enjoy. "We didn't even have a building," Le Doux remembers, so "we could design one" that reflected the learning science the engineering professors were beginning to explore.

A typical academic structure might fill a good portion of itself with large lecture halls. Instead, "we devoted half of our instructional space to so-called PBL rooms," Le Doux noted. In these small areas, eight people could sit around a table with "white board" surfaces covering everything in sight. Students could write on any wall space in the room as they struggled with a problem, then erase it and start over again when need be.

"We put students in the deep end of the pool," Le Doux noted, "and give them a whirlwind tour of the engineering design cycle."

Meeting in groups of eight in those special PBL rooms, students begin to wrestle with the problem. A slightly more advanced undergraduate who has taken the class previously joins them to help guide the process, to ask questions, but to avoid explanations.[6] A faculty mentor circulates between all the rooms, meets with the peer facilitators, and contributes to the work of all the groups. "The eight students receive a problem statement that is no more than half to three-quarters of a page long," Le Doux explains. Facilitators must begin to model the behavior they want their younger charges to adopt. "Don't lecture. Don't tell. Model the problem-solving process and team skills."

They begin with "how to introduce yourself to each other." How can they ask each other open-ended questions? How can they be curious about one another? "We want them to learn enough about their colleagues to begin to see that everyone is unique and that each one has special skills to bring to the problem," Le Doux explains. As we listened to the Georgia Tech professors explain their process and philosophy, we could hear Paul Baker's approaches and ideas from his Integration of Abilities course rambling in the background.

After students read the problem statement, the facilitator marks off an area on one wall where they can list everything they think they know about the issue. As that area fills, another section invites the class to identify what they don't know that needs to be answered. As they build that second list, the fledgling engineers also begin to speculate about possible solutions and to keep records of their ideas. Early in the process each student picks some aspect of the overall question and begins to develop an in-depth expertise around that subtopic. Much of the content learning occurs as students do individual research outside of class on their special aspect of the overall problem and then begin to share with one another.

The group meets twice a week for ninety minutes, and for several weeks each session begins with the same process. What do they know? What questions are still relevant? What have they learned since the last session? "Each student," Le Doux summarizes, "takes ownership of one or more of the key issues, whatever they are most interested in studying, and commits to boning up on that material before the next session."[7]

In this course, students learn a lot of science and engineering content, but that isn't their primary learning objective. Instead, they work on four skill areas: They learn to engage in inquiry, solve problems, build knowledge, and work in teams. Their assessment depends on how well they do in each of these areas. "We're not trying to create disciplinary experts, but a new kind of engineer," a faculty member explained. "We want people who understand biology deeply so they can integrate engineering with a clinical perspective to improve health care." They will need "cognitive flexibility, and truly integrative thinking," and the ability to look at a problem from multiple perspectives. To get there, students will require numerous "opportunities to practice this integration, not just in some capstone course."

The Atlanta protégés receive a steady flow of feedback from the facilitators, their colleagues, and each other. Each person keeps an "engineer's logbook" that records the work he or she does "outside the group meetings." They make an entry every time they do anything to advance their own learning and contribute to the group process and date it, reflecting the "ongoing record" of their work. The students jot down every source they consult, questions and ideas that pop into their head, and major information they pick up. "As an engineer's design notebook," their syllabus tells them, "it should provide a history of the development of your knowledge, ideas, and problem solving, as you move toward a product." Several times throughout the semester each person writes a reflection on his or her work during that section of the course.

In multiple ways, the faculty constantly emphasizes a chance to grow, to move from novice to expert. The final assessment tries to capture the abilities that have matured by the end of the process and not just some average of where they have been, but it also attempts to encourage steady and regular progress, daily habits that build over time, and not just an eleventh-hour mad scramble to throw something together. That's part of what the logs do, but the peer evaluations also contribute to that end, building a community in which students feel responsibilities toward the group. Each part of the feedback from every source centers around rubrics that spell out what is expected, helping these emerging engineers focus on their own growth toward clear goals rather than on what kind of grade they are making.

All the students do a great deal of writing. They make formal presentations and "actively participate in the writing of all reports." At the end of the semester, each person writes an essay in class tackling "a complex problem in a limited amount of time." It is the final opportunity to demonstrate all that any one individual has learned.

Yet it is not such details that mark this course as super. We've included it in our collection because of the way it uses problem-based learning, building the entire experience around questions that people find important, intriguing, beautiful, and even fun. Newstetter's course fosters deep learning with an important and intriguing problem, then puts people in groups where they can learn from each other as they struggle to create something new. The experience gives everyone a chance to do the discipline before they fully understand it or have packed their brains with knowledge.

We also appreciate that this course illustrates how a department can bring someone into their faculty to help colleagues explore the learning sciences.

Motivation Matters

The key to its success or failure lies in how motivated and engrossed students become in the problem they tackle and the degree to which they feel like they are working on the frontiers of engineering, doing important and original work that could help other people. A fuzzy intriguing and important problem; a chance to try repeatedly, receive feedback, work with others; the opportunity to live a creative life: all propel the class members into deep approaches and achievement. From the beginning, people in this special learning environment have found stimulus in the respect that comes their way.

It first appears in that opening exercise in which students introduce themselves and learn that other people respect them for the unique perspectives they bring to the project.

How PBL Can Become Too Routine
and How to Revive It

The problem-based approach is still spreading, although not as rapidly as one might expect. It often flourishes at new institutions rather in older ones. Maastricht University didn't emerge in the Netherlands until 1974, but it has used PBL from the beginning. The medical faculty employed it first. Then it spread to every aspect of the growing institution: law, economics, arts and culture, psychology, humanities, science, engineering, and other fields.

After thirty years of rising academic reputations, however, some faculty began to notice how the program had frayed around the edges. In medicine, the students went through the process as a kind of ritual, but the original spirit had seeped out of the community. Students were "increasingly unwilling to share information and ideas" with one another and "assumed a 'free-rider' attitude," we were told by one faculty member. By 2001, some professors were publishing exposés on how the tutors had adopted "a more teacher-directed rather than student-directed teaching style."[8] Rather than fostering problem solving, the burned-out tutors actually lectured to their charges.

To address that turn of events, Katarzyna Czabanowska and her colleagues undertook a reexamination of their PBL pedagogy in the public health program at Maestricht. What they found is important. Although they never use this language, they discovered something we have already discussed. Students will come to the problem-based environment with deeply rooted mental models of reality. To stimulate growth, you must put them in a situation where their paradigms don't work, and they must care that they don't. As the Dutch scholars put it, learners should "become cognitively and emotionally involved with the subject."[9] Or, as we have put it, they must intend to learn deeply.

People are most likely to take that approach when faced with questions and problems that fascinate and concern them, that perturb their applecart of mental models. They will be highly motivated if they have confidence they can solve the problem (receive the right kind of assistance), the freedom (autonomy) to control their own learning ("self-directed learning" as the Maestricht teacher phrased it), and the chance to contribute to a larger good (relatedness). That's what Georgia Tech accomplished that made such a positive difference in their results.[10]

An Incubator

As we mentioned earlier, Newstetter's Super Course became an incubator for other innovations. After working with the cognitive scientist for several years and developing deep insights into human learning, Joe Le Doux tackled one of the major challenges bedeviling higher education. In the process, he and his colleagues created a Super Course of their own that has enormous potential for other fields. Joe had noticed something that other educators have recognized: students don't always learn conceptually, even when they make high grades. As a result, they often can't solve complex problems, or transfer what they learn in one area to new and only slightly different conditions.

In many fields that has meant students often look for fixed steps they can follow, some formula they can memorize. All they need to do, they think, is find the right prescription and insert the proper numbers to get the solution. Yet in life their "plug and chug" approach can't handle the messy and ill-structured challenges the Georgia Tech undergrads are likely to encounter in their careers as engineers. To address that failure Le Doux created in 2008 what he calls a Problem Solving Studio (PSS). It took problem-based learning to a whole new level of achievement (now called problem-driven learning). While the approach emerged to speak to engineering issues, it could be used in a wide variety of disciplines. At the end of this section, we'll speculate about its possible application in history and other fields.

Le Doux designed both a new kind of learning area—borrowed in major part from some much older structures used in architecture and a few other fields—and new practices within that space. His renovated classroom had twenty-four small tables and forty-eight chairs, all on wheels so they could move around. But the number of tables and chairs might vary without changing the results. Normally, four students would sit around two tables, and they would work in pairs to solve special kinds of engineering challenges. In addition to their fascination, the problems were "reasonably well-structured but somewhat complex," he told us. As we will see, the instructor could make them more or less ill-structured and complex to meet the needs of the learner. More on that in a moment.

To make their work public—one of the defining ingredients in the PSS—each pair had a pen or pencil and a seventeen-by-twenty-two-inch pad of paper—not a computer as some approaches have employed. You'll notice, no doubt, that this story well illustrates an important point from part 1 of this book: it isn't the computers that make such a huge difference in education but our increased understanding of human learning and how best to foster it on the highest levels, using whatever tools are most appropriate.

One of the students would take the marker and begin to write, explaining his or her thinking as he or she went, throwing numbers, questions, ideas, formulas, or assumptions on the paper. The other member of the team would listen and respond. After a few minutes, they would switch roles, passing off the marker to the other person. At the beginning of the semester, the students might need a little practice and coaching to master this tag-team approach to wrestling with the problem, but they soon settled into the routine with considerable comfort. It was more than a brainy rendition of tag-team wrestling that Gorgeous George and other body builders displayed from those old 1950s television shows. It was the beginning of making their intellectual exercise public.

A faculty member and several slightly more advanced students would circulate in this sea of tables and people, listening to the thinking that came out of learner's mouths and watching what splashed onto the pads.

If these roving mentors or the instructor saw or heard a team going down a wrong path, they would intervene, but not with explanations. The professor and the near-peer coaches would instead ask questions designed to get people in the class to rethink. Occasionally, students would square the pairs, bringing all four people at two tables into a conversation about the problem.

Our old friend Jerome Bruner has called this process scaffolding.[11] The term came from the temporary braces and supports employed to keep something erect during construction before it can stand on its own. With their questions, the professor and mentors provided learners with just enough intellectual support to keep them on the right track but could carefully remove that scaffolding as people learned to think on their own. Rarely, the guides by the side could say something to the entire class of forty-eight,[12] but for most of the time the pupils did the talking and thinking, building a better understanding.

Messy Problems

The problems were important and fascinating, with just enough messiness and complexity to intrigue the young engineers, but not so much as to frustrate them. In that goldilocks zone between too hard and too soft, the students would ideally find the level just right. They could work together, challenge one another, argue, and resolve—forced to defend their thinking in a publicly visible space.

But, of course, what's perfect for one table might be insultingly simple for another, or enough to prompt the gnashing of teeth and pulling of hair in a third. That's where "dynamic scaffolding" came to the rescue. In this highly fluid environment, the tutors and teacher could adjust how much and what kind of assistance they provided. When would they just listen to the struggles? What kinds of questions would they ask? That all depended on what they heard and saw on the pads.

In a traditional lecture classroom, a lot of presentation skills separated the best teachers from the mediocre. Yet the formal lecture froze the assistance in place with little room to meet the individual needs of the class members. In this new world of the PSS, quality instruction depended on good questions and the capacity to recognize the mental models that stood behind someone's approach to a problem. The best teachers had to make judgments and adjustments on the fly, to understand novice thinking, to pick the right problems, not just prepare a well-organized lecture in advance and then deliver it with flair. We want, Joe explained, to "present each team, each table, and the entire class with a problem that is [challenging], but not so difficult that" they get stalled.

The professors and peer tutor have to give "situated feedback," to know whether students are making progress or getting bored and what kind of feedback they needed. They must be able to provide a wide variety of support materials students can use on their own, including things to read or things to watch or hear.

In this Super Course, highly effective teachers also have to know how and when to create the best groups. When students first come into Joe's class, they can sit where they want. But by the third week, the team of professor and mentors fashions heterogeneous clusters of four based on their reading of students' abilities during the first two weeks. That means people with strong backgrounds benefit from explaining their ideas to someone else. Struggling students profit from working with more advanced classmates. All the students grow as they try, come up short, receive feedback (often in the form of the right question), and try again before anyone marks their work with a letter or number. Once formed, these heterogeneous groups remain together for the remainder of the term, eliminating the problem of constantly shifting personalities, and creating stability and continuity from one session to the next. With four carefully chosen people to a set of tables, the students experience enough diversity to enjoy the right measure of pressure. To balance that challenge against the need for comfort, Joe allows any student to make one anonymous request to include a specific person in his or her table of four.

Students even have the chance to test their metal. Every week or so, they can take off the training wheels and try to do the problems entirely on their own, facing the same conditions they would encounter on a test. But like everything before it, these sessions were all for play and practice. No one kept score. No one marked anyone down. Like a runner *before* the track meet, they get to learn, find out something about themselves, and continue to improve before the big event. The professors and peer tutors go to great lengths to assure students that this is a safe place where they can try, fail, and receive feedback without judgment.

In addition to the help they get in the studio, students have access to a wide variety of support materials they can use on their own. Their kit includes articles and book chapters to read, videos to watch, and recordings to hear. The professor might present explanations for out-of-class consumption, but they never take class time for an old-fashioned lecture. The studio meets for two hours twice a week, rather than for the one-hour lecture four times, and the time belongs to the students, a period when they can struggle with themselves, their colleagues, and the ideas, and get the proper assistance when they need it.

Did this need-to-know and just-in-time approach improve conceptual understanding? The simple answer is yes, and in spades. It did exactly what the learning research and theory had predicted. "Our results show," Joe Le Doux and Alisha Waller wrote in 2016, "that even though PSS emphasizes engineering problem-solving skills, the students' conceptual understanding of the material significantly improves."[13] Furthermore, conceptual understanding increased for all kinds of students, no matter their level when they entered the class. Those who came with some prior understanding improved, and so did those who arrived with little comprehension.

What more could you do to improve this experiment? Le Doux and his associates are already thinking about the next steps. When we explored their educational gem in 2018 and 2019, they planned to change the rubrics for "both the PBL course and the PSS course" to reflect a concept of fairness and justice. "Are the people in the class treating each other fairly? Are they creating a climate in which everyone has a fair chance to succeed?"

Le Doux makes it clear that the school wants "to graduate students who appreciate and even value diverse teams." How can the course promote that end? How can the rubrics help people evaluate their contributions to that end? "We want them to see that they can benefit from working with" different kinds of people, and to define diversity in multiple ways, including backgrounds, perspectives, skills, and cultures. With support from the National Science Foundation, they are now working on how they can foster a sense of belonging in the university and an appreciation for uniqueness.

"You come from a certain soil, a certain family," Paul Baker had stressed. "You were born in a certain house at a certain time. Each of you has your own philosophy, your own view point, your own physical tensions and background." We can all learn from one another.

Using the PSS in Other Disciplines

Does this experiment in Atlanta have implications and offer promise for other disciplines? We thought it would be fun and useful to speculate about its use in a discipline far afield from engineering. What would a history class, for example, look like in the Problem Solving Studio? Imagine giving students a set of Cold War documents. Numerous possibilities come to mind, including the files found years ago on various proposals to discredit Fidel Castro, or kill him. The questions would be different than those for a problem in conservation principles, but equally reflective of the discipline and some of its key concepts. What do these documents reflect about US policy making, priorities, and so forth? What other historical evidence do students need to examine to draw reasonable conclusions? If they had been a member of the Kennedy administration, how would they have responded to the proposals, and why?

If you took a historiographical approach, you could give them key small excerpts from conflicting schools of thought. What are the key differences between them? Do they answer different questions, or make some conflicting claims about the same inquiry? Do they disagree in belief or attitude, or both? If they take issue with each other's view of the facts, what kinds of evidence could help resolve the conflict? What assumptions lie behind each school of thought? Where do these documents fit into a larger calendar of events? What concepts do they employ?

Students of medieval British history might receive all the known documents referring to major fires in London in the thirteenth century. Their professor might then ask them to estimate how many conflagrations erupted, and speculate about their possible consequences before looking at ideas emerging from research historians. A class of novice sociologists might, as Chad Richardson's students used to do, examine ethnographic evidence that they and their classmates had collected, to speculate about related sociological concepts.[14] The possibilities are almost endless, but most require that we think about an inductive rather than the traditional deductive approach in the social sciences and humanities. They require also that we think about ways for students to construct their own understanding of concepts and lines of inquiry rather than simply explaining them. We will need to imagine "flipping the class" to move the delivery of information outside the meeting time, and to use the precious minutes we have with learners each week to promote deeper understanding, analysis, synthesis, evaluation, and theory building and testing.

Perhaps you can begin to imagine combining various examples from this book to capture and build your own Super Course. What if you drew, for example from Joe Le Doux's Problem Solving Studio, reconfigured it slightly, used students who had taken the seminar previously, and built an interdisciplinary experience in which multiple "seminars" flourished in a single classroom before reconnecting in a final exchange. Or not. The Super Courses in this book emerged from such "wild thinking," from a good grasp of important concepts, from far transfer,[15] from careful planning, from experimentation and careful evaluation of the results, and not from simply plugging and chugging, adopting a series of steps without any deep understanding.

CHAPTER FOURTEEN

A Personal Journey toward a Super Course

One day in the summer of 1994, we stood in line at Al's Deli near the Northwestern University campus. As we waited for our shot at corned beef on rye with coleslaw on the side, a colleague from the business school joined us. For more than a year, we'd ribbed each other about our respective disciplines.

"I have two questions for you," he chuckled, as he slid into the line. "Why would anyone want to learn history, and what would it mean to do so?" His jabs were nothing new. History had been under attack for years as irrelevant and boring. Students, so the critics charged, at best compiled a headful of isolated facts they quickly forgot. Too many struggled to pass required introductory courses, contributing to the high dropout and low graduation rates that plague higher education in the United States. At some large state universities, departmental culture seems to prize professors who flunk a higher percentage of their students. Abuses abound.

Overworked graduate students grading papers sometimes found it easier to mark the quick notes someone scribbled at the beginning of a blue book rather than to read the essay they had written further on. A professor of British history at the University of Texas Austin once lost an undergraduate's research paper placed in his mailbox, gave the student an F, then bragged that it helped him meet his quota.

Like most people in our discipline, we thought teaching history meant delivering lectures. Our colleague's questions that day, however, finally touched off a major reexamination. Over the long days of summer in a Chicago suburb, our understanding of teaching and learning underwent a dramatic shift. What we created over the next few years laid the groundwork for an important shift in history education, helping fashion another model for a Super Course.[1] Our journey began with the two questions the business professor had posed outside Al's Deli.

Why Study History?

In theory, history is an interpretive discipline and invites students into rich intellectual battles where they can master new ways of thinking. Those fresh mental skills can serve them well in multiple ways but none more important than confronting the historical claims that bombard them. We all encounter contentions about the past. They pop up in the news, political debates, advertising campaigns, song lyrics, movies, novels, jokes, and even casual conversations with friends. "I don't know or care about history" may be a common student refrain, but most people still have historical ideas that influence how they think and even the values they hold dear. Sometimes those notions drift into our minds with such subtlety that we don't even recognize they are there. Many common prejudices stem from mistaken although still vague historical notions about certain people and their cultures.

If we expect to examine thoughts and improve their quality, however, we must be aware of how historical beliefs shape how we view ourselves and other people, mold political and social ideas and attitudes, and even determine our tastes and feelings. With such powerful forces drifting around our brains, how can we learn to weigh them? How do we recognize the sometimes faint historical arguments that float through our culture. They shape views about everything from race and gender to politics and personal affairs.

But what do people learn when they study history? Everything that ever happened? Obviously not, but what? In its most powerful form, the discipline is the study of change over time, how and why it happens, and what differences those alterations make. While scientists study nature and all the tongues it speaks (chemistry, math, physics, etc.), historians explore valuable ideas about change in human affairs. History makes it possible to compare and contrast our own times with another era. ("It's a lot like seeing colors; some shades are impossible to discern unless you hold them against some other hue," as a former colleague put it.) The study of change over time provides us with rich comparisons and contrasts.

The body of knowledge existing in history as a discipline consists of ideas about the past, and unless students learn to evaluate historical claims—from popular culture and academic researchers—they haven't learned the discipline. Some colleagues do help their students tackle primary sources to reach their own conclusions. That's an admirable goal, but it's not enough. After all, no professional historian does original research on every question he or she might encounter. Historians rely on the work of colleagues, and their own capacity to read other scholars critically, to compare and contrast conflicting views. Students, even the beginning learners, can master some of the same abilities.

We had no interest in controlling what our students thought but did hope their education would broaden what they noticed and influence the mental skills they use to collect and assess ideas, impressions, and attitudes. We wanted them to recognize the historical assumptions that lie behind their ideas, and realize the problems they face in accepting whatever they might believe.

As students encounter hot debates between different schools of thought in history, they can draw the most reasonable or probable conclusions from the current evidence. But they can also recognize the limits and restrictions of any historical inquiry. History can instill a burning curiosity and a lifetime habit of questioning while prompting a better understanding of how and why things change. When new information comes along, better ways of looking at the data emerge, a fresh perspective blossoms, or new tools of inquiry become available, then good learners will know how to reevaluate. History courses can foster empathy for other people. In short, they can help students learn to think like good historians.

Getting the Facts First?

Most history teachers support these goals, but many add that students must first learn "the facts" before they can think critically (although it's seldom clear which facts they should learn). Daniel Willingham, a cognitive scientist in Virginia, famously wrote in 2009, "factual knowledge must precede skill."[2] Hundreds of classes have taken that notion to heart, spending all their time filling students' heads with "things they need to remember" and then testing their ability to recall those little nuggets or at least recognize them on a multiple-choice quiz.

Of course, no one can think critically about something they've never encountered, but it does matter where and how they "get the facts."[3] It makes a world of differences if students learn the basic information *while* engaging in analysis, synthesis, evaluation, and theorizing rather than passively listening to stories (otherwise known as lectures) or through rote drilling. If students become familiar with key facts while they engage in critical analysis, they are more likely to think about implications and applications, to transfer knowledge across a host of situations, and to become adaptive in their expertise.[4]

Yes, it matters a great deal whether students understand, say, the chronological order in which events took place. But an education that merely consists of remembering that the assassination of Franz Ferdinand Carl Ludwig Joseph Maria took place forty nine years and two months after the killing of Abraham Lincoln offers little if any insight into either of the murders nor into their consequences.

Lighting Their Fires

As we contemplated these matters that summer in Chicago, we realized that to achieve any of these lofty goals, students had to take deep approaches to their studies.[5] They had to read historical scholarship deeply, to learn to "author it" as David Dunbar (see chapter 16) would argue, build good arguments, and communicate their thoughts clearly. From the beginning of their studies, students had to realize the interpretive nature of the discipline and appreciate its contingency. If they did

not learn to communicate in words, they could not formulate fully developed thoughts and would, instead, live by the vague impressions and
emotions that often substitute for ideas. To put it another way, to
achieve any of those higher objectives, students must learn to read and
write with deep intentions. A purely lecture course couldn't help that
much.

Learning to read and write in this fashion requires hard work, however. Students need to become highly motivated to get through it, and
any teacher must at least avoid discouraging them. Thus, the new Super
Course had to find new ways to move them.

As we've noted earlier, research has produced considerable evidence
that traditional extrinsic motivators (assignments, grades, and stern
looks) will actually reduce students' interest. The emerging Super
Course at Northwestern that summer in Evanston had to find methods to spark intrinsic concern, to get students to take control of their
own education. On the first day it could outline the promises of the
class and invite students to join without using the language of requirements.[6] "Our work together is an integral part of getting a liberal education at this school," we began. "But no one can force you to experience
that kind of learning. I just hope to convince you that it will be
worthwhile."[7]

Using the Arts to Raise Questions

Helping students develop a strong sense of control over their own education could pay handsome rewards, but it wasn't quite enough. Over a
thousand years and longer, the arts have learned ways to spark the mind.
Could the dominant art form of the twentieth century—motion
pictures—help engage students? After all we also wanted students to
practice reading popular culture. Setting up a film series outside of class
seemed like the perfect approach.

We selected a small group of movies for Thursday night showings,
complete with popcorn (in the first year, a single graduate student aided
in the process; in later years, as the number of undergraduates flirted
with the century mark and sometimes topped it, the department

assigned a second teaching assistant to the Cold War offering). The course was divided into a series of important questions, and each movie was chosen to stimulate interest in that inquiry—not to provide answers but to spark deep concern. Each one also reminded students that their own historical views came from multiple sources, including films.[8]

As students gathered to watch each movie, they received a list of the major questions the unit would explore. After the showing, they got a challenging checklist of scholarship they should collectively consider as they grappled with the questions at hand and some documents to analyze.[9] We divided the class into heterogeneous cohorts of six members apiece. Each group looked like a cross section of the whole class.

After watching students' eyes bulge slightly as they surveyed the commanding list of appropriate scholarship, we suggested that they divide the articles between them. At least two people on each team should read any one piece. "Take notes and share them with one another," we advised. They now created assignments for themselves and held each other accountable, making each person responsible for a certain part of the material. The groups now had a purpose, no longer just an obligation that class rules imposed on them.

Playing Roles

Even more powerful than the movies, the students played a series of simulation games. They took on roles, immersed themselves in both primary and scholarly sources, and came to class ready to do battle over some issue, playing a key person or faction in the historical drama. The students didn't just reenact history, however; they fought political and intellectual battles and even tried to find ways to change the outcomes as long as they remained true to the characters and positions they played.

In one unit, for example, the class took up two simulations around US Cold War relations with Chile. In the first, set in 1970, that South American country had elected an avowed Marxist as its leader, and President Richard Nixon had asked for advice (this was after the class had viewed and discussed Costa-Gavras's fast-paced thriller *Missing* and had read critical commentaries on the film and news accounts of the Reagan administration's campaign to discourage Americans from watching it). Each group was randomly assigned to one of the factions that actually arose in the United States that year and given a set of documents and historical studies to read. In the second game, they played Chilean political leaders and advised the Marxist president, Salvador Allende, on what to do about Nixon and the economic warfare he waged against them.[10]

In addition to the simulation and role-playing games, the class took up a series of case studies modeled after Roland Christensen's work in the Harvard School of Business.[11] Each game centered around a historical crisis and question (e.g., how to respond to Holocaust survivors, many of whom sought admission to the United States while others wanted to settle in Palestine). Outside of class, students read a twenty-to-thirty-page case providing historical background, then engaged in a discussion around five types of questions that Christensen had suggested: *exploratory* (What are the primary issues this material raises. What major concepts does it utilize?); *testing* (What are some possible answers we might consider? What problems does each entail?); *relational* (How do we compare and contrast solutions? What criteria should we use to weigh each possibility? What concepts will we employ in making such judgments?); *priority* (Which is the best solution or idea? Why? What do you reject? Why?); and *concluding* (What have we learned here? What are the implications of our conclusions? What questions remain unanswered? How do we answer those questions?) Sometimes the conversation began with a think-pair-square-share, other times with the whole group popping ideas while someone collected them on the board. We also encouraged students to see each case as highly interpretive, subject to questioning.

For several weeks, the excitement flowing out of both simulation games and cases was so intense that it seemed tangible, something you could cut with a knife. Once we stumbled onto a meeting held in the old Deering Library where two groups working on a simulation game had inadvertently claimed the same space. It was early in the morning, and nobody else was around. As the discussion began, the stained-glass windows in that collegiate gothic structure seemed to vibrate with the intellectual energy that flowed from their verbal battles.

On several occasions, students came to the office deeply engaged in debates about one issue or another. Such a group appeared one morning during the Chile games. These people had developed considerable sympathy for the economic and political reforms that Allende's administration had put forth. "But we don't think he could pull them off without heavy opposition from the Nixon administration," one person explained. "Through no fault of his own, he has become too much of a polarizing figure." With considerable detail, these young scholars laid out their understanding of the historical developments, citing matters that went far beyond any of the common readings. They struggled to find some resolution for the challenges facing both Nixon and Allende, speculating about an array of fine-tuned alternatives. Did Allende have to become a martyr to his own cause before it could triumph, they asked themselves.

When the class met at one o'clock on Tuesdays and Thursdays, the room always filled quickly with students chattering about the day's case or simulation. It was not unusual for outsiders to attend these sessions as word about the intense debates spread across campus. Rare was the day when any enrolled students missed class, while ten or fifteen extras sometimes crowded in around the edges. Still others waited outside asking, "Do you have room for me today?" The same scene unfolded on movie nights. But it was not just the chance to see a free flick that motivated strangers to join. Most of them came for the heated discussions following the screenings.

The games, cases, and movies helped generate student interest and excitement, but so did one additional maneuver. For the first reading, we picked a highly provocative selection that would draw students into the debates even if the piece came out of its traditional order. Does a Super Course need a spark plug, something that will grab interest quickly and begin to build student trust that this class will be worthy and different?

To that end, the course began with Mark Danner's gripping book *The Massacre at El Mozote*.[12] The journalist explored the events of

December 1981, when an American-trained army swept through the tiny Salvadoran village of El Mozote during the civil strife between leftists and rightists. Even though the residents of the hamlet had guarded their neutrality in the war, the army killed everyone in the village: men, women, and children, except for a woman who hid in a tree. Many were tortured before dying. Soldiers raped dozens of young girls before killing them.

The Reagan administration denied the atrocity had ever taken place, while American right-wing watchdog groups ridiculed journalists who broke the news in the *New York Times* and *Washington Post*, sometimes denying that the affair actually happened.

On the first day of class, we asked students to read the book by the following week, when they would be given a chance "to demonstrate [their] brilliant understanding of the work and its issues" (we purposely avoided the word "test"). Does Danner provide sufficient evidence that the massacre actually happened?[13] What does he mean that the killings represented a "central parable of the Cold War"?[14]

Let's Have a Party

Fully charged up after experiencing the El Mozote reading, the simulation games, the cases, the movies, and the provocative questions they raised, the Cold War students now needed practice with higher-order reading and writing skills and a chance to get feedback.[15] To that end, they engaged in a series of reading and writing parties. We gave them some carefully selected passages—sometimes a single paragraph—that they would read in class and begin to analyze together. With a great sense of dedication, students worked in groups of six to find arguments (not all statements are arguments), separate evidence from conclusions, distinguish between different kinds of agreements and disagreements (in beliefs and attitudes), and recognize whether evidence was observed or inferred.[16] They spotted common logical fallacies, both formal and informal, scouted for assumptions, and identified abstract concepts and distinguished them from concrete claims.[17] "I thought at times this was a logic class," one student reported with an approving smile.

Sometimes they tackled material in class, using some freshly intro-duced technique to analyze. They dissected passages with conflicting claims (teaching the controversies) and asked, "What's the nature of the disagreement—over beliefs or attitudes?" While they worked together in groups, we floated through the class, ready to intervene with a ques-tion or explanation if necessary. They learned to add "could be," at the end of every claim they encountered or made, a habit of healthy skepti-cism that always left open other concepts, assumptions, evidence, and conclusions. The reading parties worked well to improve students' com-prehension and to develop robust habits of the mind because we used carefully chosen passages[18] and approached each one with a sense of exploration and adventure. Nonjudgmental feedback drove the inqui-ries and stimulated deep intentions.

Using Class Time More Effectively

The instructor and the students used their valuable minutes together to do more than dispense information they could easily encounter on their own. Reading parties did, however, contain the key "facts" they might traditionally hear in a lecture.[19] One session helped students define what it meant to "think like a good historian." In that major exercise we asked students to define their own meaning for historical thinking. After a few minutes in which they collected their ideas in silence and began to cast some of them onto a piece of paper, they heard, "Now turn to one other person sitting near you and share your thoughts with them." The room would burst into conversation while we roamed through the aisles, listening to the chatter and visibly taking notes. For about five minutes, the students struggled with this strange idea of historical thinking. "Each pair should now form a square with two other people and continue your conversations. Take careful notes on your thoughts. You'll need to share your main points with the entire class in about ten minutes."

Students speculated and struggled to define a new meaning for them-selves. But they also tried to join a new community of knowledgeable peers that the professor and graduate students represented, to compare their own ideas with those coming from that group. After students had collected their thoughts and massaged them in a communal exercise, each square put their main points on the board. The public display of thinking prompted new discussions: "What do you see here? Which thoughts trouble you? Which ones do you like?" After a brief give-and-take, the students received some short definitions of historical thinking coming from historians and then spent a few moments writing out their own thoughts at that point.

Still other sessions gave the students experience in evaluating their own learning progress. Students were not just encountering a body of information and ideas but mastering the approaches of adaptive expertise and critical and creative thinking. After taking up a major new historical question, students often spent time speculating about possible answers *before* they tackled any scholarship on the matter.

Helping Students Learn to Learn

Traditional teaching in college spends hours telling students what they need to remember but little time on how they can recall, understand, apply, analyze, synthesize, evaluate, or theorize. Imagine a baseball coach who lectures on how to throw a ball or swing a bat but never gets the team to do any of those activities, let alone play a scrimmage where they can try them out and get feedback. Students need practice in getting ideas and information out of their brains.

At the time, the term "retrieval practice" was not in common use, yet the Cold War course employed several activities that foreshadowed that powerful idea. On many days, students ended class by writing for three minutes around some combination of three prompts: What major conclusions did you reach from today's discussion? Why did you draw those conclusions? What questions remain in your mind? The exercise gave people in the class practice in finding ideas and information in their memories, then associating them richly.

We now have considerable evidence that such practice helps "make it stick" far better than endless review ("quizzing is better than rehearsing"). So does another device the Cold War class used occasionally. We asked students to imagine they were teaching this course, and that they wanted to ask their student a profound question about some book or article they had been invited to read. "What would it be?"

When we suggested they prepare reading notes for other members of their group, we did so with practices that foreshadowed current retrieval research. "After you read a chapter or article, close your book then jot down the central issue or question, the major argument advanced, the chief evidence offered, the implications you see, and any important new abstract concept."

Learning the Meaning of Good Writing

In the third class session, students received four introductions that undergraduates at another leading university had written for papers. Two of them introduced work that eventually received honors, and two that got a B minus (they were mediocre but not terrible). "Your job is to decide which is which, then list the criteria by which you have made your choices."

After student groups of six worked together for fifteen to twenty-five minutes, they came back together and took a vote, and each group put their assessments on the board. After a brief discussion consisting mostly of questions rather than statements, students read a summary of the criteria by which the essays had been judged. No one ever told them the "correct answer," but after they received the criteria, they were asked to do their evaluation a second time. After that additional chance virtually all the students improved their understanding of good writing. Both thinking and writing matured significantly.

"This is the most powerful hour I've spent in college learning to think and write," one person wrote on the end-of-term review of the class. Many others expressed similar views.[20]

At the end of the term, each pupil constructed an argument, complete with supporting evidence, about the level of learning he or she had achieved and the grade he or she deserved (the class had previously constructed together a rubric of what it meant to be an A, B, C, or D thinker). They were asked what they thought their strengths and weaknesses were as a historical thinker. When it came time to hand out grades, we made our assessments first, then looked at theirs. If student and teacher agreed, case closed (which happened about 97 percent of the time). If not, we looked more deeply at their evidence and reasoning, using a portfolio approach to a wide range of a student's work rather than simply adding up scores from past papers and dividing by some predetermined number. In essence, the final grade came out of a conversation between the professor and each student.

The Project

For the Cold War course, the ultimate achievement of this revolution came in the highly personal work and progress of students. Everybody crafted his or her own historical question, investigated the matter in both scholarly treatments and primary sources, and found a way to share his or her resulting arguments with others.

"The project isn't about pursuing a topic," they heard constantly, "but about exploring and tentatively answering a question. You must find your investigation important, fascinating, beautiful, fun." Many people went to great lengths to research their query (using spring breaks and summer extensions to travel to distant archives or to do interviews—something that was not necessarily expected). Most students wrote papers but had the option to express themselves in film and other media. Several people wrote a play.

"I want to write a play about the struggles over El Mozote," Joel Feinman proclaimed the day he heard about the project. "But I'll need more time and an extension on the due date. I want to do more research." In June after the class was "over" he traveled to El Salvador, interviewed the woman who had escaped the massacre by climbing in a tree, read through the Argentine forensic reports on the carnage, came home, and wrote his play. That fall, he gathered actors, costume and prop designers, stage-lighting experts, and others and put them through a three-week seminar on the civil war in El Salvador before rehearsing them for the stage production. His play ran for two weeks on campus, playing before sold-out audiences and creating a buzz that was palpable.

But the story didn't end there. The next year Joel returned to Central America and stayed for a while in a refugee camp. There he met a woman who had walked into a cross fire between competing troops one day in the 1980s. She was carrying her baby son on her back and ran for miles to escape the gunfire. When the woman finally stopped, she discovered the boy had been shot through the head. She buried the child but lost her mind, living for several years in the high jungle like a naked animal. Soldiers in the Farabundo Marti National Liberation Front (FMLN) brought the woman to a refugee camp, where Joel met her. She made a deep and lasting impression on his life.[21]

Joel's adventure all began with a question that seemed to some like it was not in the proper chronological order, continued with collaboration, and finished with opportunities for students to take a deep approach to questions they regarded as important, intriguing, and beautiful. Along the way, Joel and other students enjoyed the "professor's prerogative" to try, fail, receive feedback, and try again. They could speculate and learn by doing history. The course appealed to their emotions and their intellect, gave them control over their own education, deliberately challenged major paradigms, provided places to learn inductively, and offered guided practice in deep reading and writing.

A New Game in Town

Around that same time, Mark Carnes, professor of history at Barnard College, initiated a revolution that is still reverberating through classrooms around the world. We had not met Mark at the time, and we had no influence on each other's work. It is sheer coincidence that we all struck on the value of role-playing games. Mark's experiment took the idea into new territory. It also shifted the learning objectives and expanded the discussion about intrinsic motivation. Carnes called his courses Reacting to the Past (with the method of the class now known as "Reacting" pedagogy). With superior organizational skills, he built a network of history teachers that carried the role-playing games into classrooms around the world.

For the New York maestro, a successful learning experience could tap three interlocking student motivations: the drive to win games, the desire to play a subversive, and the thrill of being someone else. "Most people are eager to seize every opportunity to engage in subversive play," he surmised, "even when it happens in a seemingly unlikely place such as a college classroom."[22]

In the games that he and others began creating, students took on the role of a person caught up in some key historical moment (much as the Cold War class was doing with the simulation cases). They might be Socrates at his trial. They could be Anne Hutchinson in early Rhode Island, Galileo standing before the accusations of the church, or any number of people.[23]

Each game featured two competing factions (e.g., those who wanted to kill Socrates and those who didn't) and a third group that the first two tried to convince. The vote of the "impartials" determined who won. "The very existence of such competition," Carnes would later write, "evokes subversion, because it encourages any competitor to imagine herself as a different kind of person—and that is the deepest form of subversion."[24] (The Cold War class appealed to that same sense of rebellion by calling itself an "experiment" that would "rock the foundations of education.")

The Barnard College professor had noticed that while students grew increasingly bored with class, they played video games with wild abandon. One study found that two-thirds to three-fourths of college students played video games every day, and those gamers were more likely to binge drink and do poorly in school.[25] If he could channel their competitive spirits into learning, the historical games would revolutionize education. Although he never used this language, Carnes fashioned passion-driven experiences that seduced students into doing something (playing a role-based game), in the course of which they would take a deep approach to history and develop an empathetic understanding of the people caught up in a distant controversy.

Students took over class time: no more passive attention to lectures. While the games provided little exploration of change over time or stimulated students to read historical scholarship, they did spark great interest in classic texts from the history of ideas. Driven by the excitement of troublemaking role-play and sometimes fierce competition in the game, students pored over those written relics from the past, prepared speeches, wrote articles, published newspapers set in an ancient time frame, and plunged into debates where the intellectual fever boiled over in palpable tension and excitement.

Several large and multiyear studies have found impressive learning results from Carnes's approach, all quite similar to outcomes in the Cold War class.[26] Engagement soared, and so did attendance when compared to traditional classes. Confidence surged. Students remembered and understood more information and crafted more sophisticated arguments. Oral communication skills skyrocketed. Writing abilities at least kept pace with those of students in more traditional classes (in the Cold War class, writing gains outstripped those in speaking).

A study at Indiana University South Bend found that students who played these games developed a greater belief in their capacity to learn, a reflection of their rising sense of self-efficacy. Thus, the games fostered the growth mindset that Carol Dweck and her colleagues found so essential to learning. Perhaps most important, Reacting students learned more about themselves, reexamining long-held beliefs, sometimes to build greater strength of convictions and other times to move in new directions.

While a competitive spirit bathed and coddled this intellectual exercise, it wasn't the old struggle over grades and class ranking. The games did not pit students against each other in the stupefying competition of grade grubbing. "The pedagogy leverages students' innate desires to win," wrote a trio of scholars, "to compel them to grapple with the contingencies of the past and the complexities of human agency."[27] Students said they worked harder and longer in their role-playing classes, but they enjoyed them more than they did traditional classes because their drive came from within rather than from the assignments of teachers.[28]

Stories of student excitement abound. When students at Dordt College in Iowa learned they wouldn't have time to finish a game, they volunteered to meet every morning at 7:30 a.m. in order to do so.

Professors at nearly four hundred schools now use the Reacting ped-agogy. They've written scores of games, and some pioneers are carrying the ideas into science classes and other disciplines. Skeptics have often assumed that the pedagogy can work only at highly selective universities and in small classes. Yet it has also transformed learning at more open admission schools and even in fairly large classes. Remember that the Cold War class had sixty to nearly one hundred students on board, ac-complished by having groups rather than individuals taking on roles. Bridget Ford, a history professor at California State at East Bay used a similar approach in a required survey course of 125 people. The move, along with closer monitoring of student progress, cut failure rates by more than half. At Eastern Michigan University, the Reacting classes attracted a cross section of students, many of whom struggled to stay in school and generally made lower grades than others. Yet they too thrived in and enjoyed the games.[29]

What's Next?

Much remains to be done to realize the full potential of these innova-tions and to spark and support rich natural critical learning environ-ments where students learn in magnificent new ways. The Cold War class didn't reach every student educationally. It didn't always realize the student-run classes that Mark Carnes creates nearly every session. The Northwestern course may have stressed the study of change over time and provided explicit help with specific reading and writing abilities, but the Reacting courses fostered growth mindsets and self-efficacy. As new generations of faculty members join the academy, they bring a rich set of experiences and perspectives that will allow them to use the re-search on human learning to help every student realize his or her poten-tial to learn and create, putting to rest forever the notion that school is merely a place that selects good students and rejects bad ones.

Even within the last year, we've heard from young educators who have been exploring ways to expand the applications of these new ideas to help students learn history. In August 2019 the *New York Times* inau-gurated a series of essays it called the "1619 project." The first contribution came from investigative journalist and MacArthur Fellowship winner Nikole Hannah-Jones. Her essay eventually garnered a Pulitzer Prize in the commentary category.[30] She marshaled a considerable body of recent historical scholarship to argue that Americans of African descent played the key role in pushing the United States toward a democracy and that the institution of slavery stood at the center of the American story. The article opened a public debate about a historical question, as traditionalists sprang into the arena to reject its conclusions.

Could the fight become the model for classroom debates that utilize some combination of Carnes's games and our case studies to bring students into historical controversies? Rather than centering a series of cases on disagreements that erupted in the past, could they focus—at least in part—on the debates that have emerged between historians or at the intersection of scholarly discussions and public discourse? Those historiographical debates have long been used by some teachers but often within traditional lecture or discussion courses. What if they became integrated into a simulation game or case study? Could they create the experiences in which students learn to ask questions, do research, explore a rich palette of ideas, think logically, expand their empathy and interests, and understand the problems they face in any conclusion they reached?

CHAPTER FIFTEEN

All Knowledge Is Related

Jeanette Norden spent much of her adult life studying neuroscience and helping other people explore issues about the workings of the human brain. But she also had other interests, including a lifelong fascination with both nineteenth-century European philosophy and the Second World War. "I love to go into an antique bookstore," the now-retired Vanderbilt medical school professor told us, "and rummage through bins of used books, squirreling around for something in one of those areas." On one of those expeditions, she found a thin volume, long out of print, written by an Austrian psychiatrist who spent time in two different Nazi concentration camps.

Ella Lingens-Reiner wasn't a Jew, Pole, Slav, or from any of the other major groups the Nazis persecuted, but Hitler's Gestapo arrested her and her husband for supporting Social Democracy and criticizing the Fuhrer. The police sent the young couple to Auschwitz-Birkenau and later transferred her to Dachau. Prior to the war and incarceration, Ella and her husband had a chance to leave the country but stayed to help their Jewish neighbors with the growing nightmare of a rabidly anti-Semitic government. After liberation, she wrote an exposé about day-to-day life in the brutal compounds that the right-wing dictatorship had constructed, and that's the book that Norden found.

As she purchased the used copy of *Prisoners of Fear—a Life of Resistance*,[1] the scientist probably could not yet imagine how it might play a role in a senior neuroscience course. Years later the Vanderbilt professor organized her first undergraduate offering in the College of Arts and Science and remembered her purchase of Lingens-Reiner's account. How she used that book to help create a Super Course illustrates well the ingenuity and imagination that often mark these educational inventions. Her story also exemplifies how a broadly educated person can fashion a learning environment that knocks down the walls of disciplinary focus. While this Super Course took place in a small senior seminar at a highly selective university, its core principles have more universal significance. Even someone teaching a large "lecture" class at an open admissions school can find powerful ideas nestled in this model. You must think conceptually, however, and the prize is there for the taking.

As she explained to us recently, Norden wanted to produce a capstone course for senior biology majors who studied the brain. The enterprising professor began working on the new offering after the College of Arts and Science asked medical school professors to consider teaching undergraduates. She was one of the first to volunteer.

Her goals reflected well a long devotion to rigorous and comprehensive mastery of a field. "I wanted to make sure," she explained to us, "that anyone graduating with a neuroscience emphasis could explain in a straightforward way the basic principles of" the field. But she also expected the people in her seminar "to understand that all knowledge is interlaced," that getting an education isn't just about learning one or two subjects well, but it is the integration of broad areas of knowledge and developing the capacity to transfer from one domain to another. Finally, she hoped the people who took her class could reason well, draw their conclusions from scientific evidence, defend their positions in a clear and articulate manner, and appreciate the demands they faced in accepting whatever they believed.

To promote those results, she could have chosen to "lecture" in all these areas. After all, the award-winning teacher had become legendary for her clear and stimulating oral presentations. With that prowess she had won every major teaching award in the medical school, and some of them so many times, the administration would no longer let her compete. When the university created endowed chairs of teaching excellence in the 1990s, Norden gobbled up the first of those distinctions, with her power at the podium playing a significant role in the selection. But stunning lectures were never her only forte.

Giving Undergraduates More Freedom

Norden had developed considerable understanding of how people learn deeply and how best to foster that achievement, and when she began organizing her first undergraduate course in 1999, the Vanderbilt professor drew from those insights. Most fundamental, she gave the people who enrolled in her new seminar control over their own learning and allowed them to do most of the thinking and talking. At the same time, she devised an ingenious yet simple scaffolding that kept them engaged and provided vital direction for their studies. In all, she shaped a special experience that left them with important alternatives, and highly motivated, and in the process created a course with many of the elements of a natural critical learning environment.

Most of the people who signed up for her senior seminar came to pursue one fascinating question: How does the human brain work? How does it see, hear, feel, taste, and smell? How do those several million tiny cells, living in the dark of our skull, learn a language and how to communicate with other human beings? How does that teaming city of synapses come to control an empire of other organs strewn throughout our bodies?

But students soon encountered other inquiries that grabbed them by their neurons and wouldn't let go. How and why do we enjoy music? How do humans generally develop a sense of ethical behavior, and why and how do some people violate those norms in acts of unspeakable horror? Where does evil originate? How can I navigate the moral questions that often crop up in life? Should I purchase something made with child labor? How should I react to a medical catastrophe bubbling in a distant country?

Learners Plan the Course

Each time she taught the class, Norden had no syllabus in hand on the first day of class—and that's important to know about her Super Course. Instead, over the early sessions, the participants constructed the course they would pursue. People would control their own education. "That's why it turned out so different each semester," the professor explained. But this didn't mean just going into class and saying you are on your own. Norden made significant contributions, and how she did so while still keeping them in charge played a large role in why we selected this example in a book about Super Courses.

"I went into class with a list of about fifty to sixty fascinating books and a sheet of biographical questions about the undergraduates," she explained. That little bibliography became the foundation of the house she sought to build.

Students could choose three to five of the works to read. By taking the class, they had, in essence, agreed to help their classmates grasp the key information, ideas, and issues within each of the books they chose, and to think about their broad implications and applications. Many of the items they encountered looked familiar, best sellers from a wide variety of authors. Millions of people had already expressed their interest in these works, and each item had something important to say. These books had become part of a broad intellectual conversation.

Jared Diamond appeared with his monumental smash hit *Guns, Germs, and Steel* a wide-ranging history of the world focused on why some parts of the planet have become so wealthy while others live in miserable poverty. Steven Pinker and Stephen Jay Gould found their way into Norden's bibliography. So did Candace Pert, with her *Molecules of Emotions*.[2] Susan Hunter came to the list after the publication in 2003 of her *Black Death: AIDS in Africa*. Historians, anthropologists, paleontologists, evolutionary biologists, philosophers, and others populated this collection of influential and much debated writers. But what did each of these contribute to a study of the human brain? That became a major part of what the pupils had to figure out. Most of the people in the seminar were headed to medical or graduate school. How could this bibliography help them as physicians and scientists?

Anyone could add an item they wanted to explore. All they had to do was request that a particular book be included and provide an explanation of why it should be. "Over time," the biology professor told us, "they helped build and modify the list. I included things because someone from an earlier year had recommended it."[3]

Learning about the Students

Even before selecting the books they would read, the people in the class filled out the sheet of biographical inquiries that Norden gave them. That seemingly innocent step might prove to be quite problematic with some people, even a privacy violation and a potential source for prejudice and stereotyping. But not in this case. She asked them if they would be willing to share personal information about themselves that might be used in the class discussions.[4]

Her approach said, *I'm interested in you and what you like and do.* Nobody had to divulge anything. All items were voluntary. Among the wide-ranging set of questions: What languages do you speak? What is your ethnicity? Do you come from a religious background? Do you have any special abilities or hobbies that make you proud? Is there anything that makes you distinctive? Good, bad, or indifferent? "It is amazing how much they wanted to tell me about themselves," Norden remembered.

Everyone understood that anything they put on the sheet could prompt a remark during a discussion but none of it would form the basis for prejudice and discrimination. "When we explored language and the brain," the teacher explained, "I might call on a multilingual person to share examples from one of the languages they spoke." One semester, a young woman put down that she was an accomplished musician. It just so happened that a group in the class wanted to explore music and the brain. Norden then asked the musician to bring her cello to class and play a Bach concerto. Her performance prompted a wide-ranging discussion about how the brain processes different kinds of music. Does it handle Bach differently than it does, say, the country tunes that earned fame for Vanderbilt's hometown of Nashville?

As part of that drive to make undergraduates captains of their own schooling, the professor also asked them what grade they wanted to pursue in the course. If someone sought an A, he or she chose five items from the list of books; for a B, four; for a C, three. In multiple ways, Norden gave people in her class choices, building that sense of autonomy that Deci and Ryan had stressed. They would define the topics that the seminar would pursue, and, as we will see, the learners even controlled what happened in class and the quality of those sessions in helping them to learn.

Setting Parameters with a Question

On that first day, Norden would, however, set some important parameters, but not with some rules dished out with no context. Rather she engaged people in a conversation that helped them understand certain expectations they would face constantly. The undergraduates were forming a community they would govern, but they were also joining a larger academic village of knowledgeable peers that had its own standards. That's a tricky combination. How can you help people appreciate the demands of the second part of that equation—joining an academic society that already exists and accepting its standards—without challenging and perhaps even destroying their sense of autonomy?

Norden did so with a question and the discussions that followed. It was a model of things to come, similar to the way Andy Kaufman set the tone on the first day of his class with his discussion about how works of art can influence you. Please note how both teachers stretched the disciplinary boundaries of their course, preparing the groundwork for even broader excursions later.

Here's what Norden asked: Are poor countries simply made up of people with inferior brains while rich places have more intelligent people? Are some communities and their leaders just smarter than others, and thus leap ahead? The Vanderbilt professor was capturing a debate that had emerged long ago and still raged in some minds.

For several centuries Western countries had gone to places that had less material wealth and more primitive technologies and concluded that the locals obviously had inferior brains that explained their history.

In the late twentieth century, many scholars had rejected such a fundamentally racist view. In *Guns, Germs, and Steel*,[5] Jared Diamond had wrapped up the argument against "White supremacy." But the old racist notion continued to flit through the culture. Hitler's application of racist thought had led some people to challenge the prejudices, but that didn't keep remnants of previous thinking from intruding into polite and otherwise intelligent conversations.

Norden raised this issue for two fundamental reasons. For one, it illustrated quite well how disciplines that seem far apart are interconnected. The query about inferior brains is both a historical and a biological matter. Second, she wanted to use this potentially explosive topic to model how well-educated scientists could respond to a variety of inquiries. No matter how anyone replied, the Vanderbilt professor countered with the same questions: What's your evidence? How was that data derived? What counts as proof? What are the problems any reasonable person would face in accepting your line of reasoning and the support you offer? If you have no underpinning, can you admit that your views are unsupported opinions?

Through careful and polite exchanges, the professor brought the people in the class into a world of scientific thought, with its demands for confirmation and critical thinking. Those interrogations reverberated constantly through the seminar as students took them up as their own.

These were senior biology majors who had long experienced the demands of corroboration in their scientific work, but now Norden asked them to apply the same criteria to their social, political, and cultural thinking. They had to overcome the far transfer problem that often plagued even the most sophisticated thinking. They had to recognize that knowledge doesn't just come in nice neat little boxes with disciplinary labels on them. "I wanted them to realize," the professor told us, "that what we think we know is all connected." An educated person recognizes that the division of knowledge into various fields of study may be something that schooling encourages but that it can limit our efforts to act as rational creatures. "Universities break things down into subjects, and you major in one or two of them, but our insights are related to multiple disciplines," she reminded.

Through that initial discussion and in all the exchanges that followed, Norden challenged rather than browbeat her class, and the standards she set for an educated exchange of ideas and perspectives came with respect and not with a sense of superiority. It came also with a strong faith in the abilities of class members to rise to a new standard, to examine their own thinking, to ask themselves those humbling inquiries: Why do I believe this to be true? Am I willing to change my conclusions in the face of overwhelming counterevidence? Can I admit when I have no proof but hold to a certain opinion for emotional reasons or out of an unquestioned habit of thought? That respect and faith shaped the success of the class.

All too often a similar enterprise could flounder because the class sees the professor's criteria as attempts to control and even to humiliate rather than uplift them. (If you are thinking, "My students can't become sophisticated thinkers," you may be right. But one of their biggest obstacles may be your conception of them.)

Between the first and second meeting, Norden surveyed their book choices and looked for patterns of matters they wanted to investigate: how the brain processes language, makes ethical decisions, and so forth. She also devised a schedule of when each group would take over the seminar. The class might spend several days on any one topic, and during their time in the spotlight, the group in charge could decide how they engaged their peers.

But students still had to meet certain expectations. They should help others understand the basic thesis of the reading but also ask about implications, applications, possibilities, and evidence. What are the broader questions that arise out of the book and its primary thesis? Where do you stand on the controversies that arise? And most important in each case, what are the neurological issues that emerge, and how can your knowledge about the human brain help resolve those matters?

While one group led the seminar on any given day, other people in the class had their own responsibilities to ask questions, seek clarifications, request examples and evidence, and raise additional or alternative implications and theories. In essence, Norden invited young scholars into a rich conversation about important subjects and requested that they bring important thinkers to the table.

What Could Go Wrong?

In the best of times, the experience could liberate and stimulate minds, giving these undergraduates a chance to think, explore, imagine, and expand their insights. Yet some people have been conditioned to operate strategically, to focus primarily on the grade, and to probe constantly for the easiest way to "complete an assignment." They sometimes learn to "fake their way" through a reading without taking any of it seriously. In one classic version, they simply become outspoken critics of whatever they are supposedly reading. "If I hadn't really read something carefully," one person offered about his college years, "I would tear it apart in class, attacking anything that I might imagine that the author had written. I could even make up stuff to reject."

How could Norden guard against those strategic intentions and foster deep engagement among all the people who joined her twice each week? On a fundamental level, she made clear that she had read all the books on her list and knew them well. But that alone couldn't turn the trick. The biologist had to build an intrinsically interesting learning environment that would engross her undergraduates in fascinating, intriguing, important, and beautiful inquiries. She did that in major part with the wide-ranging issues brought to the table, an interdisciplinary approach that made rich connections with a dazzling array of questions. She had a deep and genuine fascination with the human brain, and her curiosity and enchantment became contagious. "How could you not be interested in the one organ that determines every thought you have, every step you take?"

Furthermore, she had an abiding faith and interest in the lives of the people in her class and their personal and intellectual development, and she expressed those feelings in multiple ways. Even the biographical questionnaire she distributed on the first day conveyed that interest, and so did each time she called on someone to offer a personal illustration. In those little acts of attention, she helped people take pride in who they were and in their cultural and linguistic backgrounds.

But the neurology professor also had to let students carve their own path through the material. We've already noted that they could pick the number of books they would read, and even which titles and topics they would explore.[6] But freedom didn't stop there. Once during the semester, they could exercise a kind of "safety valve" to release class pressures. If someone had not read something on time, that person could admit it to the class and pick something else to read for a future date. "I wanted to impress upon people who enrolled that they had a responsibility to themselves and one another to prepare for each class."

The Professor's Challenge

Norden did pick one book that everyone would read, and at the end of the semester the entire class took up that work. But she made that choice with care, selecting something that would grab attention, even startling people, making them question their comfortable assumptions, and helping them grasp the interrelated nature of all knowledge. It was usually something seemingly far distant from the study of neurology.

One year, for example, she picked Ella Lingens-Reiner's *Prisoners of Fear*, the dusty little volume she'd found in that used bookstore some years earlier. But how did that account of the brutality of fascism spark deep insights into the human brain? Once we explore and comprehend that question, we can begin to grasp the genius, imagination, and ingenuity that defined and built Norden's Super Course.[7] Every teacher comes from a unique background and can pull from his or her own experiences to create a special environment for students. In every case, a broad set of interests, an interdisciplinary approach, can fuel those endeavors.

She always introduced the reading with a question. How does, say, a work on Nazi concentration camps provide us with any insights into the workings of the human brain? "That's for you to figure out within your groups," she would say to anyone who asked. Her response struck at a key idea that has crept into both teacher and student thinking about learning, although seldom discussed.

Many of the traditional practices of education leave people with the notion that their teachers can "give" them a better understanding of something, as if someone could turn their heads sideways and pour comprehension in their ears. Teachers can, of course, share ideas and information, but the learners must take what they hear, read, or experience and make sense of it, comparing and contrasting it with prior knowledge, thinking about its implications and applications, and transferring it to new kinds of situations.

To become highly adaptive experts, able to solve problems they have never encountered before, students must learn to think critically and imaginatively about anything they learn. No one can give it to them. It comes from practice, getting feedback, and contemplating. As John Dewey wrote "there is no intellectual growth without some reconstruction, some remaking." As we noted earlier, the American education philosopher believed "intelligent judgment" could come only when we "Stop and Think," and examine experience, to free it from "immediate whim and caprice."[8]

Yet many of our traditional practices encourage registrants simply to remember the professor's judgment long enough to spit it back on an examination. Norden was giving the undergraduates the opportunity to build a comprehension that would stand up to rigorous demands for evidence and reason. She was creating an environment in which students not only would comprehend the fundamental ideas of neurology but also would make connections with matters seemingly far afield, and, using all that, address important social, political, ethical, and other types of questions. They would decide how *Prisoners of Fear* helped them penetrate the mysteries of the brain and its operation. Their elections were astounding, reflecting the success of the learning experience Norden had fashioned.

One group, for example, wanted to look at Lingens-Reiner's account of how much food each group received from their captors. The Nazi's parceled out the daily rations according to the racist categories they had created. No one got very much, but Polish Christians received more to eat than did Jews. The students used the book's account to calculate how much each group ate versus the amount their bodies needed to survive. The brain decides how calories are distributed throughout the body. When the general supply runs low, the big operator upstairs steals nutrients from other organs. How does the human brain stay alive under starvation conditions? At what point would that master organ not get enough to maintain itself and begin the slow thefts that would leave vital parts helpless?

The group calculated that the ration for Jews would allow them to survive only about three months. Was this a deliberate attempt to starve all Jews to death even before the gas chambers began their deadly business? Were the caloric calculations enough to prove that such a diabolical plot existed from the beginning? Or did other factors encourage the Nazis to turn on the gas chambers? As the students considered the biological evidence they had gathered, they thought about implication for historical inquiries. But they also puzzled over the significance for medicine and neuroscience, for anorexia patients, for example, or the medical implications of certain diets.

These speculations arose and took on meaning largely because the class had originated them. Over the course of the semester, they had learned how to raise important questions and to ignore the usual disciplinary boundaries in doing so. The students had developed the habit of asking themselves for evidence and the presence of mind to explore implications and possibilities.

Imagine for a moment that Norden had raised the questions about nutrition and rations, say, on an examination. It might have sparked some registrants to broaden their considerations and even to question deep-seated mental models, but it might have soured others, frustrating them with the pressure of a test. In the environment of Norden's seminar, they could lay claim to their own questions, creating an experience where their sense of autonomy, competence, and relatedness could flourish.[9]

Another group asked how humans make moral judgments. What parts of the brain play a role in ethical matters? Once people make a decision about what's right and wrong, how do those assessments translate into actions? How could any humans bring themselves to accept something like the Nazi practices, let alone carry them out? They prepared a comprehensive presentation for their classmates, detailing the sections of the brain involved in all those mental acts. It was a partial course in neuroanatomy that carried far more meaning for the class than did the old-fashioned tour around brain parts.

Teacher-Led Discussions

On rare occasion, Norden would conduct a discussion to model something important, and to set a standard and tone for the student-led days. That happened when consideration of a particular book ran slightly ahead of schedule, creating a "free period," and on those days, the professor would foster a special kind of exchange that further drove motivation and fascination with the brain. It illustrated as well how she used what some would regard as unrelated activity to promote their deep learning. But she still didn't put herself front and center.

On those particular days, she used the kind of moral dilemmas that Lawrence Kohlberg had devised when he was at Harvard.[10] Although the famed psychologist didn't use this language, he had created powerful "model failures," those pregnant moments when people suddenly face a scenario in which their existing mental paradigms don't work so well. Kohlberg's dilemmas created tough moral decisions, and it was that kind of pickle that Norden brought to her undergraduate neuroscience course as part of a broader discussion about how the brain works.

Norden's moral dilemma went something like this: "You find a rug you love. Then you discover that it was made in a country where very young children are used for the labor to produce the carpet. Does an ethical person buy the rug?" Norden would give the class a brief summary of the moral problem that was not much longer than what you just read. She then left the room for fifteen minutes while students organized themselves into those who thought it would be acceptable to do so, and those who didn't, and to prepare their arguments. When she returned, they held a debate.

Some years, she might ask people to pick sides then to take the opposite position in the debates, giving the teams several days to dig through the literature. These were lively exchanges, both intellectually and emotionally charged.

But what role did such a conversation play in a course on the human brain? For Norden everything is related to neurology because we encounter the world with our noggins. In these lively class discussions the professor could encourage and feed that brain-centered perspective on life, but with practice, the students took it up, driving the inquiry. Specific areas of the brain control the making of moral decisions, and the debates sparked a plethora of neurological questions.

What are those regions and how do they function? What happens to the capacity to make ethical judgments when those areas suffer damage? How can intelligent people disagree so completely in a discussion of this nature? How can people concur in beliefs yet diverge in their attitudes? Or do the opposite? Norden was a master at dispensing information in class in a clear and comprehensive way, yet in this seminar she used her precious time with the pupils to spark imaginations, to raise questions, to build interest, and to let the learners construct connections and practice their own skills of thinking and communication.

Solidifying Knowledge in the Field

Such a freewheeling discussion sparked excitement and interest, making students masters of their own education. It helped them see how all knowledge is interrelated, and it fostered an interdisciplinary approach to learning. The people in the class often became highly imaginative and critically thinking problem solvers. But how could the course also expand their knowledge in the field and give people a chance to demonstrate to themselves and others their mastery of neuroscience?

A traditional approach might summarize key information for them in a series of lectures. But that would leave no time for the stimulating discussions. In essence, Norden "flipped" the class, although she never used that language. For each one of the major topics that they would pursue—chosen by the enrollees as they picked which books to read—the professor prepared ten thought questions and gave them to the class. They might be on evolution of the brain, perception, the making of moral decisions, the formation of language, or any number of possibilities. "Questions were designed to test how they draw conclusions and support their answers, but also to allow me *and them* to measure their factual knowledge of neurology," Norden explained.

One year, for example a key theme focused on how the brain processes sensory information. One of the thought questions read: "Since we have no blue cones in the center of the retina how is it that we can look directly at something and see it as blue." Students had to know what blue cones are and what it is that they do, and also realize how color information is processed by the central nervous system.

Students then worked in groups "outside of class" to research the questions and draft comprehensive answers, notes that they could use to quiz each other. On a special day at the end of the semester, Norden would pick one of the questions they had been studying and give each of them a chance to answer it.[11] On that occasion, they put all that they had compiled with their colleagues aside and drew only from their memory, reflecting the good habits of retrieval practice.

She would also give them one question that they had never seen before. Even in that act, Norden gave learners choices with her wording of that item. One semester, for example, she asked simply "What major paradigm did you alter as a result of your study in this class?"

Keeping the Class Small and Intimate

Such conversations could evoke deep intellectual and emotional responses as students grappled not only with grasping the workings of the brain but with comprehending their implications for a wide variety of issues. Norden had created a safe place where people could explore profound questions about the nature of life and society, about morality and justice, about the meaning of consciousness and existence, where they could help one another struggle both intellectually and emotionally as the evidence of science played roughhouse with long-standing religious beliefs and family traditions. Creating such an environment might become a central goal in any class, no matter what its size or content.[12]

"I just loved that class," Norden recalled a decade after the program ended, "and I loved the people in it." But Norden didn't take credit for its success. "It was the students who made it work," she confessed. "What the teacher does is create an environment." The key, she believed, was freedom. "There was just such an intimacy that developed because of the type of class that it was, with the discussion about issues that the students chose themselves, and they decided how they would approach each subject." On several occasions the class became quite emotional as people raised tough moral problems, or made decisions about their most fundamental beliefs. What kind of responsibilities do humans have toward one another? What are our origins? Are we creatures of a loving god or the random products of a blind evolutionary process? Can I be proud of my own heritage rather than accept the stereotyping of popular prejudices? Are we somehow fundamentally different than other animals with our feelings of moral obligations? In the face of a monumental catastrophe like the AIDS epidemic in Africa, what ethical duties do we face?

Mind you, students raised these issues, not Norden. In those moments of extreme tension, they took action, sometimes actually pulling their chairs closer to each other to pursue a more intimate exchange. Rather than shunning one another over some touchy disagreement, they grew closer together. "It is difficult for me to convey in words the richness of their discussions," Norden concluded. "I felt privileged to be present" at this nonjudgmental give-and-take.

CHAPTER SIXTEEN

The Pedagogy of Getting Out

Forty years ago, a small liberal arts college in Oklahoma took its students out of the classroom to enrich and deepen their learning. The school was not the first to do so, nor would it be the last. Like many such institutions in those days, this school had a special January term when students took only one experimental class, and, therefore, had the freedom to travel. In 1976 about fifteen people signed up for a course that mixed the study of the "Civil War culture" in the South with an exploration of racism, segregation, and the civil rights movement.

They piled into a caravan of cars, station wagons, and one old pickup truck and headed for some of the battlefields where the federal government maintained parks to commemorate the battles over enslaving human beings. While the official public histories of these places like Shiloh, Vicksburg, Chickamauga, Atlanta, and elsewhere spoke of valor and heroics mixed with a tinge of nostalgia about a "lost civilization" that the war had supposedly obliterated, these students pursued different questions and perspectives.

How did twentieth-century White and Black southerners view the mid-nineteenth-century conflict, and how did their concepts of that war shape contemporary political and social views, especially their reactions to the civil rights movement and the attacks on mandatory segregation?

The course relied on the church affiliations of this denominational university to find ways for students to stay in private homes. The faculty and students loaded into their vehicles handouts, books, and articles to read as they moved across Arkansas, Louisiana, Mississippi, and on into Alabama, Georgia, and Tennessee. By day, the moving train of cars and a truck became a rolling seminar with conversations that spilled into gas stops and roadside bistros, and, of course, the tours of the battlefields. At one point, these nomadic scholars stayed with a family near Shiloh in Tennessee that had turned their house into a civil war shrine, filled with reproduced replicas of Confederate flags and genuine relics of spent cannonballs and other memorabilia collected from the floor of the nearby battlefield park (maybe in violation of federal law).

Students slept on four-poster beds with the obligatory rebel battle flag stretched above them as a canopy. How did these people view the war? What did they think they knew about its origins and outcome, and what kind of attitudes did they have toward Martin Luther King Jr. and other civil rights leaders? The class visited the church where King began his ministry, walked near the Edmund Pettus Bridge in Selma, Alabama, where police bloodied John Lewis and other voting rights marchers not quite a decade before the Oklahoma students came to town. They noted that the namesake for the structure that spanned the Alabama River had been a former Confederate general and a grand wizard of the Ku Klux Klan.

This ragtag army of young people, now molded into a community of learners on a mission, explored questions about the rise of the civil rights movement and its interplay with politics and power, nationally and locally. Did the movement arise from strictly grassroots origins or did it spring forth and become prominent only because a significant portion of a power elite had soured on the old ways of segregation and discrimination partly because they now wished to do business with a largely "non-White" world that stretched across Asia, Africa, and the Americas?

The class might have found fertile ground for learning if it had raised those questions back in an Oklahoma classroom, but somehow to explore them on the run meant that these questions became an experience that sparked deep thoughts and reflections. It was the kind of educational environment that tore down the traditional cleavage between the "real world" and school, a giant, all-enveloping "model failure" that students sometimes experience in travel abroad programs, archeological digs, or other science class fieldwork.

CITYterm, Using the Local Landscape

David Dunbar had taught in independent high schools in New Mexico and elsewhere for two decades. In 1996 this seasoned New England educator took a special kind of teaching position in Dobbs Ferry, New York, an old Hudson River town a few miles north of Manhattan and the Bronx. After twenty years in the classroom, he had become consumed with one big educational question. How does a class become an "experience" rather than just another requirement that people must complete on their march toward graduation? How do you turn any students—good or bad—into deep learners?

"I wanted to know," Dunbar remembered one Tuesday morning in the scorching August heat of 2019, "what is the cognition and psycho-emotional disposition behind adolescent transformation? Why does some schooling become an 'experience' for students that changes them forever, both emotionally and rationally," while much of formal education leaves people flat and sometimes disenchanted? As Dunbar continued to think about those questions, he became increasingly interested in empathy and how it matures in some people and leaves others untouched.

Reading some of Barry Lopez's acclaimed works, including *Of Wolves and Men* and *Arctic Dreams*, Dunbar began to contemplate: "What is it that causes a biological reaction to the text?" Was there some special balm found in getting out in the world? Did travel, as Lopez would later write and Dunbar quoted, "turn the mind toward a consideration of context" and release "it from the dictatorship of absolute truths about humanity"? Did it help "one understand that all people do not want to be on the same road."

Dunbar, a man with a boyish expression and grin that has hidden his age as he grows older, studied at Amherst College in the early 1970s and later did graduate work at Yale in religious studies and philosophy. In the inner closets of his life, he'd collected a slew of honors, both for academic achievements and for sports glories, primarily in soccer and lacrosse, and while at Yale he'd served as assistant varsity men's soccer coach. He'd lived both a highly active physical life and a rich intellectual adventure, and those athletic experiences probably influenced his educational thinking as much as did any research findings and scholarly work.

"When students reach that level of having an 'experience,'" he theorized, "their bodies react." He wanted to know "what it is that causes a biological reaction to the text?" Dunbar subscribed to theories of "embodied cognition," the philosophical and psychological notion that thought doesn't happen independent of the whole body. When people construct high-level concepts, reason through a problem, or make a judgment, their entire bodies—their motor and perception systems, their moves through and physical interactions with an environment— all shape those mental endeavors.[1]

As Dunbar ignited this conversation between himself and the books and articles he read, he began to think about building a special learning experience that could promote and utilize that interaction between mind and body. Leaders at the Masters School in Dobbs Ferry, a residential campus for secondary students, would give him that opportunity. It had empty dormitory rooms to fill every year, and that necessity along with Dunbar's journey through human psychology and philosophy became the mother of a powerful educational invention. Over the next two decades Dunbar, his colleagues, and students fashioned a Super Course that expanded the natural critical learning environment.

Rather than trying to recruit more full-time permanent students to the suburban campus at the Masters School, he created a venue where high school seniors and juniors from around the world could spend a semester using New York City as their classroom. This "CITYterm" experience would transform scores of students into engaged and deep learners. "So many young people come here expecting that they can simply act like the good students they have always been," Dunbar explained, "but leave realizing they need to become good learners instead."

Good Students versus Good Learners

Erica Chapman came to CITYterm from Chattanooga, Tennessee, more than twenty years ago. She was a high school student from the Chattanooga School for the Arts and Sciences in Tennessee. The magnet school where she attended prided itself on its diversity and a deep and long-standing commitment to Mortimer Adler's vision of a liberal arts education rooted in a Socratic dialogue.[2] Before applying for Dunbar's program, she had been to New York only once.

After college and graduate school, she returned to Dobbs Ferry to become a faculty member in the innovative educational experience and eventually its director. "It was apparent from the very first moment at CITYterm [as a student] that learning emerged and happened in a very different way than anything I'd encountered before," she recalled recently. That difference helped her and others separate CITYterm and all it offered from the paradigms they had built about school and learning. "We were not going to be in a traditional classroom every day. Getting out into New York City felt alive and risky in a positive way. We were going to test ourselves in the 'real world.'" For this young woman who'd grown up in the shadow of Lookout Mountain, "the walls of the classroom were metaphorically opening up, and so was my mind." She and her classmates would face ambiguity and learn to live with it in mindful adventures.

So what was the CITYterm experience? Let us say immediately that it didn't mean simply taking people to New York City, or some other large metropolis, nor did it even depend entirely on the rich resources of the Big Apple. We came to believe many of its most golden features could emerge from almost any spot and time that involves getting out of the classroom. Nor does the success of such a program depend on the wealth of a well-endowed private school or the resources of a prosperous student population. We can't dismiss it as something you can do only if you have plenty of money and your students come from well-heeled families.

Masters was a private school, and many of the people in the program did pay tons of money to attend CITYterm, but the institution offered need-based scholarships that produced economically and ethnically diverse classes. They admitted only sixty students each year, thirty per term, however, and its size raises questions about what might be extracted from it to inform much larger programs and classes.

The Initial Experience and the Building of Trust

CITYterm would lead Erica and generations of students who came after her into a flood of learning and transformation that seems almost impossible to achieve in such a short sixteen weeks. When we looked at all that the students did and how they changed, we could begin to understand the former student who told us "Time felt different. In sixteen weeks we did more high-level work than most students accomplish in a year." When we asked Erica how the faculty motivated people to do so much and dig so deeply, she saw several key factors, but she focused first on one that often doesn't get much attention.

"By the time we reached the highly demanding activities in the middle and later part of the term," she explained, "students trusted us to offer them a meaningful and life-changing experience. So they went along with us in almost blind faith." That trust formed the foundation for everything that came in its wake.

If you had a favorite friend or relative when you were growing up, you can quickly understand what she meant. When Uncle Charlie or Aunt Noha came to your house on a quiet Sunday afternoon and offered to take you on a mystery trip around town, you jumped at the chance. You knew such trips would be fun and interesting and maybe life changing. Nalini Ambady, the late Harvard and Stanford psychologist, found evidence that might explain that reaction.

Humans actually have a considerable ability to make quick and accurate judgments, Ambady and her colleagues discovered in a series of experiments, and those capacities form the underpinning for the miraculous trust that sometimes emerges. As we discussed in *Best Teachers* in 2004, within ten to twelve seconds, students can often predict with great accuracy which professors will stimulate their learning and which will not.[3] That's not to say that you have only one shot to engage a class, but it does suggest that the first activity can be enormously captivating—or not.

So how did CITYterm make that strong first impression? With a scavenger hunt that was part research exercise with a big scoop of fun and games. On the first weekend, the class broke into smaller groups of six to eight people and fanned out across New York looking for a series of prompts. Each of these smaller clusters had its own unique list of clues. A teacher came along with each group, to "keep them safe," but would intervene as little as possible, leaving most of the decisions to students.

"It was really up to us to decipher a clue, to work together, to find someone on the street who might know the answer or point us toward some good resource," Chapman remembered. One prompt, for example, asked students to find the oldest wooden escalator in the city. They had to develop a method of inquiry. "What are some buildings we know that are old? Which ones would need an escalator? Where could we turn for help?" They also had to learn how to approach strangers and engage them in conversations, one of "little" goals of the course that formed a rich pallet of "learning objectives."

The Hunt, as it was called, helped these young people become good researchers, but it offered much more. From that experience, students began to change their ideas about learning. "What I realized intuitively," Erica reported, "was that this was the kind of learning the program would prize." School was no longer about "just listening in class and parroting back what the teacher wanted me to say." School, properly conceived, was about helping people to develop good reasoning abilities and other skills. The Hunt altered also her view of the instructors. They were there to encourage students, not to restrict, or even judge. They didn't provide answers, or even to tell young people they were on the right track. They let class members make mistakes and learn from them.

Former students called the day "partly social," and "bonding" and even "hilarious" and "fascinating." They used words like "connectedness," "different," and "new." The scavenger hunt "opened up questions" about history and change over time. What was it like before escalators, and elevators, and even tall buildings. In this and subsequent activities, the program began to reveal the layers of New York City, to open new questions about the metropolis, and to make "you curious, wanting to learn more."

In the afternoon on that first weekend, all the groups gathered in Central Park for a picnic. Students would report on what they had discovered, listening to and questioning one another. People began to ask each other, "how did you figure that out?" And in those exchanges they grew their repertoires of research skills and investigations.

Getting Out More

That magic weekend fed into a series of exercises that continued to stretch students' abilities. The activities became "more academic in nature and more connected to learning history, literature, or environmental science, but from that first weekend, I knew this was something different," Erica remembered many years after her initial experience. When it came time to do serious and extended research, to read a new book, to write, to make presentations, or to engage in any of the other activities of the class, the students trusted that their teachers had arranged for them deeply meaningful and productive appointments.

Over the next sixteen weeks, the young people in the program engaged in a variety of adventures in the city. Two examples illustrate well the kind of activities that drove the CITYterm experience and how the acts of getting out of the classroom changed everything.

The Building Project asked each person to select a prominent structure in Manhattan and study it. They would explore its history and nature, looking at how it was used and how it interacted with the community around it and how that changed over time. But this was far more than just an architectural, sociological, or historical probe. Dunbar had designed this endeavor as a pathway to deeper reading of any text. That's right. Deeper reading.

"Everything changed for the CITYterm kids," the soccer coach and scholar would observe, "when they realized that to read a book deeply is to author it." Dunbar was fond of referencing American author and film director Paul Auster, who Dunbar remembered had said something like "the book doesn't only belong to the writer, it belongs to the reader as well, and then together you make it what it is." If students read the way Dunbar hoped, they would no longer just decode symbols on a page as their teachers had taught them to do, but engage in a conversation and exploration, reaching that point in the text where the author is struggling, a point beyond where they not only didn't know but also didn't fully understand that they didn't comprehend. In that kind of reading, the students could embrace failure and spring free of the perfectionism that pervades many elite secondary classrooms. They could wallow in ambiguity and love it.

The young people in the program first engaged in that kind of reading while learning to "read a building." In a relatively short time, they crawled through the structure and its neighborhood, explored historical documents, took pictures and notes, read facades and hallways, contemplated their own fascination with the edifice and its interiors, and explored its setting. That mammoth enterprise led to a carefully documented paper, but it also produced a twenty-minute walking tour in which each student shared the story he or she had discovered (and often spoke of "my building"). No facts to memorize, no right and wrong answers, but a combination of carefully documented research and individual reactions to all that any one person had gathered. The approach they experienced in the building project became their new way of reading a book.

Near the end of term, the students did it all again, only this time on a larger scale and in small groups. On the twelfth Sunday night in the semester, the teachers organized the entire class into groups of fifteen students each and sent them out to study an assigned neighborhood. They had one week to explore and dissect their community. On Friday, they would present their findings and story to an audience at Barnard College that usually included people from the neighborhood, students' parents, and other "kids who had studied another area of the city." They could do whatever they wanted to tell their story. No guidelines. No stipulations. Just complete freedom to focus where they wished, using whatever means of communication they thought most appropriate. It was a massive undertaking within a short time, and "a huge experience" for the students.

Forming Strong Bonds

Chapman and her colleagues harnessed a great sense of "collective responsibility" that had emerged in the class. By that point in the semester, the students had formed strong bonds with one another and with their teachers. They trusted the leaders to provide golden opportunities, and they believed this community of learners could muster the energy, insight, and creative juices to get this done. But "everyone is needed at the table to make it work." Every voice is important and has a responsibility to the larger project.

"The publicness at the end is highly motivating," Chapman concluded. Everyone wants to "present something that is good to our friends, family, and peers." Most important, curiosity undergirded every aspect of this enterprise. The program tended to pick neighborhoods that students didn't know, and over the course of a week, they would build an intellectual and even emotional relationship with that community. "Large numbers of former students would go back to live in their neighborhood after college," Dunbar pointed out.

The Secret Sauce

At the heart of the CITYterm experience was the "getting out" into the city, but as we will see, it was much more, and those other elements can help educators turn almost any location into a similar environment. Let's look at three of the most essential ingredients.

Everybody Has Value

"At every point and in multiple ways, we say to the students, you are a mind of value," Chapman told us. That begins to happen on the scavenger hunt, because "we are constantly saying you have to decide, you have to make the decision. You are in charge of your own education." And that same approach saturates every activity in the semester, from the many interactions with the city to all the books that students read. It was almost as if Paul Baker were whispering into the collective ear of the CITYterm staff.

"You are unique. You have a particular set of strengths and weakness," Chapman and her colleagues emphasized again and again. "Your mind is valuable."

To maintain that message, they eliminated any social hierarchies that might suggest that some people were more worthy than others and that those on the bottom side of any comparisons didn't quite have sufficient value. "We maintained a 'flat social culture,'" Erica and David explained. "Everybody was on a first-name basis." Equally important, the program invited rather than commanded, arranged, and protected rather than required, and it emphasized at every turn, students control and shape their own education.

"One of our constant tag lines," Erica shared with us, "was our paraphrase of something Aldous Huxley said: Experience is not what happens to you, it's what you do with what happens to you."

Redefining Feedback

Equally important, the program defined traditional grading in a whole new way. We'll explore the full thrust of that new approach in our final chapter on evaluation and grading. For now, let's examine one key element that helped define the CITYterm experience, an aspect that is often associated almost inexorably with evaluation but more rightly belongs within the domain of helping people to improve rather than with thoughts about how to judge them.

"So much of the traditional practice on feedback," Dunbar argues, concentrates on correcting. "As teachers, we often say, 'I've got a set of papers to correct.'" That focus has helped spark anxiety and fear or has often led some students to give up, drop out, and become disengaged. "Feedback in high schools," Dunbar observed, "centers around grading, so things have to be 'corrected.'" But if you are "trying to work on transformation," you should "help them change, to help them understand that they are the authors of their own learning." That means they must learn to self-assess.

In thinking about how to do that most effectively, Dunbar turned to other professions. "Teachers are not necessarily the best people to ask about some of the things they do." On feedback, he explored the thinking of "doctors in mortality and morbidity sessions." What's your feedback loop? "I talked to choreographer Liz Lerman about how she gave feedback to her dancers."[4] As long as feedback was all about scoring then "there was no hope of learning anything about how to do it better," the soccer coach concluded.[5]

In this process Dunbar decided that Lerman's feedback "gave primacy to the person who originated the thing." Therefore, it's not corrected. It's not graded. "Ultimately, if you are looking at a paper with a student," David concluded, "you want to get to the point where the paper feels like a thing that is alive. The student wrote it, and the teacher read it, but they are both creating it, in the sense that Paul Auster described." With that kind of respect for the student, you can "have people feeling like they were creating something. But you can destroy all of that with conventional high school feedback mechanisms."

A New Way to Read

Ellen Langer's work on mindfulness made a deep impression on how Dunbar began to understand reading, and he shared those emerging ideas with his students, bringing them into a conversation about their learning, and once more making them feel like CITYterm was fundamentally different from any other schooling they had encountered.

"Mindfulness is the process of actively noticing new things," Dunbar quoted Langer as saying, "When you do that, it puts you in the present. . . . It's the essence of engagement." In a key handout to the students, the CITYterm founder pulled the Harvard psychologist into the conversation.

"We all seek stability," he quoted Langer as saying. "We want to hold things still, thinking that if we do, we can control them. But since everything is always changing, that doesn't work. Actually, it causes you to lose control." Yet if you understand reading as a mindful person, "uncertainty creates freedom to discover meaning. If there are meaningful choices, there is uncertainty," Langer wrote and the students in Dobbs Ferry read in their course materials. "If there is no choice, there is no uncertainty and no opportunity for control. The theory of mindfulness insists that uncertainty and the experience of personal control are inseparable."

Dunbar combined those ideas about mindfulness with his notion about the interaction between mind and body to produce a fresh approach to reading, and how it could become an experience, something that transforms. No longer did students read just to get facts they could remember, but to find out where they have a physical reaction to the text, where "we have a tightness in our stomach or our throat feels constricted or there is a lightness in our chest." For Dunbar, "that is our body telling us something about an interaction we are having." CITYterm students "practiced noticing those 'felt senses'" when they read. And they noticed the ambiguities that emerged, the uncertainty, the choices, and the problems they faced in believing whatever they might accept as true. They carried those approaches from the building project and neighborhood study into everything they devoured.

That kind of learning changes minds and lives. In a "Letter to a Young Poet" (something the CITYterm students read and felt), Rainer Maria Rilke, the early twentieth-century Bohemian Austrian poet and novelist, captured well the aim of that kind of education: "Be patient toward all that is unsolved in your heart and try to love the questions themselves," Rilke advised, "like locked rooms and like books that are now written in a very foreign tongue." The poet had urged, "Do not now seek the answers, which cannot be given you because you would not be able to live them. And the point is, to live everything. Live the questions now. Perhaps you will then gradually, without noticing it, live along some distant day into the answer."[6]

Chapman and Dunbar wanted students to value not knowing and the "anxiety of uncertainty." That quest for ambiguity became a central part of the whole CITYterm experience. Combined with the physical excursions into city and the systematic use of the landscape to expand everything from research skills to reading, the total environment in which students operated transformed them.

We can now begin to think about the natural critical learning environment as a rich and multifaceted situation that would have made little sense at the beginning of this journey. But to grasp the full scope of the educational revolution underway, we have one more stop to make, and we go there in the final chapter.

CHAPTER SEVENTEEN

Grades

We were having lunch one day at NYU when a colleague joined our conversation. She had attended one of our workshops and immediately grasped the beauty and power of a natural critical learning environment. Yet as she neared the end of her first semester using the new pedagogy, she had doubts. The students had not responded the way she expected. It was an uncommon result but certainly not unprecedented. What had caused her and a few others to stumble where so many had flourished?

At first, she blamed the problem on her students. As we talked about the class, however, the young scientist began to realize that her old-fashioned approach to grading, not her students or the new way of teaching, had undermined her otherwise brilliant and stimulating course. "I just used the same grading policies I had experienced in school," she confessed, "and didn't question them because to do so seemed like I was breaking the laws of nature and lowering standards." She laughed at herself and finally asked, "where and why did we introduce grading into education?"

The answer to that question could unlock some of the secrets to more powerful teaching and learning. If we take a historical perspective, we can begin to see our own thinking against other possibilities and understand that what we educators do—almost without thought—hasn't always existed. To make changes will not violate natural law or undercut quality.

Our modern grading system emerged with the coming of the industrial revolution. Society wanted to know how much learning was taking place. That became especially important in fields like medicine, engineering, and architecture. Would someone be able to build a bridge or house that didn't collapse? Does your physician know enough to make a decent prediction about your health? Yet, surprisingly, the first attempts to put a score or letter on someone's thinking came in the humanities and social sciences. A few classes in English at Cambridge in the 1790s apparently were among the first to do so. The old Chinese imperial examination system had a kind of pass-or-fail scoring structure (get the *jinshi* degree, or not), but the great medieval universities in Europe didn't.[1]

In essence, with the coming of an industrial economy, society began to impose a new set of responsibilities on educators. The old list said, simply, educate the young. The new job description added, while you're at it, please certify how much learning you think has taken place. So we invented grades as a kind of shorthand to fulfill that new charge.

It was a radical step to put a number on someone's thinking, so unusual that the practice didn't spread rapidly at first. Previously, people might debate and discuss the merits of a thought or action, testing it against the dictates of some ancient text and later against the demands of logic and evidence. But giving it a score? How odd. Through most of the nineteenth century, many schools in the United States and Europe simply gave someone "credit" if that person successfully completed a course or line of study, or they didn't. Universities that cropped up in China, South America, Africa, and elsewhere apparently followed the same pattern. This pass/fail approach seems to have satisfied most people until near the end of the nineteenth century.

As society became more industrial and scientific, pressures presumably grew to make the system precise. Humans were measuring everything from time to space with greater detail and accuracy. Why not do the same for intellectual activity? Or so the thinking went.

Schools began using a system of either letters or numbers. In the United States, they employed A to F (yes, there was even an E originally, which didn't fade until well into the twentieth century, now preserved at only a few institutions).[2] But such precise details about this history can obscure the heart of what was taking place. The emergence of grades meant that humans thought they could tell you the exact quality of someone's thinking abilities with the scientific accuracy they might measure time or space and the objects within it.

Mind you, this was the same period—the late nineteenth century—when the followers of eugenics thought they could tell you something important about human beings by measuring the size of noses, heads, and other body parts and classifying people into different "races." We're not saying that grades are racist, but we recognize that the ideas for "scientific" racism and our grading system came out of the same social, political, economic, and intellectual milieu.

As Carol Dweck reminds us in her classic *Mindset*, the nineteenth and early twentieth century saw everyone and their intellectual dog debating the origins of something we call "intelligence." Was it the product of some inner and immutable quality or the child of experiences? Did nature or nurture determine how *smart* someone would be and what abilities he or she could muster? Alfred Binet, a French psychologist, thought conditioning played a large role, perhaps bigger than the size of your brain. But in one of the great stories of unintended consequences, this champion of the nurture side of the debate helped spark the twentieth century notion of "good students" and "bad" ones, the ideas of a fixed intelligence that determined "how well" you would do in school.

Three years into the twentieth century, the French Ministry of Education wanted to find a way to help students who might not score so well with the standard instruction in the public schools. To do so, they reasoned, they needed to intervene early, and to do that, they had to predict with some accuracy who might face trouble down the road. The ministry contacted the forty-seven-year-old Binet, already an accomplished psychologist working at the Sorbonne, and asked him to devise a method to make those projections. Binet then produced the first widely used "intelligence test." Even though it came from a man who believed that humans could grow their capacity to remember, reason, invent, and do other tasks we now associate with what we call intelligence, many people who used it began to assume the test measured something fixed, like the size of a person's eyeballs.

With IQ tests and a system of letter or number grades, educators could more easily put people into broad categories. They decided some students were "good" and others were "weak." In the early twentieth century, some people used "race" to determine who belonged in which categories. At least one notable mathematician concluded that African Americans couldn't possibly understand his discipline and reportedly tried to bar them from his classroom even after his university ended required segregation. But wait, you might plead, grades, tests, and other apparatus of assessment don't imply that anything is frozen for life while an IQ test often does. We assume you can improve your marks from one assignment to another, from one term to the next, while intelligence remains remarkably stable (although not as constant as we long assumed, James R. Flynn and others discovered).[3]

While that's a nice assumption, the research on how teachers react to students suggest another reality. Instructors often tend to put their pupils into broad categories of ability, subconsciously deciding that some people have what it takes to shine in class, and others don't. Those impressions affect how teachers assess the people in the class.

Substantial evidence of this phenomena comes from systematic research. A group of Australian investigators, for example, randomly assigned faculty members and teaching assistants to watch one student giving either a "poor" oral presentation or a "good" one. Both groups then assessed unrelated written work from that same student.

You might think that the oral performance would have no substantial influence on the grade for the essay, but you would be wrong. The people who saw the polished speech generally gave high marks to the written work while those who suffered through a bad talk awarded much lower grades to the essay. Keep in mind, both groups were marking the same paper from the same student.[4]

This so-called halo effect is but one of the major problems with rewarding grades. Several factors suggest that academic marks have less legitimate meaning than we've traditionally thought. Some observers have fought for several decades about whether males or females face the biggest discriminations in school when it comes to the grade book. Yet it seems increasingly clear that both sides in the debate are right and both are wrong.

Gender often matters, sometimes to the benefit of women and in other ways and times to reward men. The general pattern has changed over time. At the beginning of the twentieth century, women usually faced a tough time, and relatively few entered higher education, let alone completed work toward degrees or achieved distinction. A hundred years later the broad scale had flipped. In the United States by 2016, less than 45 percent of university students were men.[5] Yet in some fields—like physics—males continue to outnumber females.[6]

Social and economic class influences academic standing, and so does our definition of race. The latter may have no biological meaning, an illusion invented in the sixteenth century, but the victims of racial discrimination and their families are real people who get bounced around. So do the children of the poor, regardless of how thoughts about "race" classify them. As we noted in chapter 2 (and examined more thoroughly in chapter 4 of *What the Best College Teachers Do*), if someone is a member of a group in their society about which there is a pervasive negative stereotype about their intellectual or physical abilities, those popular prejudices can and often do adversely affect their performances, even if they personally reject that popular view of "their kind." As we noted earlier, such "stereotype threats" attack victims of racism and poor people who feel the sting of notions that poverty somehow stems from laziness or stupidity.

Making Evaluations More Precise . . . and Less Meaningful

Some people have tried to address the capricious nature of grading with tests that seem factual. "There is a right answer to the questions I ask," shouts the precision-seeking professor, "and my students either get it right or they don't." Yet a system that puts people in a room to see how many correct answers they can muster in a fixed time doesn't always identity who can think critically, creatively, or even accurately. We say that the assessment system isn't "authentic" because it doesn't really ask people to do what their schooling is supposed to prepare them to do.

As Howard Barrows pointed out, the goal for a medical student is to learn to do an accurate and useful differential diagnosis; it isn't to impress patients with how many facts they can recite or new terms they can sprinkle into the conversation. In history, we want people to think historically with all that entails, not just spout names, dates, terms of treaties, and so forth, or find correct answers on a multiple-choice test. Yes, they must display accuracy, not some fairy-tale version of the past, but merely measuring their temporary ability to recall some fact doesn't tell us if they can analyze, synthesize, evaluate, distinguish, theorize, and make connections.

Even a field like mathematics has its problems on this score. People can learn to reach correct answers, using the "proper" formula or procedure yet never understand basic concepts. Students then can't solve different-sounding problems even though they involve the same principles. Even the old-fashioned timed examination in any field often introduces elements that are not authentic.

We're Not Always That Accurate

To put it simply, as a profession we've never been consistently good at identifying the best student work, or predicting who will live highly productive and creative lives. Grades are supposed to tell us something useful about future performances in school and afterward. We use them to decide who gets to the next level of study. We often assume that grades will tell us something important about the life trajectory of our students. Yet in most cases marks are little better than random predictors, especially when looking at the differences between the supposedly "best students" and those in the middle.

Grades in one class or level can tell us who will make similar scores in another course, but they indicate little about how those people will perform outside of school. What kind of conversations can they enter? With whom? What ideas and information can they bring to the table? How can they measure their own thinking? How creative can they become?

While it may be, as some charge, that not everyone is cut out to go to college, become a lawyer, physician, scientist, leader, or whatever, it could also be that we are selecting the wrong people to advance in a variety of areas. Maybe, as the French Education Ministry and Alfred Binet suspected, our methods of helping students learn and our means of picking out the best of the bunch may skew the whole system toward people who display only mediocre imagination, creativity, critical thought, or whatever it is that we supposedly value, rather than toward those who shine. Think of the implications that the Clemente Courses we discussed back in chapter 5 have for how we traditionally select who gets to go to college.

Grades may tell us how quickly and accurately people can recall information they've encountered, but it's not clear how well they can recognize implications or applications, or how effectively they can engage in far transfer. We often have little evidence about creative thought or diligence, or whether the people in our classrooms are likely to engage in a lifetime of deep learning and adaptive expertise. What does school tell us about who can pass the marshmallow test in the middle of an isolation response to a major pandemic?[7] Schools often test for one ability while expecting their graduates to perform in completely different ways.

Anyone who has sparkled under the current system (and that includes many of the people who might read this book) will probably find great difficulty entertaining such thoughts. But consider them we must if we want to improve our efforts to help anyone learn and to identify those who do. We must also examine other major failures of our system of grading.

As marks in school and class rankings emerged, they became more than how we weighed students' achievements. They also turned into our favorite way to stimulate learning. Teachers used grades to punish, reward, and prod, and students responded like Pavlov's dog. As this extrinsic stimulus rose in importance, intrinsic fascination declined. Many people became strategic learners with all the threats to deep learning that we've noticed earlier. The almighty grade emerged as the supreme deity of the classroom while old-fashioned and natural curiosity reeled from the blow.

The Problem of Grade Inflation and Good Teaching

For decades, lots of folks—from educators deep in the trenches to editorial writers and some politicians—have fussed over what they have called "grade inflation."[8] During those same years, a band of progressive-minded people have pushed and pleaded for better learning environments. This entire book belongs in that second category. Yet few people have noticed or widely discussed the possible conflicts between the battle against the evils of "easy grades" and the struggles to use research on human learning and motivation to improve and spread deep learning.

Part of the problem stems from the two ways we might define grade inflation. For some people, the term means simply that more students are getting A's. But is that because teachers are applying lower standards, or is it a result of deeper and more extensive learning that comes from improved environments? If schools produce better classes designed to foster deeper learning, shouldn't they expect that more enrollees will learn more deeply? How else would you identify good teaching except in terms of the sustained, substantial, and positive influence it has on the way students think, act, and feel? If classes reach more people, stimulating them to think critically and creatively and understand deeply—without doing them any major harm—wouldn't they expect more individuals to get the highest marks? Otherwise, the whole exercise is a sham.

You could, of course, redefine the meaning of each grade, raising standards, and ensuring that we're still picking only the best of the best for the highest scores. With that approach, schools would then recalibrate their scale and double-down on their role as judges who help employers or someone else decide who gets the rewards in some kind of meritocracy—jobs, positions, honors, opportunities for additional education, and so forth. If we've learned anything from the research on human motivation, however, it is that such a system of extrinsic rewards threatens to undermine the quest for deeper learning—and does so with little promise of accuracy.

Universities would become little better than the dog that chases its tail. Credentials would outrank actual human development. We might then expect some wealthy parents to risk imprisonment and public humiliation to ensure their children get into the schools they think will give them the most golden credentials regardless of the quality of the learning involved.

Derrick Bell struggled with this problem until the day he died. The brilliant constitutional scholar and lawyer, civil rights leader and thinker, writer and educator created a phenomenal learning experience for his students.[9] He didn't lecture. Instead his class became a supreme court where students argued both real and hypothetical cases in which ordinary people became embroiled in important constitutional issues. That approach resulted in highly impressive academic and legal performances and deep understanding by a sizeable chunk of his students. Yet the dean's office strongly objected to the high number of A's that came out of those classes even though those school leaders never examined the quality of Bell's students' thinking.

Highly ranked schools of law like that at NYU, where Bell taught his last twenty years,[10] were reluctant to jeopardize the Faustian bargain they had struck with top legal firms. Without ever saying so, they had agreed to help those businesses screen applicants for jobs. If a growing number of law students received the highest marks, how could the firm easily distinguish between competing candidates for contract specialist or some other lucrative position? They couldn't, and therein lay the rub.

At the same time, Professor Bell didn't want to grade on a curve, putting scores on someone's thinking that did not really recognize significant achievements, and thereby creating fierce grade competition. Pitting students against each other in competition for a limited number of A's undercut the hope of building a collaborative learning environment.

Ultimately, he resolved the dilemma with a personal letter to each student, explaining his assessment of their strengths and weaknesses and sometimes telling them that the school quota system prevented him from awarding the supreme grade. The last time we saw him before his death at the age of eighty-one, he still anguished over this worry.

Grades Are Still with Us

Despite their limitations and undesirable side effects, however, marks are unlikely to disappear any time soon. Society still wants to know how much learning occurs—and rightfully so. In recent years, the push to find out has grown, not diminished, especially as some critics have begun to question the value of a college education. In the United States, schools compete with other demands for precious public or private dollars, and skeptical leaders demand "accountability." That means educators have to find more ways to prove they are making a sustained, substantial, and positive difference in the way their students think, act, and feel.

In the last half of the twentieth century schools even tried to make their marking system more precise, as if letters with a plus or minus behind them could tell you more about the nature of learning than could the naked A, B, or C of yore. Students could now fret over a whole new level of petty concerns, imposed on them by the system, while their professors sometimes dismissed such students by labeling them with a newly coined phrase: grade grubber.

A few institutions tried to move in the opposite direction. They eliminated letters and numbers and asked professors to write detailed analyses of strengths and weaknesses for each of their pupils. In such places, the transcript grew into a stack of detailed comments. But that system was difficult to maintain. Medical, law, graduate, and other advanced institutions wanted something simple, a quick way to separate winners and losers.

We watched years ago as a department's graduate admissions committee considered applicants they might admit. Their last slot came down to two candidates. One came from a traditional institution and sported a transcript with a precise grade point average; the other, from a liberal arts college that offered reams of detailed comments, rehearsing past academic performances and summations of strengths and weaknesses. In short, the committee had considerable information about the latter but only a few numbers on an unknown scale for the former.

Most of the committee, however, sided with the colleague who kept asking, "How do you translate all of those words into a GPA." No amount of effort from a lone dissenting voice could convince them that the real challenge was the exact opposite. What do the grade averages tell you about anyone's abilities to do advanced studies and thinking? By the end of the century, most schools had abandoned any attempts to provide more meaning to the letter or number grade.

Grades and Evaluations in Super Courses

How then do our Super Courses address these issues? No one approach prevails, and some of our samples make only slim attempts to adjust anything. We'll admit at the outset that nobody has found a perfect remedy for all the grading problems. Yet some of our innovators have toyed with steps around the edges of this complex matter, and still others have actually dug into the heart of this issue, finding sometimes creative ways to address its basket of complex puzzles. In the process, they have challenged traditional thinking on assessment. Let's explore some of the major practices and thoughts that constitute this revolution.

1. Perhaps most fundamental, the Super Courses have created ways for students to try, fail, receive feedback, and try again. While some interested parties may fret that so many extra chances dilute standards, making it easier for students to learn, our subjects recognize that they are merely seeking to duplicate the environment that every scientist, scholar, artist, artisan, and deep learner expects for him- or herself—the pleasure of failing, taking risks, and developing a better mind and body.

As for the bit about being too easy, "that's nonsense," one instructor told us. "Every level of learning has its challenges and people learn to persevere in their struggles if they can grapple over and over again, get help when they need it, and find success." When professors create arbitrary difficulties just for the sake of doing so, they reinforce the notion that they can punish and reward with a whim, leaving students with little sense of control over their own education.

But who has time to give people multiple "Do Overs," as one colleague dubbed them? Anyone does, if the class helps students learn to critique their work by giving one another feedback. And that's what many of the Super Courses do. That means everyone learns how to think about their own thinking, to recognize places where growth and better understanding can emerge. Implicit in this approach is the idea that deep learning occurs only when students have thought a great deal about the nature of their intellectual and personal growth and have begun to formulate profound ideas about its meaning. If students leave a class without any experience or ability to assess themselves, they emerge minus a key ingredient for lifetime learning. What are they to do for the rest of their lives? Constantly return to their mentor to ask repeatedly, "How am I doing, how am I doing," never able to take control of their own learning?

Part of the feedback does originate with the teacher, who offers what we sometimes call "formative assessment" rather than "summative judgment."[11] In the end, the system may force these educators to put numbers or letters on someone's thinking, but that comes reluctantly and only after students have had lots of chances to try, come up short, hear ideas about how to improve, and go at it again.

Indeed, as we interviewed people for this book, we noticed a marked rise in teachers who recognized that such practices don't represent some lowering of standards, but rather an extension to students of the same kind of learning environment that faculty members have always valued for themselves. "If I have an idea for my research and take it down the hall to a colleague," one person told us, "I'd be terribly insulted if they just looked me in the face and said, 'you're making a C thus far.' But that's exactly what we do to students all of the time."

We suspect that years ago, Richard Light helped spark a more enlightened view of formative feedback. Derek Bok, then president of Harvard, had asked the Kennedy School professor to find the key qualities of the courses that students regarded as most meaningful. After interviewing scores of current and former undergraduates at the Ivy League university, Light concluded that these "highly respected courses" included "high demands" coupled "with plentiful opportunities to revise and improve their work before it receives a grade, thereby learning from their mistakes in the process."[12]

"In an ideal world, I would never get to a 'final grade,'" one person explained, reflecting a sentiment we heard often. "That closes the book on learning, and I want my students to grow even after the class is over. Feedback and discussion helps people learn; giving them some mark doesn't." As David Dunbar put it to us, "It isn't about 'correcting papers,' but opening a conversation where everyone can grow."

2. In one of the most important and ingenious aspects of the Super Courses, many teachers have decided that effort counts from the beginning while results matter only after repeated chances to grow. These educators generally encourage students to experiment, to risk failure and benefit from it. Their assessment scheme rewards people who do. Yet they give no room to those who would see how little they can do and still survive.

Every student is expected to participate fully throughout the semester, but they have lots of opportunities to fail, receive feedback, and try again without lowering their grade. Failure does not sink their boat, but lack of effort and engagement does. Rewards abound for those who take feedback and improve their thinking and performance. In that way, the class can establish even higher intellectual and professional expectations than usual, not lower ones. Only in the end do performances translate into something that goes on a transcript.

3. In multiple ways the courses say to students that no one is attempting to control them. The learners remain in charge of their own education while the instructors invite and tease, appealing to curiosity, fascination, promise, a sense of concern for others, and a desire to display competence and creativity.

That can be a hard sell. As long as grades remain, teachers still have enormous power. They can make or break someone enrolled in the class. So how do the Super Courses help learning feel like it did for the DIY Girls, keeping the five-year-old alive and flourishing?

We came to believe that it began with the way the person in charge thought about grades. If you talk to many traditional professors, they will tell you that scoring is necessary to push learning, yet the Super Course architects don't believe that anymore. Indeed, they think the marks probably hurt deep learning, cultivating extrinsic motivation at the expense of the intrinsic. They stress formative feedback and tell their students that the summative judgments come reluctantly. Those different conceptions shine through to the pupils and influence their attitudes, helping them to feel that all-important sense of autonomy. When we asked learners what aspects of their Super Course motivated them most, they usually included some version of the following: I'm in charge; my teacher is trying to help me but isn't attempting to control my life.

Students also often spoke about the novel and enticing objectives they pursue. "This was different. It invited me into an adventure and goals that excited me." All our Super Course designers had thought deeply about what people should be able to do or become by the end of the term, often redefining standards, stretching them upward and outward. That has meant far less emphasis on simply remembering stuff and more stress on the decisions people can make, or the conversations they can join, the data they can bring to those exchanges—even if they have to look it up—and the adaptive expertise they can display.

The Super Course typically wants to know what concepts students understand and what kinds of problems they can solve. Can learners think about implications? Can they transfer ideas and insights from one area to another, even when these ideas seem to have little connection? What can people create? Do they comprehend what facts are important and know where anyone can find the precise details when needed? The objective in Super Courses is sometimes about how anyone has developed as a human being, how he or she has matured as a thinker, creative person, professional, learner, and ethical individual, not just about how many facts anyone can make stick in his or her brain. Super Courses have learning goals that even defy any attempt to put a number on that objective.

The upshot of all this is that Super Courses are unlikely to use the standard timed big examination in which students either write essays or pick out factually correct answers from a short list of choices. Even when these classes use something that at first glance seems traditional, it often isn't. Eric Mazur's ConcepTest may appear to be just an ordinary multiple-choice quiz, but it measures how his students understand and can apply threshold concepts and how they can learn from mistakes, and it is a way to help them learn, not judge them. The final grade doesn't come from those exercises but from the ability to take chances, grow, and achieve. Jeanette Norden administered a comprehensive final examination, but it didn't shroud itself in some deep mystery while students tried to guess what might be asked. Everyone received all the questions long before test day.

In short, the trick seems to begin with learning goals the people in the class will embrace as valuable. Students don't see the marks as a way to control their behavior but as a means to help them grow. That's most likely to happen when people in a class are pursuing an objective they regard as beautiful, important, and intriguing, not because it would boost their GPA, but because it enables them to live creative, competent, compassionate, challenged, and critically thinking lives. If those objectives also help students flourish socially, economically, and professionally, so much the better. With all that, they maintain a strong sense of autonomy.

Many of the evaluations in Super Courses are highly authentic, that is, they measure how well anyone can do what they are ultimately expected to do. The evaluation doesn't just add up how many facts students can recall in an hour but how well those people can work with others to do a differential diagnosis, unravel some historical mystery, solve a social problem, apply a scientific understanding, contribute to a conversation, design and build something new, analyze, synthesize, theorize, and evaluate. When we teachers embed all that in a system of try, fail, receive feedback, and try again, we can keep the five-year-old alive, nourishing curiosity, imagination, and excitement. If students believe their mentors want to help each person succeed rather than just fill a quota of who gets to shine, that seals the bargain.

Epilogue

How do we evaluate Super Courses?

Sometimes, we simply want to know whether students like the experience. But that's not the only question. When our super professors assess, they are usually asking if people learned. Do they understand physics or history? Are they likely to remember what they have come to comprehend? Can they use it in multiple situations, realizing its implications and applications, often across a broad range of possibilities?

Did the course engage students educationally? Did more pupils take a greater interest in the material and keep up with the readings? Did learners' new understanding stick with them? Did it help them become better problem solvers, or more empathetic people, or adaptive experts, critical thinkers, inventive writers, or whatever the learning goals happen to be? Do the graduates of a Super Course engage in far transfer more often than do the alums of conventional classes? Does the experience foster more lifetime learners, people who will contemplate the questions long after the class is over and will seek out new evidence and ideas?

We all recognize these as important issues. But the inquiry about liking isn't irrelevant. Student attitudes can influence their learning. If people intensely dislike a class, that experience can sour their feelings toward the whole discipline. "I've hated chemistry since taking a boring lecture course my freshman year at state college." Those visceral reactions can, and often do, influence motivation and learning in the long term.

Both perspectives (liking and learning) often do have one thing in common. Answers can vary from student to student. Thus, educators will ask about both the range and the distribution of responses. In our case, they might want to know whether Super Courses get the same distributions that traditional offerings do. "When I try something new," one professor might note, "I'll get some students who like it, and others who don't." When Professor Song Ailing served food to her class, it might have tickled the pallets of some but soured those of others.

We think we can safely say, as one instructor told us, "you will never reach every single student educationally unless it is an extremely small class, and even then that's rare."[1] When you do something in a class, a plethora of conditions can influence the outcome, including all the things that are happening in the lives of some students—the sleep they didn't get because of the job they lost (or must try to keep), a death or illness in the family, the breakup with a romantic partner, an illness, a wave of depression. So we play the odds, and those distributions become important, but it is the distribution of both attitudes and learning outcomes that should capture our attention.

But what evidence do we have about the Super Courses? Throughout this narrative we have noted multiple systematic studies of specific courses. They have told us repeatedly that in a natural critical learning environment most students learn more deeply by every measure we might value, and that a wide variety of people benefit, regardless of ethnicity, gender, or previous knowledge. But there is one qualification we should note.

Robert Kamei at the medical school in Singapore captured it well, but his observations apply more broadly: students will more frequently like and learn if they understand the logic and evidence behind the new experience. When the medical school spent time in orientation sessions briefing students "on the learning sciences and why the process of [team-based learning] is consistent with optimal learning," they responded well.[2] If such orientations were dropped, however, more students complained about the "amount of extra work" they had to do.

Kamei's observations are consistent with two major studies. The first we noted in *What the Best College Teachers Do* but is important here too. Two Scottish researchers, Hilary Tate and Noel Entwistle, found that ratings of professors depend in major part on whether the teacher expects to and does help those in the class to learn deeply, and in part on whether the students have deep intentions.[3] Pupils who think their goal is only to memorize lots of information and get high grades (strategic learners) will glorify professors who help them do so and reject those who emphasize critical thinking. Classmates who value higher-order abilities and adaptive expertise will do the opposite even if they are sitting in the same class: cookies for the people who sponsor deep learning and jeers for those who don't.

The second is a study that Louis Deslauriers, Kelly Miller, and their colleagues did at Harvard in 2019. In short, they found that people often cannot recognize accurately what kinds of experiences will help them learn deeply. Some will see the wisdom of the Super Course approach, believe that they learn more with them, and demonstrate that they do in independent measures. Yet an annoyingly large number—sometimes even a majority—will say they most "enjoy" highly passive lecture classes that feed them the key information. They will even report that they "learned more." But independent measures of how much they understand and of their ability to apply strongly challenge those easy assumptions: The Super Course approaches fostered deeper learning for more people. Even in comparison with the best of lecturers, active pedagogies produce the best result.

Does that mean that professors must commit to displeasing students in order to serve their educational needs? Absolutely not. First, the people in the Harvard study did not say they hated the active learning classes; they just gave them lower (but still positive) marks than they gave the good lectures. Second, and most important, much as Robert Kamei found in Singapore, professors can help their classes appreciate the high quality of the Super Courses.

Here's what the Harvard research group did. Somewhere near the outset of a physics course, they reported, the professor spent twenty minutes explaining active learning, sharing evidence that it worked better, and showing the class the data that students often could not accurately predict what would best help them learn deeply.[4] Did that help?

When the researchers surveyed students at the end of the class, nearly seven out of ten said that their faith in active learning had grown during the semester. Three-quarters said that "the intervention at the beginning of the semester helped them feel more" favorable. Deslauriers and his colleagues recommend that instructors intervene early. Explain that anyone may need to struggle more with Super Courses and that it may feel like they are learning less at first, but the results will pay off in the end. Show them the evidence: no pain, less gain. To clinch the deal, give students an assessment of some sort as early on in the course as possible so they can see what they are actually learning. (We might say that early intervention can help transform strategic learners into deep ones. But make it a formative, not a summative judgment.)

To create a Super Course we must help students to understand and appreciate new definitions of learning and the evidence about how these new kinds of courses are best designed to serve their needs. Andy Kaufman did that. So did Robert Kamei, Derrick Bell, Wendy Newstetter, Eric Mazur, Joe Le Doux, Erica Chapman, David Dunbar, Paul Baker, Kate Walker, Jeanette Norden, Song Ailing, Fan Yihong, Li Hao, Charlie Cannon, Mark Carnes, Kelly Miller, Melissa Harris-Perry, Evelyn Gomez, Jonathan Stolk, Robert Martello, and all the other super professors in our study.

Final Thoughts

We know some people will dismiss much of what they read here because they think it would never work for their students. "Not at my school" becomes an anthem for defeat. That's too bad. Everyone deserves better. We have considerable evidence that the ideas of the natural critical learning environment will stimulate students broadly, although each Super Course needs to ask the right questions to make it work for any specific person. An inquiry or challenge that appeals to one group may fall flat with another. The great teachers will adjust accordingly, probing and experimenting until they get it right.

The revolution we've tried to capture in its infancy has enormous potential to spark even more growth if we are willing to explore. Each of us brings valuable personal perspectives to the struggle for deeper and more meaningful learning. Yet we must recognize that great ideas are most likely to emerge from a swirl of perspectives and a broad willingness to explore, to test and examine, but not from dark corners where people wallow in their isolation from each other.

Education and life offer us the chance to participate in at least four great conversations. You really can't engage fully in any one of them, however, without partaking on some level in all of them.

The first conversation is the dialogue with the natural world. "Nature speaks in many tongues," Nobel laureate Dudley Herschbach once told us. "Chemistry is but one of them." So is physics, biology, math, and each of the other sciences.

The second is the discourse with ourselves and with other human beings about our common humanity. Who are we? How can we give life meaning? How can we examine our values? What's the right thing to do?

Third, we can plunge into a rich discussion with all the things we've created. That includes the gadgets, organizations, institutions, traditions, cultures, ideas, sounds, music, works of arts, and regulations.

The final is a kind of metaconversation about change and stability in all these matters. How do things transform over time? How do they evolve? How did we get where we are? How will the world shift in our own lifetime and in the years of our collective offspring?

Why do we engage in those exchanges? Because we want to. Because we get depressed if we don't. Because the world is better off when we do. Because we have this insatiable longing to know and to live creative lives. The Super Courses we have reviewed and the natural critical learning environments they have captured recognize those opportunities and obligations, inviting us to the table.

In recent years, we've placed a great emphasis on the discussion within and about STEM courses, but that has come at the expense of all those other possibilities and even to the disadvantage of our love affair with science, engineering, and medicine. When we join the conversation in the humanities, we have an opportunity to jump into the discussion about ourselves and other humans, to explore things that can't be proven, to enter the realm of ambiguity and uncertainty, to examine what we value and the kind of life we want to live, and to experience beauty and the challenges of any work of art. Our greatest hope comes in breaking down the barriers between the disciplines we've created, and recognizing how all knowledge and ideas are related. That's what the Super Courses do most magnificently.

In the hands of Andy Kaufman, Fan Yihong, Li Hao, and others, we can revive the humanities and with them pump new vitality into the sciences, the social sciences, professional studies, and the arts.

Each of us can build our own Super Courses. If we don't, no one else can muster exactly what we might have done, and the world will have lost an important asset. Yet we should all be willing to pull from the rich mustard of ideas and practices that others have produced and from the research on human learning and motivation.

For decades, we have educated people to memorize all the important facts. At best, they could solve conventional problems by remembering some set routines. Our top graduates could perform other people's creations. At worst, we bored students who dreaded memorizing details they quickly forgot. For the latter, schools became a burden. Some dropped out. Others stuck with it and graduated but benefitted little from their experiences in the classroom.

In today's world, we need deep learners and adaptive experts. No longer can we make do with the "good students" of the past who learned all the material and could spit it back on an examination. Our world is changing rapidly, and it needs creative and curious individuals who can solve new kinds of problems that no one has faced before; who can respond effectively to pandemics, economic collapse, and environmental disaster; who can grasp the promise—or threats—of new inventions and ideas. We need adaptive experts, not just routine ones. We can no longer afford an educational system that leaves so many students disenchanted and unproductive. Humans cannot even afford a system that simply produces strategic or surface learners who may shine in school with their emphasis on making good grades, but who have not learned to build creative, productive, and moral lives, filled with beauty and intrigue.

We now understand the importance of adaptive growth for the individual. People can live richer and more fulfilling lives if they develop the dynamic powers of their own minds.

APPENDIX

RUTR 3340
Books Behind Bars: Life, Literature, and Leadership

"To be able to affect others, an artist must be an explorer, and his work of art has to be a quest. If he has discovered everything, knows everything, and is just preaching or entertaining, he makes no effect. Only if he keeps searching, then the viewer, or listener, or reader fuses with him in his search."

—FROM LEO TOLSTOY'S DIARY, DECEMBER 1900

"He who opens a school door, closes a prison."

—ANONYMOUS

Who am I? Why am I here? How should I live? In this course you will grapple in a profound and personal way with timeless human questions by reading and discussing classical works of Russian literature with youth at a maximum-security juvenile correctional center. By learning to facilitate meaningful, authentic conversations with peers, you will gain a deeper understanding of the purpose and relevance of literature studies and an appreciation of the power of literature to create community, inspire personal insight, and affect social change. The course can also help you develop essential professional and personal leadership skills.

At a time of social divisiveness, the course provides you with the opportunity to build community by leveraging the power of conversation, collaboration, and creativity inspired by great works of literature. We will focus on Russian works that have proven successful at deepening personal insight, breaking down social stereotypes, and encouraging authentic dialogue about life's "accursed questions" among people from diverse backgrounds. Authors read will include Leo Tolstoy, Fyodor Dostoevsky, Anton Chekhov, Karolina Pavlova, Nadezhda Mandelshtam, Alexander Solzhenitsyn, and others. The course is open to all students regardless of major, and we welcome applications from students of all years. You will receive 4 credits.

What Will You Learn?

"Books Behind Bars" has several learning objectives. Some focus on tangible knowledge and skills while others are more abstract and of long-lasting benefit. Some of these objectives relate directly to the subject matter—Russian literature—while others are more broadly related to your professional and personal success in life.

<u>Foundational Knowledge</u>: What knowledge can you obtain in this course?

In this course you should learn to:

- Recognize key authors, works, themes, and characters from nineteenth- and twentieth-century Russian literature
- Understand some of the social, economic, and cultural forces that shape an author's world view
- Learn enough about classical Russian writers to decide which ones you might like to pursue further

<u>Application</u>: What skills can you acquire in this course?
This course will help you to:

- Analyze a literary text as both a reader and discussion leader
- Gain practical professional leadership skills in diplomacy, planning, creative problem-solving, and relationship-building with diverse audiences

<u>Integration</u>: How will this course help you see connections?

This course will help you to:

- Discover connections between your study of literature and issues in your own life and the world around you

Human Dimension/Caring: Why should you care about this course? In this course you will learn to:

- Be more self-reflective and gain a deeper understanding of yourself
- Develop increased empathy for the experiences of others

Learning How to Learn: How can this course help you be a better learner?

This course should help you to:

- Take more responsibility for your own education now and in the future
- Read literature in a way that is more personally useful and relevant
- Realize your creative potential as you explore teaching and learning from various points of view

What Will You Do When?

To prepare you for this experience, during the first three and a half weeks of the course you will spend time gaining knowledge of the literature and of the skills necessary to lead discussions with correctional center residents.

First, you will be discussing the literature itself. You will focus on the themes, specific passages, and other aspects of each work, much in the way that you would expect in a traditional literature class. Some of these discussions will be facilitated by the instructors, while others will be facilitated by students in small groups. This second element will give you practice with leading discussions. You'll learn how to formulate stimulating questions and activities as well as gain other skills, such as learning how and when to ask follow-up questions, how to follow the thread of a discussion, and how to handle other issues that might come up. The goal of these first few weeks is not to have you "master" the art of facilitation, but to give you enough tools and exposure to facilitation that you will feel more comfortable and competent when you begin meeting with the residents.

The third and final element of your preparation involves gaining some understanding of the people you will be working with and the world you'll be going into. To that end, you will attend an orientation at Bon Air Juvenile Correctional Center, during which you will learn more about the residents and learn about specific issues that might come up during your meetings, such as how to set boundaries and deal with unforeseen circumstances. You also will be asked to submit your fingerprints for a required volunteer background check. If you have any concerns about this, please let us know right away.

Once these preparations are complete you will begin a series of ten weekly literature discussion meetings with the residents, travelling to Bon Air on Tuesday afternoons. The meetings last approximately one hour and a half, and it takes about an hour and ten minutes to travel there each way. No student is expected to lead a discussion by him- or herself. You will be paired with a facilitation partner for the duration of the course and the two of you will meet with the same group of residents each week. The class will continue to meet on Thursdays at UVa to debrief and explore additional course material.

In addition to periodic writing assignments in Collab and regular group discussions, you will keep a reflective journal. This is the place for you to explore your thoughts and feelings about the readings and other experiences during this class. You will be asked to reflect frequently and explicitly on your interactions with the correctional center residents, as well as on what you are learning. You will be given the opportunity to write about your assumptions, expectations, and apprehensions. You will explore how your discussions affect your ideas not only about the literature, but about juvenile offenders, yourself, and what it means to read and study literature in a community context.

At the end of the semester, you will produce a Learning Portfolio and a Reflective Essay. The portfolio represents your intellectual and personal evolution in this course. The reflective essay describes what this experience has meant to you and how your portfolio reflects your unique journey through the world of Russian literature, juvenile justice, and self-discovery. In other words, you and your learning experience are the subject of this essay.

During the semester we will have guest speakers who will talk to us about various aspects of this learning experience. Professor Dorothe Bach of the German Department and Associate Director of the Center for Teaching Excellence at UVa will give an experiential workshop on listening. Later in the semester Deron Phipps, Director of Policy and Planning at the Virginia Department of Juvenile Justice, will speak to us about salient issues in the juvenile justice world, and how the Books Behind Bars course fits into those efforts.

How Will You Be Supported along the Way?

Because this will be a small class, and Ms. Patterson will work closely with me as both a teaching assistant and program coordinator, you will have the opportunity to work with and receive frequent feedback from experienced and caring teachers. We will provide you with constructive ongoing feedback on both your written work and your facilitation, and are always ready to meet with you and/or you and your partner should you want to discuss anything. You will also have ample opportunity for self-reflection and self-assessment throughout the semester, and the journey itself, not the end "product," will be the focus of our attention. Although this course is not part of the residents' regular class schedule, they will have the opportunity to meet weekly on Mondays with Julia Fisher, English Ph.D. student at UVa, who will lead them in an informal prep session in advance of your Tuesday meetings.

Readings

In this class you're going to have the opportunity to read slowly, carefully, and deeply. We'll be reading only around ten to twelve short works (a portion of a short novel, short stories, and poems). These carefully chosen readings are among the acknowledged classics of Russian literature. Experience has shown that the residents find them largely interesting, accessible, and provocative.

From the bizarre to the beautiful, the gritty to the godly, these works and the characters that inhabit them, should inspire, challenge, and enlighten both UVa students and Bon Air residents. The works have at least three features in common:

(1) They are entertaining, powerfully written, provocative and have stood the test of time. They are classics.
(2) They are short and thus you and the residents will be able to delve into them deeply.
(3) They radiate with a moral-spiritual intensity and emotional boldness, encouraging readers to ponder timeless human questions, or "The Accursed Questions," as Russians often refer to them:

- What makes for a successful life?
- What is happiness?
- Is spiritual wealth more valuable than material wealth?
- Is selfless love possible?
- What does it mean to be a hero?
- How can I be true to myself?
- Who *am* I?
- How much should I care what society thinks about me?
- What is my responsibility to others?
- Does evil exist in the world? Inside me?
- Given that I am going to die, how should I live?

Primary Works of Fiction

All of these readings are available in Collab under Resources/Literature: Primary Works:

STORIES

Anton Chekhov, "Ward No. 6" (1892)

Fyodor Dostoevsky, "An Honest Thief" (1848)

Karolina Pavlova, A selection from *A Double Life* (1848)

Nadezhda Mandelshtam, "Last Letter" from *Hope Abandoned* (1974)

Varlam Shalamov, "My First Tooth" and "Handwriting" from *Kolyma Tales* (1970–76)

Leo Tolstoy, "How Much Land Does a Man Need?" (1885)

Leo Tolstoy, "The Death of Ivan Ilyich" (1886)

Ivan Turgenev, "Living Relic" from *Notes from a Hunter's Album* (1852)

POEMS

Anna Akhmatova, "Three Things in This World He Loved," (1911) "We're no good at saying good-bye" (1917)

Alexander Pushkin, "To a Poet" (1830), "I loved you . . ." (1829)

Marina Tsvetaeva, "On Parting"

Mikhail Lermontov, "Native Land/Motherland" (1841), "Bored and Sad" (1840)

Fyodor Tiutchev, "Silentium!" (1830), "You cannot understand Russia with your mind . . ."

Karolina Pavlova, "Strange, the Way We Met" (1854)

Secondary Literature

You will also be assigned to read short selections from *A History of Russian Literature* (D. S. Mirsky) and *Handbook of Russian Literature* (Victor Terras, ed.), as well as some background material from other sources. These readings will be available in Collab under Resources.

Other Readings

In addition to the primary literature and secondary literature, there also will be some short readings about teaching, education, and juvenile justice. All of these readings will be available in Collab under Resources.

Reflective Journal

In this class you'll have the opportunity to keep a journal, which should be separate from your class notes. This will be the primary venue for regular writing exercises. At various times during the semester, you will be asked to hand in your entries.

Given that writing longhand is more tactile, and perhaps stimulates different senses than composing on a computer, I suggest you purchase a notebook and write entries by hand. You may also keep your journal electronically, if you prefer.

The journal is your opportunity to respond to suggested discussion questions, to reflect, to analyze, to integrate, to explore, and to test the boundaries of your thoughts and feelings related to the contents of the class. For some of the entries, you will be asked to respond to specific, prompted questions, or do short creative writing exercises (e.g., a personal letter to an author, an alternate ending to a story). And for some of the entries you'll have the flexibility to write about whatever you wish.

You'll have one entry per week (except for the first week and week of spring break), around 250–300 words per entry. Some weeks you might write a little less, others a little more depending on your level of inspiration and time availability. But try for somewhere in that range, which usually comes out to at least a page or more of prose per week. By the end of the semester you should have 14 entries total.

Finally, please remember to *date* each entry. This will help you when you prepare your Learning Portfolio and Personal Reflection Essay at the end of the semester. Also, although it's not required, I encourage you to come up with a *title or theme* for each entry you've written. Past students find this to be an enjoyable creative exercise, as well as a useful tool for grasping the bigger picture, the patterns, and the overarching thrust of your thoughts.

Collab Responses

We will sometimes ask you to prepare short written assignments that you will post in Collab, no later than 9 am on the day of Tuesday's class or 9 am on the day of Thursday's class. Note that these Collab responses are separate from your weekly journal entries.

Mid-Semester Essay (3–5 Pages)

The description will be forthcoming.

Final Essay: Learning Portfolio and Personal Reflection (5–7 Pages)

For the final paper you will start by creating a portfolio of your (written) work to represent your own intellectual, creative, and emotional evolution in this course. Then you will write a reflective essay explaining what this collection as a whole means to you and how this portfolio reflects your own journey through the world of Russian literature and juvenile justice. You will receive more detailed instructions at the time of the assignment.

Summary of Course Requirements

ACADEMIC COMPONENT

- Class attendance and active participation
- Weekly Journal (14 entries total for the semester)
- Collab Responses
- Mid-Semester Essay (3–5 pages)
- Learning Portfolio and Personal Reflection Essay (5–7 pages)

- Regular attendance of meetings at Bon Air, and preparation ahead of time
- Responsibility to the class (completing travel and materials sign-ups, fulfilling roles as a speaker at final event)

Assessment

In this class our focus is going to be on learning rather than on grading. I have designed the class in such a way that grades are not the primary motivation for your work. Additionally, each one of you has been chosen for this class on the basis of a university-wide application process. We already know that you have a strong desire to be here, that you want to learn and work hard, and that you will succeed.

You will take responsibility for your own learning and will be actively involved in the assessment of your own work. Self-assessment is a core principle of the Books Behind Bars class.

How will you know that you're learning?

You'll know because you can observe growth yourself—in your facilitation skills, in your evolving insights into Russian literature, into yourself, the world of juvenile justice, into life itself.

Did you notice something about the literature, about yourself, about life, that you hadn't noticed before? Have any of the expectations or paradigms you previously held been disrupted? Did you have an experience in class, while reading, while writing in your journals, while meeting with the residents that stimulated, excited, or provoked you? And did you process that experience in your journal and/or in class discussion in such a way that you gained some insight from it? If so, then learning has taken place.

You will know that you're learning, because you did a better job facilitating a discussion at Bon Air than you did in previous weeks, and you can articulate the reasons why. And if you weren't as successful, then what did you learn from that failure that you will use next time? Whether the result was positive or negative, what did the experience teach you, and how will you apply those lessons to the next discussion? Reflecting thoughtfully about such questions is the essence of experiential learning in this class.

You'll know you've learned, because your final essay contains ideas and insights that you didn't have or couldn't have articulated fifteen weeks earlier. And perhaps, as many students of the course have reported, you will know because you have been permanently changed in ways you did not foresee.

Grading Principles

For better or worse, I am required to assign grades at the end of the semester, so you might find it helpful to know some of the general principles guiding the final grading decision:

- **Growth and Improvement** over the course of the semester are more important than your performance on any single assignment. I am most interested in where you are at the end of the semester in comparison to where you were at the beginning. This helps to ensure that you continue to take intellectual and creative risks, without the fear that a "failure" on any given assignments will negatively impact your grade. It also ensures that you focus less on what you think is best for your grade than on what you believe is best for achieving your own learning goals, helping your Bon Air residents, and enhancing your group experience. We are here to support you and help you discover and leverage your strengths, while at the same time identifying opportunities for growth.
- **Effort** counts more heavily in this class than in many other classes. In an experiential learning class many things are beyond your control. One thing *within* your control, however, is the effort you put into your work and the diligence with which you address challenges and opportunities. Granted, not every challenge you face will be fully resolved to your satisfaction, nor every assignment you complete a home run. I don't expect

perfect solutions to facilitation challenges; nor do I expect each Collab response or journal entry to be a polished piece of writing. (The mid-semester essay and final reflection, however, should be more polished.) What I do hope to see, however, is a pattern of effort and diligence over the course of the whole semester.

- **Reflection on successes and failures**. More important than whether you "succeed" or "fail" during the facilitation of a discussion is whether you reflect honestly and deeply on those successes and failures, and then incorporate those reflections into your future meetings. You will have multiple opportunities for such reflection: in your team self-evaluations, journals, discussion with the instructors after class, and during in-class debriefings.
- **Unique learning outcomes for each student**. Although there are a number of course objectives, as described above, not all of them will be equally applicable to every student. Each of you brings a unique set of skills, passions, and perspectives to this class, which will be reflected in your unique learning outcomes and demonstrated in the things you choose to write about, the risks you take, and the areas in which you grow the most. There is no one type of "successful" BBB student.
- **The totality of your work** in this class will be taken into consideration, and, as mentioned above, I will always look for opportunities to reward growth and improvement as well as emphasize your strengths rather than weaknesses.

Excerpts from the Books Behind Bars Syllabus of Andrew David Kaufman, University of Virginia. We invite readers to examine and weigh concepts involved in the approaches reflected here for their own work. But we remind readers to adhere to all copyright laws. Copyright 2018 Andrew David Kaufman.

- learning by doing rather than by listening
- exchanging ideas with others
- seeing how science applies to the real world, and enjoying
- working in teams to solve problems and build things

As the instructors for this course, we are ready to help you gain a better understanding of how science applies to the real world and develop skills that will be useful in your career. Our goals are to promote self-directed study of basic physics, explore physics in the context of real-world applications, improve collaborative and communication skills in team-driven activities, and develop research skills by working on projects.

What this course promises you

Most likely, the majority of the courses you have taken so far involved you listening to lectures and taking exams. As you are progressing in your studies here at Harvard, you might have a number of important questions. How does what you learn relate to the real world and to your future career? What are the skills that will make you successful in your career? How can the work you do now help you continue to grow after you graduate?

In this course, we will help you obtain answers to these questions. You will have an opportunity to explore physics by engaging in physics through projects. In the process, you will obtain insight into the thought processes that underlie most of science and engineering. You will also hone skills that will be beneficial to you, regardless of your career path. How do you design something? Take data and analyze them? Convince others of your thought processes? How do you learn on your own, for your own benefit? How do you work with others and convince them that what you are doing, or thinking, is relevant and important?

How will these promises be fulfilled?

There are no lectures and no examinations in AP50. Instead, to realize these promises, you must take responsibility for your own learning and actively participate in the learning process—what you get out of this course depends very much on what you put in! In general, the best way to learn something is by engaging in the material and by interacting with others. For this reason, the core of the course is a set of three, month-long projects on which you will work in teams. During the course of the semester, you will apply electrostatics to build a generator, design and build an electromagnetic safe, and design and build an imaging spectrometer. At the same time, the best way to develop important skills, such as collaborative skills, is by engaging in these skills. In other words, you will be learning by doing and I promise you that it will be both rewarding and fun!

Course Goals

After successful completion of this course, you will be able to . . . (within the context of introductory physics)

1. Engage in **self-directed learning** by:
   - identifying and addressing your own educational needs in a changing world, including awareness of personal attributes, fluency in use of information sources, planning, and problem solving
   - using independent study and research to tackle problems, especially ill-defined or open-ended ones
   - using a variety of techniques to get a handle on problems: represent the problem visually or graphically, perform order of magnitude estimates, use dimensional analysis and proportional reasoning, recognize symmetries, evaluate limits, and/or relate the problem to cases with known solutions
   - explaining and justify any assumptions made
   - "thinking critically," both positively and negatively, about any situation or the solutions to any problem
   - evaluating the correctness of a solution

2. Demonstrate **content mastery** by:
- meeting the content learning goals specified in the project briefs
- applying your knowledge of physics to solve problems
- taking data, analyzing, and interpreting them

3. Engage in productive **team work** by:
- contributing effectively in a variety of roles on diverse teams
- conveying information and ideas effectively, using written, oral, and visual and graphical communication

4. Exhibit **professionalism** in your conduct by
- acting in a manner that is respectful to your teammates and the teaching staff
- being punctual and participating fully in all classroom activities
- taking decisions and executing actions that are fair and honest, and that are consistent with accepted standards of conduct

The activities in AP50 are designed to contribute to the development of the following general competencies:

- **Qualitative Analysis**: The ability to analyze and solve problems in science and engineering and other disciplines qualitatively, including estimation, analysis with uncertainty, and qualitative prediction and visual thinking.
- **Quantitative Analysis**: The ability to analyze and to solve problems in science and engineering and other disciplines quantitatively, including use of appropriate tools, quantitative modeling, numerical problem solving, and experimentation.
- **Diagnosis**: The ability to identify and resolve problems within complex systems through problem identification, formation and testing of a hypothesis, and recommending solutions.
- **Design**: The ability to develop creative, effective designs that solve real problems though concept creation, problem formulation, application of other competencies, balancing tradeoffs, and craftsmanship and which integrate knowledge, beliefs and modes of inquiry from multiple and diverse fields of study.
- **Teamwork**: The ability to contribute effectively in a variety of roles on teams, including diverse teams, while respecting

everyone's contributions. You will develop collaborative skills that may include questioning, listening, and identifying multiple approaches and points of view.

- **Communication**: The ability to convey information and ideas effectively, using written, oral, and visual and graphical communication.
- **Lifelong Learning**: The ability to identify and address your own educational needs in a changing world, including awareness of personal attributes, fluency in use of information sources, planning, and self-directed learning. The ability to "think critically," both positively and negatively, about any situation or the solutions to any problem.
- **Ethics**: The ability to take decisions and execute actions that are fair and honest, and that are consistent with accepted standards of conduct.

Getting Help

Because we are not lecturing you, we can make our time available to help you and provide personal assistance, both in and out of the class. Never hesitate to contact us—our contact information includes our numbers and you are free to call us anytime; you will never disturb us. We all hold office hours (see Teaching Staff list), but we are happy to schedule a meeting at any time that is convenient to you and to us. In addition to our office hours, your team will be assigned a Team Mentor for each project cycle. The Team Mentor will be your go-to person for help with any aspect of the course. You will check in with your Team Mentor twice weekly in class, and s/he will be offering you and your teammates feedback throughout all aspects of the course.

Teamwork

Teamwork creates synergy. Because the combined effect of an effective team is significantly greater than the sum of individual efforts, teams can tackle problems that are too big to solve for any individual. In the professional world, effective teamwork is paramount. For this reason, AP50 uses a team-based approach that will help you develop collaborative skills, that will help you work effectively in a team, and that will maximize your learning. As in the professional world, three important features affect your productivity and success in a team: your own effort, the effort of people you depend on, and the way you work together.

Throughout the term, you will work closely with three or four of your classmates, as part of a project team. The teams will change for each of the projects, so as to provide an opportunity for you to become better acquainted with your peers and also to develop the interpersonal skills you need in the professional workforce where you are likely to encounter a diverse ensemble of people.

The activities in AP50 are designed so that no one individual can successfully complete them alone. It is therefore very likely that on the parts you work on alone, your performance will be significantly worse than in a course that does not involve teamwork. Don't let that discourage you, as individual activities are always followed by a phase where you get to work as a team on that same activity, permitting you to improve your performance with others (and learn in the process).

To be successful in AP50, therefore, you need to first try your best on each of the activities on your own and then tackle those activities and the projects as a team. While it is expected that you will divide and conquer when working as a group, each individual is responsible for the whole product.

Research on teamwork suggests the following good team practices:

- **Come to class prepared**. Before working as a team, read any relevant material(s) and formulate your own approach to the task at hand.
- **Actively participate** and contribute to all activities when the team is together (both in and out of class). When even one team member checks out and starts working individually (or starts checking email, text messages, etc.) instead of engaging with the team, the overall performance of the team is adversely affected.

- In all team activities, be prepared to **share** three things with your teammates: (a) what approach you chose as an individual, (b) why you chose that approach, and (c) how confident you are about your approach.
- Be **respectful** and listen and evaluate other people's points of view.
- **Deliberate as long as time permits**. Regardless of the make-up of the team, teams that deliberate longer do better in team activities.

FAILURE—THE UNAVOIDABLE PRICE OF SUCCESS

Throughout your education, you have probably been led to view mistakes and failure as something that is unfavorable and that negatively affects you—something to be ashamed of. However, success is not possible without taking calculated risks, which inevitably means failing sometimes. The road to creativity and innovation, in particular, is littered with failure. "If you haven't failed, you're not trying hard enough," goes a well-known saying. Failure is a problem only if it is your end point. On the way to finding a solution, failure can be very productive as it can teach you a lot (what doesn't work, what might work, and what you might want to explore in greater detail) and lead you to success.

In AP50 we want to create a culture that encourages creativity and calculated risk taking. Also, we design all of the activities in AP50 so that they leave ample room for errors for anyone (including the staff) and your intermediate scores may be lower than you are used to in other courses. Only then can we guarantee that everyone's learning will be maximized and that you will learn to feel comfortable with the (productive) failures that go hand-in-hand with creativity. See them as learning opportunities, not negatives, as stepping-stones to success, not the end point. So be bold and take risks, both as an individual and as a team— failure, even repeated failure, is a healthy and necessary part of becoming successful. Also, rest assured that the assessment in AP50 does not penalize you for the failures you may encounter on the way to success!

PEER ASSESSMENT

It is important to provide positive feedback to people who truly worked hard for the good of the team and to also make suggestions to those you perceived not to be working as effectively on team tasks. Three times during the semester you will provide an online assessment of the contributions of the members of your team (including yourself) to all the activities in class and to the project. The feedback you provide should reflect your judgment of each team member's:

preparation—were they prepared when they came to class?
contribution—did they contribute productively to the team discussion and work?
respect for others' ideas—did they encourage others to contribute their ideas?
flexibility—were they flexible when disagreements occurred?

Your teammates' assessment of your contributions and the accuracy of your self- and peer-assessments play an important role in your final grade for the course—see *Assessment*.

Course Activities

I. PRE-CLASS: reading assignments and annotations (*Perusall*)
Purpose: Provide you with a first exposure to the material so we can spend the class time doing activities that help you better understand the concepts
What you need to do: Read the chapters according to the class schedule and enter your questions, comments, and/or responses to others' questions and comments in *Perusall* (see *Technology* above)
Evaluation: Your annotations will be evaluated on quality (thoughtfulness), quantity, timeliness, and distribution. See the *Annotation Rubric* for details

Details: Because there are no lectures in this class, you are responsible for familiarizing yourself with the physics principles involved in the projects by reading the relevant sections of the textbook before coming to class. The course schedule includes required weekly readings—you are free to study ahead, but the schedule ensures that you are prepared for the activities in class and any assignments.

The goal of the pre-class reading is to gain sufficient knowledge to be able to participate in the class activities in a meaningful way. Annotate the text in the *Perusall* system to interact asynchronously with your classmates and to get help when other people are not nearby. From the data we have obtained over the past years we find that people who do the following tend to do better in AP50:

- read for **understanding**, not memorization
- interact with others online by contributing **thoughtful** annotations
- help others by **upvoting** good questions and helpful answers
- don't wait until the deadline, but **start reading early**
- don't read the entire assignment in one sitting but **come back often** for shorter readings.

The goal of the pre-class reading is not master every little detail—the in-class activities are designed to reinforce your understanding of the important principles before you begin to apply them in the projects. And you certainly won't ever need to memorize any information because we will never deprive you of access to the text (or any other source of information, including the Internet). However, by reading with attention and with an inquiring mind, you take ownership of your learning. Additionally, your annotations help us determine how to best tailor the in-class activities to improve your understanding of the material.

II. In-Class Activities

Instead of presenting the textbook content to you, we will use the time in class to expand on your initial reading of the text and address any difficulties you express in the annotations using six types of interrelated activities that build on each other: Learning Catalytics, Tutorials,

Estimation Activities, Experimental Design Activities, Problem Set Reflections, and Readiness Assurance Activities (details below). In addition, time will be allocated for project work. The class schedule shows the scheduled timing of these activities (white = project work).

LEARNING CATALYTICS (LC)

Purpose: Probe and deepen your understanding of the course content

What you need to do: Bring your laptop or other compatible device so you can log on to LC.

Evaluation: Your performance on these questions is recorded and can be reviewed by you. While the correctness of your responses to these questions is never considered in the evaluation scheme, your participation contributes to your professionalism score.

Details: During this activity, which lasts 90 minutes, the instructor will pose questions, which you first answer individually using your device, then discuss with your team members (effectively teaching each other), and then answer again. If an issue remains, you can always review the work done in class later or ask someone from the staff for a clarification. The skills you develop in this activity will improve your performance on the Problem Sets and Readiness Assurance Activities.

TUTORIALS

Purpose: Address common misconceptions in the course content

What you need to do: All materials for this activity will be supplied.

Evaluation: Your work is neither corrected nor scored, however your active participation in this activity is evaluated by both your teammates and the teaching staff and this evaluation will factor into your professionalism score.

Details: During this activity, which lasts 60 minutes, you will work with your team on a worksheet that will explore your thinking about the more difficult concepts in the material. The teaching staff will contribute to the team discussions. Check in with your Team Mentor before ending this activity to make sure that you and your team members have resolved any misunderstandings. The skills you develop in this activity will improve your performance on the Problem Sets and Readiness Assurance Activities.

ESTIMATION ACTIVITY (EA)

Purpose: Develop estimation skills that are essential for problem solving

What you need to do: All materials for this activity will be supplied.

Evaluation: The activity is run like a competition among teams, and while it is not graded, your active participation in this activity is evaluated by both your teammates and the teaching staff and this evaluation will factor into your professionalism score.

Details: Your team will receive a list of two or three unknown quantities to be determined to the nearest order of magnitude (see Chapter 1 of the text). You should estimate (not guess or Google!) the quantities using the estimation procedures discussed in the text. Spend the first five minutes thinking *individually* about a strategy, then go at it with your team. There are only 20 minutes, so think fast! One or two teams will be selected at the end of this 20-minute period to present their estimates to the class. The skills you develop in this activity will improve your performance on the Problem Sets and Readiness Assurance Activities.

EXPERIMENTAL DESIGN ACTIVITY (EDA)

Purpose: Develop experimental and/or analytical skills that are important for the current project

What you need to do: Bring your laptop or other compatible device.

Evaluation: Your work is neither corrected nor scored, however your active participation in this activity is evaluated by both your teammates and the teaching staff and this evaluation will factor into your professionalism score.

Details: The projects require you to take measurements, analyze data, carry out simulations, etc. The Experimental Design Activities help you master the skills that are required for successful completion of the projects.

PROBLEM SETS (PRE-CLASS) AND PROBLEM SET REFLECTION (IN-CLASS)

Purpose: Develop problem-solving skills; self-assessment of your knowledge and skills

What you need to do: Before class: solve all problems, giving them your best effort and following the instructions given on the Problem Set Rubric. In class: work with your team to correct your solutions, resolve conceptual difficulties, and identify areas that need to be reviewed.

Evaluation: Your work is evaluated on the effort you put into the application of problem-solving steps and the accuracy of your self-evaluation. You will receive a Problem-Solving Rubric with the first Problem Set.

Details: Learning to develop problem-solving strategies is an important goal for this course. Good problem-solving practices include:

- articulating your expectations for the solution to a problem before diving into the details
- breaking down longer problems into smaller, more manageable pieces
- checking your solution by justifying the reasonableness of your solution, checking the symmetry of your solution, evaluating limiting or special cases, relating your solution to situations with known solutions, checking units, dimensional analysis, and/or checking the order of magnitude of the answer.

You can hone these skills on five problem sets, each of which involves two phases:

1. You work on the problem set **ALONE**, before coming to class when it is due, giving it your best effort.
2. You work in class with your team members on correcting your work, comparing it to the solutions we hand out to you, and completing a self-evaluation form. You hand in this form together with your marked-up work.

Treat the problem set as an open-book take-home exam, even though **you will not be evaluated on the correctness of your answers**. Instead, your work will be assessed on the individual effort you put in solving the problem set before coming to class and the correct evaluation of your own level of understanding.

You should see the problem sets as an opportunity to learn. For example, you might give the entire problem set your best effort without getting it all correct, but by accurately identifying your difficulties in understanding, you will earn full credit and we can put you on a productive path forward that will maximize your learning. Please note that completing the individual portion of the problem set in class (rather than before coming to class) will be considered academic dishonesty.

READINESS ASSURANCE ACTIVITY (RAA)

Purpose: Assessment of content-specific goals and problem-solving skills

What you need to do: Bring your laptop or other compatible device so you can log on to LC.

Evaluation: Your RAA performance is determined by a combination of your individual score (50%) and your team's score (50%).

Details: To assure that everyone is on track in the learning of the basic concepts we will have five RAAs over the course of the semester. During the first half hour of each RAA you will work alone to solve a set of problems similar to the preceding problem set (individual round).

You are free to consult the text or the Internet, but not other people. During the remaining hour of the RAA you get to discuss the problems with your team members (team round). The goal for your team is to use the combined knowledge of the team to maximize the entire team's RAA score. This team round provides an opportunity to learn in a collaborative environment, consolidate your knowledge, hone your team-building skills to achieve the best possible scores, and receive immediate feedback on your performance.

We design the RAAs in such a way that the average score in the individual round is around 50% and nobody can score 100%. Typically, teams figure out the correct answers to all questions in the team round. The team round thus provides an opportunity for everyone to improve their scores and—most importantly—to learn.

If you fully participate in all in-class activities, and if you are fully conscientious with the relevant problem sets and annotations, then you will be well prepared for the RAAs without having to "study" for them like you do for a traditional exam. If you do wish to practice your knowledge, be sure to review the Checkpoints in the text (solutions are in the back of the textbook), try the Worked Examples in the text, and above all use the Practice Volume. Typically, there are around 60 Checkpoints and 30 Worked Examples for each unit. The RAAs also draw from the Tutorials and involve at least one estimation problem, so you may want to review those as well. The Practice Volume contains many examples.

III. Projects

Purpose: Transfer your learning and understanding of concepts to a real-world context

What you need to do: Work with your team to produce a project presentation and a project report

Evaluation: Your team's project presentation and project reports will be evaluated separately. In addition, your team members will evaluate your relative contribution to the project. A rubric will be distributed with each project.

Details: There will be three month-long projects over the course of the semester. At the beginning of each project, you will receive a project brief that describes the learning goals and guidelines for that project. Be sure to carefully read the entire project brief before embarking on your project. The project brief includes project requirements and evaluation rubrics for the project presentation and the project report. Project materials will be made available in class. In certain cases, you will receive a budget for your project and your task is to stay within that budget. At the end of each monthly project cycle we will have a project fair where teams present their results.

Approximately a week after each project fair your team must submit a project report, using guidelines detailed in the project brief. After the report is evaluated and returned to you, you will have a few days to improve your report and your evaluation of the report.

ETHICAL CONDUCT

We expect everyone to adhere to the highest standards of ethical conduct. For every action/decision you take, subject yourself the "headline test": if your action were printed as the front-page headline in the newspaper and those you care about—your friends, family, your team members, peers, the teaching staff—would read it, how would you feel? If the answer is anything but "good", you are probably not adhering to the highest ethical standards and your Ethics score is likely to be affected. In the extreme, copying work of others, using material found online or in books as your own without proper attribution, interfering with the performance of others or other teams, plagiarizing ideas or work that are copyrighted or in the public domain, communicating in person or electronically during the individual parts of the RAAs, constitute academic dishonesty. Any such dishonesty will be reported in accordance with University policy. Any single such occurrence of academic dishonesty immediately drops your ethics score to 0, which according to the policy outlined in the figure on the previous page **automatically drops your final grade to a C or lower**. Also, bear in mind that for any team assignment plagiarism by one team member affects the score *for the* *entire team*, as every team member is responsible for the entire content of the assignment, even if the tasks for that assignment were divided among team members.

RAA APPEALS

If your team feels strongly about the correctness of an item on an RAA, the team may submit a written appeal. This appeal process must occur immediately following an RAA and only teams, not individuals, may write appeals. Only teams that write successful appeals get credit for that appeal, even if another team missed the same question(s). Appeals are not simply an opportunity to dig for more points. Rather, they are an opportunity for teams to make scholarly arguments for their collective positions. All arguments must be supported by evidence from the text or other source. If the appeal is based on an ambiguously phrased question, the team must suggest wording that is less ambiguous. The decision to grant or refuse an appeal will be made by the instructors after class via e-mail. The following is an example of a successful appeal:

Argument: "We feel that A, rather than B, should be the correct answer to question 8."

Evidence: "According to Figure 12.42 in the text, friction affects the motion of the objects. The speed of cart 2 decreases over time. Because friction cannot be excluded in question 8, we would expect the same decrease in speed to occur for the cart in this question."

Excerpts from Eric Mazur's course syllabus for Applied Physics 50 at Harvard University illustrating the natural critical learning environment.

MA 255
Spring 2017

Dr. T
e-mail: diana.thomas@usma.edu
Office: TH254

The Three Laws of Mastery

1. **Mastery is mindset**. Our beliefs about ourselves and the nature of our abilities determine how we interpret our experiences and can set boundaries on what we accomplish.
2. **Mastery is a pain**. The best predictor of success is a non-physical trait known as perseverance and passion for long-term goals.
3. **Mastery is an asymptote**. You can approach mastery. You can home in on it. You can get really, really close to it. But you can never touch it.

Taken from the book "Drive" by Daniel H. Pink

What this course promises you

The literature on learning and motivation indicates that our ability to excel is dependent on a variety of factors. I promise to foster the incremental theory of intelligence which is founded in the belief that intelligence is something you can increase through opportunities for growth rather than something you demonstrate. In this course we will focus on learning goals that are structured around the incremental theory of intelligence. As stated in the book "Drive"

> *"Getting an A in a French class is a performance goal. Being able to speak French is a learning goal."*

This course promises to

- ***Engage you*** through current applications of multi-variable calculus
- Improve your ability to ***recognize*** when to use mathematics, how to ***analyze*** problems using mathematics, ***identify*** the limitations of a mathematical model, and ***improve*** models beyond their current limitations
- ***Foster mastery*** of mathematical skill.

What you will be doing to reach these goals in combination with standard MA255 course-wide activities (WPR, Project, Tech Lab, Application Days, TEE)

Laboratory Notebooks: Mastery of skill requires repetition. To do a good cross-over you need to practice your cross-over many times before an actual game. To provide support, drill problems will be assigned through WebAssign and will be completed successfully through the computer with work recorded in a composition notebook. If there are issues with the successful completion of any problem, you can turn the notebook in to me for review. After receiving feedback you can retry a modified problem or receive one-on-one assistance as required. *The laboratory notebook will help you build strength in mathematical computations. The laboratory notebook will help you recognize mathematical errors and learn from them.*

In Class Assignments: We will work in groups on material presented in the course during the semester. The comfort of access to the professor and other students is essential to building confidence and understanding of mathematics in general. Mathematics and science are not solo sports. *The in class assignments will help you master concepts and solve problems in teams.*

Exams: Exams will be designed to measure retention of material. All exams will be comprehensive. We will always conduct a pre-examination where you will identify topics that require further work.

How will you and I know how you are doing?

[Some material omitted]

Characteristics of Successful Mathematicians

1. **It's okay to be wrong!** *Not all of our calculations are perfect* every time. Many times we head down the wrong path. Keeping a log of our errors and past computations helps us gain experience with the mathematics involved in the problem. At times, these computations become useful at a later date.

2. **It's okay to ask for help!** *There is no "smartest mathematician".* We all collaborate with other mathematicians and scientists when the need arises. We love mathematics and love talking about mathematics. I think we like asking questions even more than answering them. A good problem is very tasty!

3. **It's okay to be slow!** *You are not judged by how fast you solve a* *problem* but by how beautiful the problem and solution is. IT'S OKAY TO BE SLOW!

4. **It's okay to work hard!** *Successful mathematicians work very* hard.

This is an excerpt from the syllabus in Calculus I taught by Professor Diana Thomas in the Department of Mathematic at the United States Military Academy. It follows the Invitational (or Promising) syllabus model that has three major components: (1) The promise or invitation; (2) an introduction to what the students will be doing to accept the invitation (or realize the promise); and (3) how teacher and student will best come to understand the nature and progress of the student's learning. Used with permission from Professor Diana Thomas.

NOTES

Chapter One. Pinning Our Hopes on Our Machines

1. Sugata Mitra, "The Hole in the Wall Project and the Power of Self-Organized Learning," Edutopia, accessed February 14, 2018, https://www.edutopia.org/blog/self-organized-learning-sugata-mitra.

2. Joshua Davis, "A Radical Way of Unleashing a Generation of Geniuses," *Wired*, October 2013, accessed January 5, 2018, https://www.wired.com/2013/10/free-thinkers/.

3. Davis, "Radical Way of Unleashing a Generation of Geniuses."

4. Our conversations with teachers and other professionals from various fields have taken place over the course of many years of research and teaching, via email and in person.

5. Quan Chen and Zheng Yan, "Does Multitasking with Mobile Phones Affect Learning? A Review," *Computers in Human Behavior* 54 (January 1, 2016): 34–42, https://doi.org/10.1016/j.chb.2015.07.047. See also Douglas K. Duncan, Angel R. Hoekstra, and Bethany R. Wilcox, "Digital Devices, Distraction, and Student Performance: Does In-Class Cell Phone Use Reduce Learning?," *Astronomy Education Review* 11, no. 1 (December 2012), https://doi.org/10.3847/AER2012011; and Yu-Kang Lee et al., "The Dark Side of Smartphone Usage: Psychological Traits, Compulsive Behavior and Technostress," *Computers in Human Behavior* 31 (February 2014): 373–83, https://doi.org/10.1016/j.chb.2013.10.047, and, in contrast, "Some Schools Actually Want Students to Play with Their Smartphones in Class," NPR.org, accessed March 6, 2018, https://www.npr.org/sections/alltechconsidered/2012/10/03/162148883/some-schools-actually-want-students-to-play-with-their-smartphones-in-class.

6. James M. Lang, "The Distracted Classroom: Transparency, Autonomy, and Pedagogy," *Chronicle of Higher Education*, July 30, 2017, https://www.chronicle.com/article/the-distracted-classroom-transparency-autonomy-and-pedagogy/.

7. Adam Gazzaley and Larry D. Rosen, *The Distracted Mind: Ancient Brains in a High-Tech World* (Cambridge, MA: MIT Press, 2016).

8. Patrik Edblad, "Intermittent Reinforcement: How to Get Addicted to Good Habits," December 6, 2019, https://patrikedblad.com/habits/intermittent-reinforcement/.

9. Gazzaley and Rosen, *Distracted Mind*, 166, Kindle ed.

10. See, for example, Jessica S. Mendoza et al., "The Effect of Cellphones on Attention and Learning: The Influences of Time, Distraction, and Nomophobia," *Computers in Human Behavior* 86 (September 1, 2018): 52–60, https://doi.org/10.1016/j.chb.2018.04.027; "Just Having Your Cell Phone in Your Possession Can Impair Your Learning, Study Suggests," *PsyPost* (blog), May 15, 2018, https://www.psypost.org/2018/05/just-cell-phone-possession-can-impair

-learning-study-suggests-51228; Iqbal Ahmad Farooqui, Prasad Pore, and Jayashree Gothankar, "Nomophobia: An Emerging Issue in Medical Institutions?," *Journal of Mental Health* 27, no. 5 (September 3, 2018): 438–41, https://doi.org/10.1080/09638237.2017.1417564; Seunghee Han, Ki Joon Kim, and Jang Hyun Kim, "Understanding Nomophobia: Structural Equation Modeling and Semantic Network Analysis of Smartphone Separation Anxiety," *Cyberpsychology, Behavior, and Social Networking* 20, no. 7 (June 26, 2017): 419–27, https://doi.org/10.1089/cyber.2017.0113. For a brilliant examination of how and why people get distracted and how distractions can influence learning, see James M. Lang, *Distracted: Why Students Can't Focus and What You Can Do about It* (New York: Basic Books, 2020), https://www.basicbooks.com/titles/james-m-lang/distracted/9781541699816/. Lang makes the important point that distracted minds didn't originate with cell phones, the internet, or iPads. See also Gazzaley and Rosen, *Distracted Mind*, 2016.

11. See, for example, Bernice Andrews and John M. Wilding, "The Relation of Depression and Anxiety to Life-Stress and Achievement in Students," *British Journal of Psychology* 95, no. 4 (2004): 509–21, https://doi.org/10.1348/0007126042369802; "Anxiety in Teens Is Rising: What's Going On?," HealthyChildren.org, accessed August 4, 2020, https://www.healthychildren.org/English/health-issues/conditions/emotional-problems/Pages/Anxiety-Disorders.aspx; Jocelyne Matar Boumosleh and Doris Jaalouk, "Depression, Anxiety, and Smartphone Addiction in University Students: A Cross Sectional Study," *PLOS ONE* 12, no. 8 (August 4, 2017): e0182239, https://doi.org/10.1371/journal.pone.0182239.

12. William Stixrud and Ned Johnson, *The Self-Driven Child: The Science and Sense of Giving Your Kids More Control over Their Lives* (New York: Penguin, 2019), Kindle location 101, Kindle ed.

13. Yu-Kang Lee et al., "The Dark Side of Smartphone Usage: Psychological Traits, Compulsive Behavior and Technostress," *Computers in Human Behavior* 31 (February 2014): 373–83, https://doi.org/10.1016/j.chb.2013.10.047.

14. Gazzaley and Rosen, *Distracted Mind*, xv.

15. Video, "Game Changer: Teacher Sergio Juárez Correa," accessed March 8, 2018, https://www.youtube.com/watch?v=VLI0EXn2eSY.

16. Sugata Mitra, "Build a School in the Cloud," accessed March 6, 2018, https://www.ted.com/talks/sugata_mitra_build_a_school_in_the_cloud.

17. Sugata Mitra, "The Child-Driven Education," accessed March 6, 2018, https://www.ted.com/talks/sugata_mitra_the_child_driven_education.

18. Mitra, "Hole in the Wall Project."

Chapter Two. How We Learn

1. Sam Wineburg, *Historical Thinking and Other Unnatural Acts: Chartering the Future of Teaching the Past* (Philadelphia: Temple University Press, 2001).

2. Ibrahim Abou Halloun and David Hestenes, "The Initial Knowledge State of College Physics," *American Journal of Physics* 53 (1985): 1043–55. See also Ibrahim Abou Halloun and David Hestenes, "Common Sense Concepts about Motion," *American Journal of Physics* 53 (1985): 1056–65, at 1059. For further examples and discussions of this phenomenon in physics,

see Jose P. Mestre, Robert Dufresne, William Gerace, Pamela Hardiman, and Jerold T. Ouger, "Promoting Skilled Problem Solving Behavior among Beginning Physics Students," *Journal of Research in Science Teaching* 30 (1993): 303–17.

3. G. Hatano and Y. Oura, "Commentary: Reconceptualizing School Learning Using Insight from Expertise Research," *Educational Researcher* 32, no. 8 (2003): 26–29; T. Martin, K. Rayne, N. J. Kemp, J. Hart, and K. R. Diller, "Teaching for Adaptive Expertise in Biomedical Engineering Ethics," *Science and Engineering Ethics* 11, no. 2 (2005): 257–76; G. Hatano and K. Inagaki, "Two Courses of Expertise," in *Child Development and Education in Japan*, ed. H. Stevenson, J. Azuma, and K. Hakuta, 262–72 (New York: W. H. Freeman, 1986).

4. Manu Kapur, "Productive Failure in Learning Math," *Cognitive Science* 38, no. 5 (June 2014): 1008–22, https://doi.org/10.1111/cogs.12107.

5. Marshall and Albert are pseudonyms for composite figures based on observations of many students learning and acquiring second languages in a variety of situations.

6. Stephen Krashen and others make a distinction between "learning" and "acquiring" a language, and Krashen argues from his research that most approaches to language teaching foster the first at the expense of the second. Stephen Krashen, *Explorations in Language Acquisition and Use* (Portsmouth, NH: Heinemann, 2003).

7. Julia Ingram, "Q&A: Carol Dweck, First Winner of the Yidan Prize," *Stanford Daily*, November 9, 2017, accessed March 28, 2018, https://www.stanforddaily.com/2017/11/09/qa-carol-dweck-first-winner-of-the-yidan-prize/.

8. See Carol S. Dweck, *Mindset: The New Psychology Success* (New York: Random House, 2006).

9. Claude M. Steele, "Thin Ice: 'Stereotype Threat' and Black College Students," August 1999, http://www.theatlantic.com/issues/99aug/9908stereotype.htm; Claude M. Steele, "A Threat in the Air: How Stereotypes Shape Intellectual Identity," in Eugene Y. Lowe, ed., *Promise and Dilemma: Perspectives on Racial Diversity and Higher Education* (Princeton, NJ: Princeton University Press, 1999), 116–18; Claude M. Steele, *Whistling Vivaldi: How Stereotypes Affect Us and What We Can Do* (New York: W. W. Norton, 2011); J. Aronson et al., "When White Men Can't Do Math: Necessary and Sufficient Factors in Stereotype Threat," *Journal of Experimental Social Psychology* 35 (1999): 29–46.

10. Margaret Shih, Todd L. Pittinsky, and Nalini Ambady, "Stereotype Susceptibility: Identity Salience and Shifts in Quantitative Performance," *Psychological Science* 10 (1999): 80–83.

11. We once mentioned Shih's research to a former provost at a major state university who dealt with its implication by simply telling us he didn't think we were telling the truth. It is difficult for humans to give up their existing mental models.

Part II. The Courses

1. In 2004, in Ken Bain, *What the Best College Teachers Do* (Cambridge, MA: Harvard University Press), we offered a shorter list of the five elements of the natural critical learning environment. We think the two lists complement each other. Marsha Marshall Bain was part of a research and writing team that produced the 2004 book. In the body of that book her contributions are noted, but she chose not to be listed as a coauthor. Nevertheless, the 2004 book uses

the plural first-person pronoun throughout, and we continue to follow that practice in referring back to that earlier work.

2. Readers can also look at an explanation of the natural critical learning environment found in Ken Bain, "What Makes Great Teachers Great," *Chronicle of Higher Education*, April 9, 2004, https://www.chronicle.com/article/What-Makes-Great-Teachers/31277.

3. Cathy Davidson, "The Single Most Essential Requirement in Designing a Fall Online Course," HASTAC, May 11, 2020, accessed May 12, 2020, https://www.hastac.org/blogs/cathy -davidson/2020/05/11/single-most-essential-requirement-designing-fall-online-course.

Chapter Three. A New Kind of University

1. Albert Bandura, "Self-Efficacy: Toward a Unifying Theory of Behavioral Change," *Psychological Review* 84, no. 2 (1977): 191–215.

2. Anna Zajacova, Scott M. Lynch, and Thomas J. Espenshade, "Self-Efficacy, Stress, and Academic Success in College," *Research in Higher Education* 46, no. 6 (2005): 677–706.

3. Jonathan D. Stolk and Robert Martello, "Can Disciplinary Integration Promote Students' Lifelong Learning Attitudes and Skills in Project-Based Engineering Courses," *International Journal of Engineering Education* 31, no. 1 (2015): 434–49, https://www.researchgate.net/profile /Jonathan_Stolk/publication/272564676_Can_Disciplinary_Integration_Promote_Students' _Lifelong_Learning_Attitudes_and_Skills_in_Project-Based_Engineering_Courses/links /56133ae708aec7900afb1d93.pdf.

4. We talked to both Stolk and Martello about their approach. See also Stolk and Martello, "Can Disciplinary Integration Promote Students' Lifelong Learning?"

5. Edward L. Deci and Richard M. Ryan, "Facilitating Optimal Motivation and Psychological Well-Being across Life's Domains," *Canadian Psychology / Psychologie Canadienne* 49, no. 1 (2008): 14–23, https://doi.org/10.1037/0708-5591.49.1.14. See also Edward L. Deci and Richard M. Ryan, *Handbook of Self-Determination Research* (Rochester, NY: University of Rochester Press, 2002).

6. Deci and Ryan, "Facilitating Optimal Motivation and Psychological Well-Being."

7. Bain, *What the Best College Teachers Do*, 78–79.

8. Elizabeth A. Canning et al., "STEM Faculty Who Believe Ability Is Fixed Have Larger Racial Achievement Gaps and Inspire Less Student Motivation in Their Classes," *Science Advances* 5, no. 2 (February 1, 2019): https://doi.org/10.1126/sciadv.aau4734.

9. Canning et al., "STEM Faculty Who Believe Ability Is Fixed."

10. In the original study, Bain, *What the Best College Teachers Do*, we explored the research on these tensions at length in chapter 4. We'll not attempt to rehash everything we said seventeen years ago, but we recommend those passages to you.

11. Canning et al., "STEM Faculty Who Believe Ability Is Fixed."

12. Stolk and Martello, "Can Disciplinary Integration Promote Students' Lifelong Learning?," 434.

13. As the class syllabus indicated, in a rich and multifaceted journey, the people in the class examined possible "cultural, economic, or political consequences" of the technology, learning to think like good historians and engineers. "Environmental impacts can pertain to any phase of your technology's production and use," the professors explained, "such as raw material inputs,

energy costs or benefits, recycling opportunities, or environmental damage." When you examine ethical impacts, you have many questions to consider. "Can you identify larger ethical questions that are raised by the use of your technology? Who makes decisions about the design and deployment of your technology, and which values guide these decisions," the faculty asks in the syllabus. "Which interests are served or harmed by this technology? Has it had any unintended impacts?" The students dug both into scholarly studies in history and engineering and into the raw historical evidence. They also designed "laboratory experiments to measure relevant material properties or behaviors" of their technology. They applied their "understanding of materials science theory to build connections among structure, properties, and performance." In the process, they developed an "understanding of how this material (technology) works, from a materials science perspective."

Chapter Four. Books Behind Bars

1. Justin Stover, "There Is No Case for the Humanities," *Chronicle of Higher Education*, March 4, 2018, https://www.chronicle.com/article/There-Is-No-Case-for-the/242724.

2. J. K. Rowling, "The Fringe Benefits of Failure, and the Importance of Imagination," speech delivered at Harvard University, June 5, 2008. You can read the entirety of this remarkable speech at https://news.harvard.edu/gazette/story/2008/06/text-of-j-k-rowling-speech/.

3. "Opinion | Are Millennials to Blame for the Decline in English Majors?," NBC News, accessed July 27, 2019, https://www.nbcnews.com/think/opinion/are-millennials-really-blame-decline-liberal-arts-ncna911941.

4. Since the publication of Bain, *What the Best College Teachers Do* in 2004, we've been invited to consult with and speak at more than six hundred schools around the world, including institutions across the United States, Canada, Latin America, Europe, Australia, and China, and to participate in Europe's Bologna Process, and to consult with the European Union among other front-row seats for this historic process.

5. Students learn by tackling real-life problems in their community.

6. A. W. Astin, H. S. Astin, and J. A. Lindholm, *Cultivating the Spirit: How College Can Enhance Students' Inner Lives* (San Francisco: Jossey-Bass, 2011), 3; see also Ken Bain, *What the Best College Students Do* (Cambridge, MA: Harvard University Press, 2012). Marsha Marshall Bain also served on the research and writing team that produced the 2012 book although she chose not to be listed as a coauthor.

7. We will examine some of research and resulting evidence in later chapters.

Chapter Five. Diverse Classes

1. Susan Svrluga, "Tolstoy behind Bars: Why U-Va. Students Are Reading Russian Literature in a Prison," *Washington Post*, July 5, 2018, accessed September 9, 2018, https://www.washingtonpost.com/local/education/tolstoy-behind-bars-why-u-va-students-are-reading-russian-literature-in-a-prison/2018/07/05/882dad60-5e8f-11e8-a4a4-c070ef53f315_story.html.

2. "The Internet Classics Archive | Nicomachean Ethics by Aristotle," accessed October 25, 2018, http://classics.mit.edu/Aristotle/nicomachaen.2.ii.html.

3. John Dewey, *Experience and Education*, 1938, chapter 5, accessed October 25, 2018, http://archive.org/details/ExperienceAndEducation--JohnDewey.

4. This is unless, of course, you count all the scholarly commentaries as part of the content.

5. Students then grind through thousands of pages as if this were their only chance in life to explore the field, while their professors seem to assume that no one in their class will ever read a lick in the area once they are no longer required to do so in a formal course.

6. Each pair meets with the same group of residents each week.

7. We originally called it the Promising Syllabus (2004). You start with the promise of what the course will help students learn to do (intellectually, physically, emotionally), then show them what they will need to do to achieve their new abilities (in the old traditional pedagogy called "assignments" or "requirements," but now meticulously avoiding those words). The idea is catching on. Hundreds of teachers have built such syllabi around the notion, and William Germano and Kit Nicholls have used the idea of planning backward in their new book *Syllabus: The Remarkable, Unremarkable Document That Changes Everything* (Princeton, NJ: Princeton University Press, 2020). The invitational syllabus emphasizes the act of issuing an invitation. Grant Wiggins and Jay McTighe discussed the idea of planning backward in *Understanding by Design*, 2nd expanded ed. (Alexandria, VA: Association for Supervision and Curriculum Development, 2005).

8. Not to mention the juicy tomatoes, brown sugar, oregano, salt, basil, thyme, and bay leaf.

9. Parker J. Palmer, *The Courage to Teach: Exploring the Inner Landscape of a Teacher's Life* (Hoboken, NJ: Jossey-Bass, 2017).

10. It's an approach that's quite close to what Richard Miller did as the founding president of Olin College of Engineering.

11. As we put the finishing touches on this chapter, a Twitter fight erupted in social media between several professors over whether to have a mandatory attendance policy or not. Meanwhile, a biology professor in Texas called the cops after a student came late, propped her feet on a chair, and refused to take them down. Both the Twitter debate and the classroom episode in San Antonio form parts of a long-standing controversy.

To maintain the decorum necessary for a productive educational experience must the teacher maintain a stern and strict classroom of tightly enforced rules? As we thought about Andy Kaufman's class, it occurred to us that he has answered, "none of the above." It isn't the rules that make a difference; it's the invitation and the understanding entailed in that invitation, although it often helps if students spell out behavior expectations to each other, or if the behavior is couched in a concept of professionalism, as Eric Mazur does in his applied physics class at Harvard. See chapters 8 and 9 for details.

12. "Students don't want to let their UVA classmates [or] the residents down," Kaufman argues. "Rudeness, disrespect, being unprepared, being late, [and so forth], would all be forms of hurting their community, which they value, and so they just don't. It's built into the very structure of the class."

13. Earl Shorris, "II. As a Weapon in the Hands of the Restless Poor," *Harper's*, September 1997, https://harpers.org/archive/1997/09/ii-as-a-weapon-in-the-hands-of-the-restless-poor/.

14. Shorris, "II. As a Weapon in the Hands of the Restless Poor."

15. Shorris, "II. As a Weapon in the Hands of the Restless Poor."

16. Shorris, "II. As a Weapon in the Hands of the Restless Poor."

17. Shorris, "II. As a Weapon in the Hands of the Restless Poor."

18. "The Clemente Course in the Humanities," https://clemente.bard.edu/.

19. The Clemente Course is named for the Pittsburgh Pirates baseball player Roberto Clemente, and the Clemente Center in the Bronx where Shorris held the first program.

20. "The Clemente Course in the Humanities."

21. Quote on Walker's death is from email to author from reporter Susan Markisz. See also Paul Vitello, "Earl Shorris, 75, Dies; Fought Poverty with Knowledge," *New York Times*, June 2, 2012, https://www.nytimes.com/2012/06/03/us/earl-shorris-who-fought-poverty-with-knowledge-dies-at-75.html; Robert Worth, "Bring College Back to Bedford Hills," *New York Times*, June 24, 2001, https://www.nytimes.com/2001/06/24/nyregion/bringing-college-back-to-bedford-hills.html; Susan Markisz, "Call My Lawyer," *Digital Journalist*, May 2001, http://digitaljournalist.org/issue0107/assign/SM_PRISON.htm.

Chapter Six. From Charlottesville to Singapore and Beyond: Searching for Super Courses

1. Robert K. Kamei et al., "21st Century Learning in Medicine: Traditional Teaching versus Team-Based Learning," *Medical Science Educator* 22, no. 2 (June 2012): 57–64, https://doi.org/10.1007/BF03341758.

2. Michelle Miller, "A New Replication Study Revives the Question: Is Taking Notes by Hand Really Better for Students?," Medium (blog), February 6, 2019, https://medium.com/@MDMillerPHD/a-new-replication-study-revives-the-question-is-taking-notes-by-hand-really-better-for-students-2f61d0bcd89f.

3. Students can write an appeal on any test question they think is poorly worded or offers misleading answers, or if they think their answer is better. Faculty members then immediately rule on those appeals. That process helps improve the quality of questions over time. More on the nature of the questions later. We would argue that it also contributes to students' sense of control over their education.

4. The quote appears in the video "TeamLEAD at Duke-NUS," https://www.youtube.com/watch?v=BlVPLYGdBLg.

5. Student facilitators must evaluate the questions that are asked. If someone poses a question that has "low learning value (i.e. easily found on the internet/easily looked up in a text book)," the facilitators ask their peers to rephrase a question into a higher-order inquiry or remove it.

6. As the Singapore educators surveyed their work, one other important issue sprang to mind. If students consistently got perfect scores or nearly so on the readiness exams, the questions didn't challenge them. If the marks fell too low, the students were not learning on their own and the testing might even discourage their commitment. In practice, they found the students averaged around 65 percent on the individual tests and near 95 percent on the team scores. Robert Wilson, a cognitive scientist at the University of Arizona, and his colleagues used studies in machine, animal, and human learning to argue that "there is a sweet spot in which training is neither too easy nor too hard, and where learning progresses most quickly." Wilson pegged that "Goldilocks zone" at approximately 85 percent correct. Robert C Wilson et al., "The Eighty Five Percent Rule for Optimal Learning," *BioRxiv*, January 27, 2018, https://doi.org/10.1101/255182.

7. Their experience also reflects the memory research around a question that seldom gets much attention from educators but has potent implications for most fields of study. If you want to foster deep learning that has a sustained and substantial influence on how students will subsequently think, act, and even feel, is it better that they focus on one skill or concept at a time until they've achieved mastery, or bounce from one to another and back again? Conventional wisdom often picks the former, a technique called "blocking." Yet a still small but rapidly growing body of research favors the later, something called "interleaving" (the term comes from putting pieces of paper between pages in a book). Much of the early research emerging in the 1980s looked at interleaving in sports. But some recent studies have examined the phenomenon in other areas, including medicine and math, and have found a complex pattern. Interleaving works best when "learners . . . have some familiarity with subject materials before interleaving begins," Steven C. Pan, a learning scientist in the University of California system argues, "or, [when] the materials [are] . . . quickly or easily understood."

The clinical cases the students tackle in the afternoon at Duke-NUS seem ideally suited to interleaving and even naturally adapted to that process. As students move from one case to another, they encounter an almost jumbled mix of key principles, and they get valuable practice in picking which ones apply to a given situation. If they did a string of cases all resting on the same concept (in other words, followed blocking), their brains wouldn't need to search for possible solutions, and they would lose a valuable practice. With interleaving, the students are constantly bringing new ideas into short-term memory, strengthening connections to each one of them, and forcing themselves to make fine distinctions between the principles they recall. The diagnosis and treatment become more creative and appropriate, moving far beyond the apocryphal physician of old jokes who has but one answer: "take two aspirins and call me in the morning." Steven C. Pan, "The Interleaving Effect: Mixing It Up Boosts Learning," *Scientific American*, accessed January 20, 2019, https://www.scientificamerican.com/article/the-interleaving-effect-mixing-it-up-boosts-learning/.

8. Kamei et al., "21st Century Learning in Medicine."

9. J. Conroy et al., "AAMC Readiness for Reform: Duke-National University of Singapore Case Study; Implementing Team-Based Learning for Medical Students." Association of American Medical Colleges, https://www.researchgate.net/publication/234017647_AAMC_Readiness_for_Reform_Duke-National_University_of_Singapore_case_Study_Implementing_Team-based_Learning_for_Medical_Students/citation/download. Quote is from interview with Kamei.

Chapter Seven. Self-Directed Learning and Big Questions: From the DIY Girls to Hurricane Katrina

1. "In the San Fernando Valley, a Homeless Crisis Remains Hidden," *Los Angeles Daily News*, September 26, 2015, https://www.dailynews.com/2015/09/26/in-the-san-fernando-valley-a-homeless-crisis-remains-hidden/.

2. Brittany Levine Beckman, "All-Girl Engineer Team Invents Solar-Powered Tent for the Homeless," *Mashable*, June 15, 2017, accessed February 11, 2019, https://mashable.com/2017/06/15/diy-girls-solar-powered-tent-homeless/.

3. Gabriele Steuer and Markus Dresel, "A Constructive Error Climate as an Element of Effective Learning Environments," *Psychological Test and Assessment Modeling* 57 no. 2 (2015): 262–75.

4. Kristin K. Wobbe and Elisabeth A. Stoddard, eds., *Project-Based Learning in the First Year: Beyond All Expectations* (Sterling, VA: Stylus, 2019).

5. Ken Bain, "Understanding Great Teaching," Peer Review 11, no. 2 (2009): 9–12.

Chapter Eight. Peer Instruction and Then Some

1. These examples came from materials that Mazur shared with us.

2. Catherine H. Crouch and Eric Mazur, "Peer Instruction: Ten Years of Experience and Results," *American Journal of Physics* 69, no. 9 (September 2001): 970–77, https://doi.org/10.1119/1.1374249.

3. Crouch and Mazur, "Peer Instruction: Ten Years of Experience and Results," 971.

4. Eric Mazur and Jessica Watkins, "Just-in-Time Teaching and Peer Instruction," 41, https://mazur.harvard.edu/files/mazur/files/rep_634.pdf.

5. "Eric Mazur Wins Minerva Prize," Harvard Gazette (blog), May 20, 2014, https://news.harvard.edu/gazette/story/2014/05/eric-mazur-wins-minerva-prize/.

Chapter Nine. Remaking a Super Course

1. In addition to Mazur, the creative group for Perusall included Kelly Miller, lecturer at the Paulson School of Engineering and Applied Sciences at Harvard; Gary King, Weatherhead University Professor at Harvard and director of the Institute for Quantitative Social Science; and Brian Lukoff, an educator, entrepreneur, and engineer, and lecturer in the McCombs School of Business, University of Texas at Austin.

2. See the website of Perusall, https://perusall.com/about.

3. The activities are listed in the second syllabus in the appendix, in the section headed "II. In-Class Activities." For several years, Miller has been responsible for the first part of Physics AP50 in the fall while Mazur does the second half in the spring. Some students stop the sequence after only one semester, but many of them continue through the full year.

4. Chris Quintana, "Students Are Weary of Online Classes, but Colleges Can't Say Whether They'll Open in Fall 2020," *USA Today*, April 19, 2020, https://www.usatoday.com/story/news/education/2020/04/19/coronavirus-college-universities-canceling-fall-semester/5157756002/.

5. With distance learning, you might not have the machine shops that students have had at their disposal on campus, but those facilities are not the secret to the success of Mazur and Miller's class.

Chapter Ten. Soup of Interdisciplinary Learning

1. In 2018 we went to Chengdu and interviewed these students about their experiences in the class.

2. When Olmsted was eighteen, he gave up plans to study at Yale University after some poison sumac leaves irritated his eyes. He then worked as a journalist, traveled in England

and the American South, and came home convinced that slavery impoverished a whole region of people. On his journeys, this son of a wealthy Connecticut merchant had exercised his father's abiding interest in nature and the outdoors, acquiring a deep appreciation for the lavish and beautiful parks he saw in Birkenhead, near Liverpool. He became convinced that everyone should have equal access to such green spaces. The summation comes from materials that Professor Cannon wrote and supplied us. It reflects how he viewed Olmsted and his work.

3. This is an inclusion that led a Korean student to knock on Cannon's office door some years later. When he answered, she announced, "I just wanted to see what you look like in person."

4. Bain, *What the Best College Teachers Do*, 64.

5. Bain, *What the Best College Teachers Do*, 64

6. Such feelings are a major part of what Edward Deci and Richard Ryan called "relatedness."

7. Bain, *What the Best College Teachers Do*, 65.

8. Bain, *What the Best College Teacher Do*, 65.

Chapter Eleven. Integration of Abilities

1. Paul Baker, *Integration of Abilities* (Woodstock, IL: Dramatic, 2012), 11–12, http://www.dramaticpublishing.com/integration-of-abilities. Other material and quotations from Paul Baker came from notes taken in his class and from subsequent interviews with him.

2. Baker told us several years before he died at the age of ninety-eight that Baker Brownell (again, no relation) had influenced his interest in creating the course. The Northwestern University philosophy professor had devised in the 1920s a class called Contemporary Thought that sought to help students integrate the often fragmented ideas they encountered in college into a coherent personal philosophy. Paul Baker thought he could offer a learning experience that would surpass anything Brownell had mustered and would help people live the creative life. Brownell's ideas about good "cultural activities" and what constituted a work of the mind did influence the Texas professor. See Baker Brownell, *Art Is Action* (New York: Harper and Brothers, 1939).

3. "Telephone Spotlight on Texas, Baylor Theater (1958)," Texas Archive of the Moving Image, accessed May 6, 2019, https://www.texasarchive.org/library/index.php/2012_04249.

4. "What Life Means to Einstein: An Interview by George Sylvester Viereck," *Saturday Evening Post*," October 26, 1929, 17, 110, 113, 114, 117.

5. In the early 1960s, Baker, then founding director of the Baylor Theater, signed a contract with Eugene O'Neill's widow to stage the first amateur production of *Long Day's Journey into Night*. Under the agreement, Baker could make no cuts in the largely autobiographical play. When a woman from Uvalde, Texas, complained about the "raunchy" language and story line, Abner McCall, the president of the Baptist university in Waco, closed the show. The script, McCall argued, included a son's account of his visit to a brothel. You couldn't depict that excursion into the sex industry, the Baylor president contended, so you couldn't include someone's

description of it either (he obviously never saw Neil Simon's *Biloxi Blues*. Perhaps he never saw Hamlet. Too much killing). Baker and eleven colleagues in the Drama Department resigned and went to Trinity University in the fall of 1963.

6. Junyeon Won et al., "Semantic Memory Activation after Acute Exercise in Healthy Older Adults," *Journal of the International Neuropsychological Society* 25, no. 6 (2019): 557–68, https://doi.org/10.1017/S1355617719000171.

7. K. I. Erickson et al., "Exercise Training Increases Size of Hippocampus and Improves Memory," *Proceedings of the National Academy of Sciences* 108, no. 7 (February 15, 2011): 3017–22; E. Mo, "Studying the Link between Exercise and Learning," *CNN Health*, April 12, 2010, http://thechart.blogs.cnn.com/2010/04/12/studying-the-link-between-exercise-and-learning/.

8. Albert Bandura, "Self-Efficacy: Toward a Unifying Theory of Behavioral Change," *Psychological Review* 84, no. 2 (1977): 191–215, https://doi.org/10.1037/0033-295X.84.2.191.

9. Ellen J. Langer, *The Power of Mindful Learning* (Boston: Da Capo, 2016).

10. We first explored Baker's ideas and class in Bain, *What the Best College Students Do*, throughout that book, but especially in chapter 1. We recommend that work to you for a fuller understanding of what he did.

11. We've tried to help you understand the concepts lying behind this simple yet complex course and how important it became in the lives of thousands. We hope our discussion promotes thoughts about building an educational experience around the pursuit of a creative life. Where does it belong? Perhaps in an engineering department, or as part of everything from history to chemistry. But to recreate such a Super Course, you need far more knowledge about the workings of Integration of Abilities. You can get detailed information about each exercise in two ways. In *What the Best College Students Do*, we spent the first chapter exploring Baker's course through the eyes and experiences of several people who took it and discussed it throughout that book. In the 1970s someone recorded most of what Baker and his students said in the course when he was a faculty member at Trinity University in San Antonio (although this person could not capture the dialogues that emerged between students and inside each one of them). A transcript of those recordings became the basis for a book in which Baker outlined each of the exercises. A recent republication of that work has made the ideas available to new generations. Baker, *Integration of Abilities*.

Chapter Twelve. Fostering Growth Mindsets

1. Here are two college courses that carry the legacy of Baker's thinking: At both Indiana University in Bloomington and Appalachian State University in Boone, North Carolina, professors have tried to bring Baker's insights into an experience designed to help people become better students. Both have used Bain, *What the Best College Students Do*, with its account of the Integration of Abilities class, as a textbook. Joseph Gonzalez, a history professor at Appalachian State, asks students to think about their own thinking and creativity while they study and then rewrite the United States Constitution, for example. In the hands of Andrew Koke, Laura Clapper, and their colleagues, the seminar at Indiana has made more extensive and direct reference to the Baker content. Students in College and Lifelong Learning do a series of writing exercises

around Baker prompts, such as this one: " 'I realized,' one of [Paul Baker's students] reported years later, 'that an important part of being creative was recognizing good ideas and beautiful creations when I encountered them and finding ways to integrate them with my own. But it also meant—and this was crucial—rejecting the obvious first answers that tradition has given us and pushing for something fresh.' "

The exercise asks students, first, to think and write about a "beautiful" idea or "creation" they have come across that influenced them. How was the experience "humbling, moving, and/or awe-inspiring?" They next wrote about a different "beautiful creation" that they integrated into their own thinking. It might be "a book, song, movie, or some comment a friend once said or a famous quote you really liked." Students were asked how they made the beautiful creation their own, and how that experience affected them and their creative life. In a class that met for only half the semester, students often underwent a deep transformation, sparking far better academic performances and increased ability to examine and expand their own creative abilities.

2. Paul Baker, *Integration of Abilities*, 12.

3. Twyla Tharp and Mark Reiter, *The Creative Habit: Learn It and Use It for Life* (New York: Simon and Schuster, 2006).

4. Jean Houston, *The Possible Human: A Course in Enhancing Your Physical, Mental, and Creative Abilities* (New York: Tarcher Perigee, 1997).

5. Liz Lerman and John Borstel, *Liz Lerman's Critical Response Process: A Method for Getting Useful Feedback on Anything You Make, from Dance to Dessert* (Takoma Park, MD: Liz Lerman Dance Exchange, 2003).

Chapter Thirteen. A Super Course Department

1. Howard S. Barrows and Robyn M. Tamblyn, *Problem-Based Learning: An Approach to Medical Education* (New York: Springer, 1980).

2. Barrows and Tamblyn, *Problem-Based Learning*, viii.

3. Barrows and Tamblyn, *Problem-Based Learning*, ix.

4. Georgia Tech was not the first engineering school to go down this road. When Ken arrived at Northwestern in 1992, he paid a visit to Jerry Cohen, then dean of the McCormick School of Engineering, and suggested that the school get undergraduates involved in "doing engineering" early in their schooling. Traditionally, they had to take a series of prerequisites before touching a real engineering project late in their undergraduate work. Cohen and his colleagues had already been thinking about similar ideas and over the next few years tinkered with ways to implement them.

Launched in 1997, the Engineering First Program in the McCormick School of Engineering at Northwestern has no learning scientist at the helm. It begins with a team-taught course offered by engineering professors and instructors from the College of Arts and Sciences Writing Program. Students do tackle authentic engineering projects while learning "presentation skills needed to thrive in a competitive marketplace." But with the guidance of a learning scientist faculty member, the PBL approach in Atlanta offered more than just a chance to do "some engineering" in your freshman year. It helped students develop a systematic method for problem solving while it became much more integrated into the thinking and practices of the department, transforming both students and professors.

5. When we came to Northwestern in 1992, we learned that new kinds of classrooms require not only innovative spaces that recognize new research and ideas on how to foster deep learning but also a concerted effort to educate subsequent generations of faculty and administrators on how to use those rooms and why they were designed as they were. Somewhere in the not too distant past, the school had built an ingenious large classroom that recognized the power of group work.

Rather than sitting in typical theater seats, arranged in rows across the room and focused on the lecturer at the front, students sat at tables where six people could work together. Imagine tiered rows of those tables rising in a large "lecture" hall. The designers obviously wanted to move the old presentation room toward a new kind of pedagogy where students would spend at least some of their time working together on problems and questions before their group shared their thinking with the four hundred other people engaged and sitting in the room. In that environment, the professor could use "think-pair-share-square" exercises with ease, engaging a large class in a highly active learning practice.

We don't know what uses the room witnessed in its early days or if many professors moved from old-fashioned oral presentations to more interactive pedagogies, but by the time we got to Northwestern, no one seemed to remember why all the tables were there, and people simply stood behind a podium and said stuff to the class or employed PowerPoint slides to communicate at least part of their message. The original idea behind the architecture had long since been lost as newer professors and deans speculated about how many more people they could stuff into the room if they tore out the wooden tables with their attached seats and replaced them with rows of padded fold-down theater seats where students could be quite comfortable while they listened to someone talk.

In the late 1990s the dean of the business school acquired control of the room and used his considerable financial resources to rip out the tables and build a room that would hold nearly 50 percent more students than the old space. The opportunity for easy use of innovative and highly interactive practices was gone, but larger crowds could gather to see the show—like the time Bill Gates came to say a few words to an overflow crowd and someone plastered his face with a meringue pie.

Something similar happened in another room on campus—this one created to hold small classes with flexible needs. It was a round room with glass walls, filled with chairs on wheels that could spin completely around. The room could be arranged in almost unlimited numbers of ways. That highly adjustable space also became a victim of higher planning, this time with considerations that had nothing to do with either teaching, learning, research, or service. One day the library—which controlled the room—had all the rolling and spinning seats removed and replaced with stationary ones that could be bolted to the floor. Why? Custodians found it difficult to sweep easily between rows when "you never knew where the chairs would be moved on a given day." It never seemed to occur to anyone that chairs were often scattered about because the various classes needed different seating arrangements, exactly what the rolling chairs were meant to provide and the bolted ones never could.

6. The department originally used faculty members as facilitators but switched to undergraduates, recognizing and reflecting the notion that people who are only slightly ahead of you in their learning are better equipped to help you learn than are the experts.

7. Once a week, all the groups will come together for a joint session, but those large meetings are not the driving force in the class, and they are not typical "lecture sessions." The small problem-solving sections remain the key element in the experience. "We could even do away with the large meetings," Newstetter explains. "What is important is the research students will do, and their problem-solving sessions."

But those general sessions with all the people in the class do offer several opportunities. Students can hear from an expert on Parkinson's, for example, or from a member of the Parkinson's community that has suffered from the disease. "One session could deal with technical details of the disease," Newstetter notes. "The next one could be on team dynamics to help the teams work more effectively together." When it is time to design a new device, they might get technical explanations that they will need to understand. "They are ready to hear those lectures because they have already been down in the guts of the problem."

8. Noted in Katarzyna Czabanowska et al., "Problem-Based Learning Revisited: Introduction of Active and Self-Directed Learning to Reduce Fatigue among Students," *Journal of University Teaching and Learning Practice* 9, no. 1 (2012), https://ro.uow.edu.au/jutlp/vol9/iss1/6.

9. Czabanowska et al., "Problem-Based Learning Revisited."

10. Many years after she designed her Super Course in Atlanta, Wendy Newstetter found an explanation of motivation that captured the principles she wove into her course. She now uses that model to explain what she had in mind. It captures well what makes her course so successful and other less so. It comes from Brett Jones, a professor of education at Virginia Tech who took Deci and Ryan and other motivational scientists and pushed them into a memorable acronym: MUSIC (although it's a bit of a stretch to get the first letter): to become strongly motivated to take a deep approach, people in school must feel *eMpowered* (they believe they can do it). They see the course as *Useful* (to something—human good, future careers, etc.), a place where they can be *Successful*, composed of *Interesting* ideas and things to do, and filled with *Caring* assistance (from teachers, tutors, and peers). Brett D. Jones, "Motivating Students to Engage in Learning: The MUSIC Model of Academic Motivation," *International Journal of Teaching and Learning in Higher Education*, 21, no. 2 (2009): 272–85, MUSIC is explained on 273.

11. In the early 2000s, both Ken and Jerome came to New York University. Jerome was nearing ninety years old at the time and lived "on campus." His bedroom was on one side of a wall, and Ken's office was on the other. While neither Ken nor Jerome tapped out messages on the plaster that separated them, or dug tunnels to the other side, they did become friends and exchange views on how people learn. Ken later named the library in the Center for Teaching after Jerome, while the distinguished psychologist gave some of his personal collection of books to help populate the center's bookshelves.

12. "We call this 'just-in-time discussions,'" Le Doux explains. "We use them sparingly and strategically. They are important for helping students make sense of what they are doing, and we time it for those inevitable times when most of the class kind of needs it and is ready for it, now that their brains are firing with an intense desire to solve the problem!"

13. Le Doux and Waller used "Shallcross's material and energy balances concept inventory" to make their measurement in "an entry-level course at Georgia Tech called "Conservation

Principles of Biomedical Engineering (BMED 2210)." Alisha A. Waller and Joseph M. Le Doux, "The Problem Solving Studio: An Apprenticeship Environment for Aspiring Engineers," *Advances in Engineering Education*, 5, no. 3 (Fall 2016): 1–26.

14. Remember, from Bain, *What the Best College Teachers Do*, 60–63, that Richardson took this approach for introductory classes in sociology.

15. "Far transfer" occurs when people are able to understand and use the implications and applications of some idea or information in a quite different context from which they learned, and to do so without direct instruction. A student, for example, learns about geometry and then applies that insight to a pool game; a student applies what he or she learns in a trigonometry class to doing work as an intern in an architect's firm. Albert Bandura watches people learning to handle snakes and uses that experience to develop his theory of self-efficacy.

Chapter Fourteen. A Personal Journey toward a Super Course

1. The redesign emphasized ways to motivate students to take a deep approach to their learning and exercises that would be fun while helping them to develop specific learning goals, including deeper reading and writing.

2. Quoted in Pooja K. Agarwal, "Retrieval Practice and Bloom's Taxonomy: Do Students Need Fact Knowledge before Higher Order Learning?," *Journal of Educational Psychology*, June 7, 2018, 1.

3. I suspect that Willingham knows better and is not calling for the "drilling" of facts or rote memorization before students take on problems. After all, he says, "we must ensure students acquire background knowledge *parallel* with practicing critical thinking skills." Furthermore, he told his campus magazine he did not support UK secretary of education Michael Gove's plans to boost "rote learning" as a way to improve creativity and critical thinking. But his discussion remains muddy and misleading. It comes in a book entitled *Why Don't Students Like School*, but he never admits that many students hate school because of the many ways traditional classes attempt to "stuff" them with the facts before ever engaging them in fascinating problems. "Rethinking the Way We Learn: UVA Psychologist Debunks Myths about How the Brain Works," *Virginia Magazine*, accessed August 1, 2018, http://uvamagazine.org/articles/rethinking_the_way_we_learn.

4. This exercise probably would not work well if it did not come amid the movies and games, the initial fascinating reading, the great sense of fun that ran through every session, or, most important, the big question that each unit raised.

5. We taught the class described here five times, each time trying new approaches, modifying some important element of the experiment. The description you have here emerged in the second iteration and continued with some variation over the next two years. Those were the most successful versions, stimulating deep approaches and thinking. The first attempt, however, had major flaws and sparked widespread student displeasure. Only a willingness to keep trying, to experiment in new ways, to question, and to consult the emerging literature on human learning produced the version that proved to be so successful.

6. We had used the same approach for years, even in "required" classes, and we now adapted it to the new Super Course.

7. Over the years, we alternated using that opening with some other appeal. When it was used, attendance soared, and the quality of student work improved significantly.

8. The list varied from year to year but often included *The Godfather, Missing, State of Siege*, and three or four other films. *The Godfather* was the most unusual choice. Director Francis Ford Coppola claimed his film was a microcosm of the broader society, not just a gangster flick. Did it encapsulate in miniature the affairs between nation-states? After all, we pointed out, the five fictional crime families in the film had wars, spies, peace conferences, and the like. The character Michael Corleone claims, "My father is no different than any powerful man, any man with power, like a president or senator." Are nation-states any different than a group of thugs, each one out to protect its personal (national) interest? While students were quick to draw such a conclusion, we made a counterargument.

Our questions led to a rich discussion of international relations and a body of theoretical literature that students would otherwise have found too abstract and tedious.

9. For instance, students were prompted: "If someone found these documents in a mayonnaise jar a thousand years from now, what would they conclude? What questions should they ask?"

10. We held elections to select someone to represent the American leader and another person to take on the character of Allende. With devilish fun, the class sometimes named the most leftist individual to represent the American Republican chief and the president of the Young Conservatives to act as the Marxist political leader.

11. C. Roland Christensen and David A. Garvin, *Education for Judgment: The Artistry of Discussion Leadership*, ed. Ann Sweet, reprint ed. (Boston: Harvard Business Review Press, 1992).

12. Mark Danner, *The Massacre at El Mozote: A Parable of the Cold War* (New York: Vintage, 1994).

13. He bolstered his case with reports from an Argentine forensics team that dug up the bodies in the 1990s.

14. Christopher Lehmann-Haupt, "Books of the Times; the Nature of One Particular War," *New York Times*, May 9, 1994, C15, https://www.nytimes.com/1994/05/09/books/books-of-the-times-the-nature-of-one-particular-war.html.

When students came to class a week later, we asked who had not finished reading Danner's work. A few hands rose slowly. "If you didn't read the entire book yet, you have another chance next Thursday with no questions asked. We'll keep no records of who leaves the room now, or who stays." We talked briefly about a simple fact of life: No teacher can give you more time. Only the grim reaper can do so. Everyone who takes extra days to finish a reading must borrow from the rest of their lives. Take control of your time and plan accordingly. "No one requires you to take this class, but if you decide to do so, it means you've committed to do the reading so you can engage in discussions. You've joined a community, and, if you plan to stay, you have obligations to your colleagues." About a quarter of the class took this "second chance," some because they hadn't finished, others because they hadn't started. That next week, all of them came to the makeup session having read the book. For the rest of the term, nearly every student finished the readings on time.

El Mozote happened in 1981, and the Cold War had begun by at least 1945. But once the students read and contemplated Danner's account, they could go back to the beginning with greater interest and motivation. They now explored with deep intentions the debate about the nature of the "Cold War," an inquiry that seemed silly to some of them when the course began.

15. While nearly all students take classes on how to read plays, novels, poems, and short stories, few experience any explicit help with digesting advanced historical (or scientific) scholarship. Instead, they wade through boring textbooks put together by a publishing company more interested in avoiding controversy and selling books than in exploring a plethora of ideas. No wonder students often don't complete assignments, find them tedious and useless, or build strategies for "faking their way" through a reading quiz.

16. People can, for example, have similar beliefs but hold conflicting attitudes. If historical evidence is observed, then we may want to know who saw or collected it and from what perspective; if inferred, from what other evidence did it come.

17. We prepared a succinct summary of key vocabulary from logic and the kinds of agreements and disagreements students might encounter.

18. Each passage was only slightly above the reading level of the selection before it, challenging and moving students' capacity to read.

19. That's not to say that we never made any oral explanations. We did but sparingly. Each extended explanation ("lecture") came in the form of an argument with these elements: A question; an effort to help students understand the significance and implications of the question; an interactive learning activity in which students searched for possible answers (sometime in a think-pair-square-share model); an explanation of a possible tentative answer (resolution); and a follow-up question.

20. Thanks to Craig Nelson, a biologist at Indiana University, for suggesting this exercise.

21. He later went to law school and became a public defender to bring justice to people who often never experience it. We told this story in more detail in Bain, *What the Best College Students Do*, 255–56.

22. Mark C. Carnes, *Minds on Fire: How Role-Immersion Games Transform College* (Cambridge, MA: Harvard University Press, 2014), 65.

23. While the Reacting and Cold War classes both pioneered the use of role-play, they differ in several ways. None of the Reacting teachers we interviewed extended any concerted effort to teach reading and writing skills; the teachers of the Cold War classes did. Reacting courses focused on reading primary sources; the Cold War classes emphasized the reading of historical scholarship *and* original documents. The study of change over time was an integral part of the Cold War curriculum, while all the Reacting teachers argued that the structure of their games did not lend itself to such a learning objective. Reacting class contained a more specific game structure (Reacting games had "winners" and "losers"; the games in the Cold War class did not). Reacting classes have been the subject of far more extensive research and flourish to this day at scores of institutions; the Cold War classes existed for only a few years at Northwestern and New York Universities.

24. Carnes, *Minds on Fire*, 43.

25. Carnes, *Minds on Fire*, 56–57.

26. To begin to explore this research, see C. Edward Watson and Thomas Chase Hagood, eds., *Playing to Learn with Reacting to the Past: Research on High Impact, Active Learning Practices* (London: Palgrave Macmillan, 2018), https://doi.org/10.1007/978-3-319-61747-3.

27. Thomas Chase Hagood, C. Edward Watson, and Britanny M. Williams, "Reacting to the Past: An Introduction to Its Scholarly Foundation," in C. Edward Watson et al., *Playing to Learn*

with Reacting to the Past—Research on High Impact, Active Learning Practices (London: Palgrave Macmillan, 2017), 2.

28. "Students and teachers," Mark Carnes proclaimed, "deserve an academic world that is as exciting as intercollegiate football, as enchanting as World of Warcraft, as subversive as illegal boozing, and as absurd as fraternity initiations." Carnes, *Minds on Fire*, 298.

29. Watson et al., *Playing to Learn with Reacting to the Past*, 201.

30. Nikole Hannah-Jones, "Our Democracy's Founding Ideals Were False When They Were Written: Black Americans Have Fought to Make Them True," *New York Times*, August 14, 2019, https://www.nytimes.com/interactive/2019/08/14/magazine/black-history-american-democracy.html.

Chapter Fifteen. All Knowledge Is Related

1. Now available on the Internet Archive at https://archive.org/details/in.ernet.dli.2015 .203691/page/n3/mode/2up.

2. Pert's work brought more than scientific studies into the discussion. In 1978 the work to which she contributed won the prestigious Albert Lasker Award, but the citation did not mention Pert, who had played a major role in the research, nor any others besides the head of the lab. Pert protested to the head of the foundation that gave the award. Her letter raised issues about "the burdens and barriers women face in science careers." John Schwartz, "Candace Pert, 67, Explorer of the Brain, Dies," *New York Times*, September 19, 2013, sec. Science, https://www .nytimes.com/2013/09/20/science/candace-pert-67-explorer-of-the-brain-dies.html.

3. She even took things off because of student reactions. In the first iteration of the course, she had included Francis Crick's *Astonishing Hypothesis: The Scientific Search for the Soul* (London: Scribner, 1995). But over time, his major conclusions had become such an integral part of educated thinking that "there was nothing astonishing about what he had to say." Students already thought the way Crick had projected. "By the time I had taught the course several times," Norden remembered, "I could substitute other more cutting-edge works while still asking students what evidence they had to support Crick's beliefs."

4. To further guard against any possible prejudice, Norden asked that students identify their own work—papers and other items they "handed in"—with a code rather than with their names. The departmental secretary kept track of who belonged to each code. Thus, Norden never knew who had composed any of the material they submitted for evaluation.

5. Jared M. Diamond, *Guns, Germs, and Steel: The Fates of Human Societies* (New York: W. W. Norton, 1999).

6. Norden had thought in detail about various scenarios that could emerge, and she carried into each consideration a primary emphasis on helping and encouraging students to learn rather than thinking only about measuring learning outcomes and awarding points in some academic game. What if someone didn't read all the books they had agreed to master, or a person raised his or her ambitions after initially choosing, say, only three or four books? In eleven years of teaching the course, Norden told us, "I remember one student who failed to adequately discuss the number of books he had chosen to receive a B, and he received a C." Norden could not, however, remember "a single case" in which "a student who wanted an A did not meet up to the

expectation." On the other hand, "a few more [people] did BETTER than what they had chosen," she explained in an email. They might put down a B at the beginning of the semester, and "later approach me and say that they really wanted to read more of the books—with the agreement that if they did and did it well . . . they could receive a higher grade."

What if a student came to class unprepared? If you had "not read the book, or could not discuss it, you had to admit this in front of the class," she explained. "Basically, I wanted the students to feel some responsibility to their group in terms of the book that was to be discussed. In order for such a student (and yes, it did happen) to maintain whatever grade they wanted, they had to [choose] another book. A student could do this only once in the class."

7. We often hear professors say that the sciences have it easy engaging students because they can blow up stuff to get their attention. Scientists and engineers make the counterclaim, arguing that the humanities have the easy job because they can raise controversial matters and issues of values. Yet both sides are ignoring the opportunities that lie within their own domain and the chance to "cross the border" in a multidisciplinary manner. Norden's success and the achievements of others in this study came because these teachers recognized how disciplines are interrelated.

8. John Dewey, *Experience and Education*, chapter 5, accessed October 25, 2018, http://archive.org/details/ExperienceAndEducation--JohnDewey.

9. As we put the finishing touches on this chapter in the summer of 2019, a horrifying story broke about concentration camps along the US border with Mexico. According to both news reports and testimony from congressional delegations, children struggled for survival in filthy cells, sometimes sleeping on concrete floors without adequate food. Meanwhile, grown women inmates reported that they had to drink water from latrines to have enough liquid to survive. "Women Held in Border Patrol Custody Say They Were Told to Drink Water from Toilets," accessed August 5, 2020, https://www.buzzfeednews.com/article/adolfoflores/immigrants-drinking-toilets-water-aoc-border-patrol; Jenifer L. Costello, Office of Inspector General, Department of Homeland Security, "Management Alert—DHS to Address Dangerous Overcrowding and Prolonged Detention of Children and Adults in the Rio Grande Valley, July 2, 2019, https://www.oig.dhs.gov/sites/default/files/assets/2019-07/OIG-19-51-Jul19_.pdf; Adam Serwer, "A Crime by Any Name," *Atlantic*, July 3, 2019, https://www.theatlantic.com/ideas/archive/2019/07/border-facilities/593239/.

10. S. A. McLeod, "Kohlberg's Stages of Moral Development," *Simply Psychology*, October 24, 2013, https://www.simplypsychology.org/kohlberg.html; Lawrence Kohlberg, *The Philosophy of Moral Development: Moral Stages and the Idea of Justice*, Essays on Moral Development 1 (New York: Harper and Row, 1981).

11. We have deliberately avoided calling this aspect of the course a "final examination," although that's the language that tradition might apply. We're not trying to be cute nor to hide important details from anyone, but we are hoping to promote a deep reexamination of testing and grading. Students had to prepare answers to all the questions that their professor raised, but she picked only one of them for the final.

12. Originally, Norden restricted enrollment to twenty students, all of them biology majors with a concentration in neuroscience, but as fame of the course spread, other majors and concentrations lobbied for admission. One year, a clerical error allowed forty people to register, but

that size proved unwieldy, compromising the opportunity for all enrollees to participate fully. In subsequent semesters, Norden set the enrollment at twenty-two, but many people still lobbied just to attend and hear the discussions even if they couldn't join them.

Chapter Sixteen. The Pedagogy of Getting Out

1. Arthur M. Glenberg and his students at Arizona State University had also been playing with this notion, and they had found physical evidence of embodied cognition. In several experiments, they discovered that the muscles you use while reading can influence how rapidly you can process certain texts. What are the implications of Glenberg's research and the growing body of inquiries coming from the psychology labs that explore embodied cognition? "Arthur Glenberg | Department of Psychology," accessed August 13, 2019, http://psychology.asu.edu /content/arthur-glenberg; Arthur M. Glenberg, David Havas, Raymond Becker, and Mike Rinck, "Grounding Language in Bodily States: The Case for Emotion," in Diane Pecher and Rolf A. Zwaan, *Grounding Cognition: The Role of Perception and Action in Memory, Language, and Thinking* (Cambridge: Cambridge University Press, 2005), 115–28.

2. Adler called his ideas the "Paideia" plan and argued that while a vocational underpinning for secondary education might prepare students for jobs that could disappear in a changing economy, a liberal arts education had lasting value, preparing young people for work, citizenship, lifelong learning, critical thinking, and creative thought. With that kind of background, Adler argued, people could better weather the challenges of a changing world. The same ideas emerged in the Clemente Course for the humanities we discussed back in chapter 5. Jim Boles, the current principal of the Chattanooga school that adopted Adler's ideas, wrote in an email: "There are no test score requirements to be a student at our school. Students from all walks of life enter our halls and we do everything we can to meet them where they are and prepare them for whatever is next. I often say that we are the closest thing you can get to the real world inside a school. Through seminar and civil discourse, we teach students to read, write, listen, speak, and think! We believe we are changing the world one graduating class at a time!"

3. Bain, *What the Best College Teachers Do*, 14; Nalini Ambady and Robert Rosenthal, "Half a Minute: Predicting Teacher Evaluations from Thin Slices of Nonverbal Behavior and Physical Attractiveness," *Journal of Personality and Social Psychology* 64 (1993): 431–41.

4. Lerman was one of the people we explored when we examined the origins and cultivation of creativity in Bain, *What the Best College Students Do*, 21–23, 28.

5. Dunbar explored the work of Chris Argyris, the feedback researcher in the Harvard Business School who had stressed treating people positively and with respect for their abilities, and always asking "why am I doing it this way." Dunbar found a long history of people in various professions who were asking questions about feedback. Those people were often using what Argyris had called "double loop learning." They didn't just ask, how can I practice some aspect of what I'm doing so I can get better at it, but also began to explore why they offered feedback. What paradigms shaped their practices? How did they think about the people with whom they were working? "The only problem," Dunbar observed, "is this [double loop learning] generally isn't happening in high schools, and maybe not in college." Kenneth D. Benne and Chris Argyris, "Intervention Theory and Method: A Behavioral Science View," *Administrative Science Quarterly*

16, no. 4 (December 1971): 548, https://doi.org/10.2307/2391772; Chris Argyris, "Single-Loop and Double-Loop Models in Research on Decision Making," *Administrative Science Quarterly* 21, no. 3 (1976): 363–75, https://doi.org/10.2307/2391848.

6. This widely cited letter is quoted in many sources including Tasneem Zehra Husain, *Only the Longest Threads* (Philadelphia: Paul Dry Books, 2014), 171.

Chapter Seventeen. Grades

1. Good histories of grading in universities and other levels of schooling are hard to find. Even the histories of major universities often shed little light on the subject. We pieced this story together from multiple types of sources including memoirs, interviews with education historians, university handbooks, and an eclectic collection of books, articles, and webpages. Our major point, which we hope will be the main focus of any reader, is that from all we can tell, the modern system of grades is a relatively recent development in human history and that the idea of putting a number or letter on someone's thinking represents a radical turn of events.

If this note and our discussion of grades in the text provoke some intense debate about the exact chronology of this tale, we will have failed miserably. We hope instead they stimulate readers to realize that with the precise stipulation of numbers and letters that could be reduced to numbers (a GPA), educators now had taken on more work and a new kind of responsibility. No longer did teachers concentrate solely on helping people learn, but they now pretended to know how to measure someone's intellectual development, not with a discussion of ideas and critical thought, but with a yardstick, with a score, with the apparatus of a professional sports league. We hope that readers will respond instead with a kind of epistemological inquiry that chases and creates ideas about what it means to learn, to think, to reason, to invent, to theorize, to conceptualize, to make connections, and so forth. Finally, we hope this discussion will cause every teacher to consider the growing chorus of thinkers and researchers who say that our system of grades may actually harm deep learning. Until we get a comprehensive examination of grades from a historical and philosophical perspective, here are some sources any reader might want to consult, including a few that offer perspectives on the practice of grading, its meaning, and its influence on teaching and learning, which, of course, is the perspective of this book. Neil Postman and Charles Weingartner, *Teaching as a Subversive Activity* (New York: Dell, 1980); Jonathan Smith and Christopher Stray, *Teaching and Learning in Nineteenth-Century Cambridge* (Cambridge, UK: Boydell and Brewer, 2001); Damian Riehl Leader, "A History of the University of Cambridge: Vol. I, The University to 1546," *British Journal of Educational Studies* 37, no. 3 (1989): 301–3, https://doi.org/10.2307/3121288; Caroline Pulfrey, Céline Buchs, and Fabrizio Butera, "Why Grades Engender Performance-Avoidance Goals: The Mediating Role of Autonomous Motivation," *Journal of Educational Psychology* 103, no. 3 (2011): 683; Alfie Kohn, *Punished by Rewards: The Trouble with Gold Stars, A's, Praise, and Other Bribes* (Boston: Mifflin, 1999); Isidor Edward Finkelstein, *The Marking System in Theory and Practice* (Baltimore: Warwick and York, 1913); Jack Schneider and Ethan Hutt, "Making the Grade: A History of the A–F Marking Scheme," *Journal of Curriculum Studies* 46, no. 2 (2014): 201–24; Louise W. Cureton, "The History of Grading Practices," *Measurement in Education* 2, no. 4 (1971): 1–8; Mary Lovett Smallwood, *A Historical Study of Examinations and Grading Systems in Early American University:*

A Critical Study of the Original Records of Harvard, William and Mary, Yale, Mount Holyoke, and Michigan from Their Founding to 1900 (Cambridge, MA: Harvard University, 1935); Alberta Teachers Association, "The History of Grading in Three Minutes," https://www.teachers.ab.ca /News%20Room/The%20Learning%20Team/Volume%202/Number%203/Pages/The%20 history%20of%20grading%20in%20three%20minutes.aspx; E. S. Leedham-Green, *A Concise History of the University of Cambridge* (Cambridge: Cambridge University Press, 1996); John R. Thelin, *A History of American Higher Education* (Baltimore: Johns Hopkins University Press, 2011); Frederick Rudolph, *The American College and University: A History* (Athens: University of Georgia Press, 1990); Jeffrey Schinske and Kimberly Tanner, "Teaching More by Grading Less (or Differently)," *CBE—Life Sciences Education* 13, no. 2 (June 1, 2014): 159–66, https://doi .org/10.1187/cbe.cbe-14-03-0054; L. David Weller, "The Grading Nemesis: An Historical Overview and a Current Look at Pass/Fail Grading," *Journal of Research and Development in Education* 17, no. 1 (1983): 39–45.

2. We learned recently that an "E" still exists at a few scattered schools.

3. Thomas W. Teasdale and David R. Owen, "A Long-Term Rise and Recent Decline in Intelligence Test Performance: The Flynn Effect in Reverse," *Personality and Individual Differences* 39, no. 4 (September 1, 2005): 837–43.

4. John M. Malouff et al., "Preventing Halo Bias in Grading the Work of University Students," *Cogent Psychology* 1, no. 1 (December 31, 2014): 988937, https://doi.org/10.1080/23311908 .2014.988937.

5. On the gender gap, see Linda J. Sax, *The Gender Gap in College: Maximizing the Developmental Potential of Women and Men* (Hoboken, NJ: Jossey-Bass/Wiley, 2008); Jon Marcus, "The Degrees of Separation between the Genders in College Keep Growing," *Washington Post*, October 27, 2019, https://www.washingtonpost.com/local/education/the-degrees-of-separation -between-the-genders-in-college-keeps-growing/2019/10/25/8b2e5094-f2ab-11e9-89eb -ec56cd414732_story.html; Alana Samuels, "Poor Girls Are Leaving Their Brothers Behind," *Atlantic*, November 27, 2017, https://www.theatlantic.com/business/archive/2017/11/gender -education-gap/546677/; Mark Hugo Lopez and Ana Gonzalez-Barrera, "Women's College Enrollment Gains Leave Men Behind," FACTANK, News in the Numbers, Pew Research Center, March 6, 2014, https://www.pewresearch.org/fact-tank/2014/03/06/womens-college -enrollment-gains-leave-men-behind/.

6. Anne Marie Porter and Rachael Ivie, "Women in Physics and Astronomy," 2019, American Institute of Physics, https://www.aip.org/statistics/reports/women-physics-and-astronomy -2019; see also Joseph R. Cimpian, Taek H. Kim, and Zachary T. McDermott, "Understanding Persistent Gender Gaps in STEM," *Science* 368, no. 6497 (June 19, 2020): 1317–19, https://doi .org/10.1126/science.aba7377.

7. Walter Mischel, *The Marshmallow Test* (New York: Little, Brown Spark, 2015).

8. A recent web search found nearly five hundred thousand entries for the phrase "grade inflation." This does not count the number of entries for similar phrases in languages other than English; https://www.google.com/search?client=firefox-b-1-d&q=%22grade+inflation%22.

9. His course at the NYU School of Law is the focus of chapter 6 in Bain, *What the Best College Teachers Do.*

10. Bell had earlier been the first African American to win tenure in the law school at Harvard and had served as dean of the law school at the University of Oregon.

11. Those were words that used to send some people into a frenzy, like the sound of fingernails scratching a chalkboard. Over the last twenty-five years our conversations have matured, however. Chemists, historians, and others no longer feel insecure and threatened by unknown concepts they can no longer dismiss as mere jargon.

12. Richard Light, *The Harvard Assessment Seminars* (Cambridge, MA: Harvard University, Graduate School of Education and Kennedy School of Government, 1990), 8–9; Bain, *What the Best College Teachers Do*, 46.

Epilogue

1. Much the same might be said about medical treatments. Some widely used procedures and medicines occasionally cause even deadly reactions in "rare" cases, as pharmaceutical television ads remind us.

2. Robert Kamei, email to the authors.

3. Noel Entwistle and Hilary Tait, "Approaches to Learning, Evaluations of Teaching, and Preferences for Contrasting Academic Environments," *Higher Education* 19, no. 2 (1990): 169–94. See also Hillary Tait and Noel Entwistle, "Identifying Students at Risk through Ineffective Study Strategies," *Higher Education* 31, no. 1 (1996): 97–116; Noel Entwistle, Hilary Tait, and Velda McCune, "Patterns of Response to Approaches to Studying Inventory across Contrasting Groups and Contexts," *European Journal of Psychology of Education* 15, no. 1 (2000): 33; Bain, *What the Best College Teachers Do*, 165.

4. Louis Deslauriers et al., "Measuring Actual Learning versus Feeling of Learning in Response to Being Actively Engaged in the Classroom," *Proceedings of the National Academy of Sciences* 116, no. 39 (2019): 19251–57.

INDEX